D0747164

GOD AND THE WORLD

JOSEPH CARDINAL RATZINGER

God and the World

Believing and Living in Our Time

A Conversation with Peter Seewald

Translated by Henry Taylor

IGNATIUS PRESS SAN FRANCISCO

Title of the German original:
Gott und die Welt: Glauben und Leben in unserer Zeit
Ein Gespräch mit Peter Seewald

Cover art: *Creation of Adam*: Detail of Adam
(Detail of the Sistine chapel ceiling)
Michaelangelo (1475–1564)
Vatican Palace, Vatican City State
Copyright Scala/Art Resource, New York

Cover design by Roxanne Mei Lum

ISBN 0-89870-868-0
Library of Congress Control Number 2002105231
Printed in the United States of America ∞

Contents

Preface

By Joseph Cardinal Ratzinger

In 1996 Peter Seewald suggested we have a conversation about the questions that people today put to the Church and that are often for them an obstacle on the path to faith. That was the origin of the book *Salt of the Earth*, which many welcomed with gratitude as a practical help in getting their bearings.

Because of the widespread and surprisingly positive response to this book, Mr. Seewald was prompted to suggest a second session of conversations, with a view to illuminating the inner questions of faith, an area that strikes many Christians as an impenetrable jungle in which one can hardly find one's way. Much of this, even what is important for the Christian, seems in the light of modern thought difficult to understand or to accept.

The overwhelming demands of my official work prevented this at first. What little free time I had at my disposal, I wanted to devote to writing a book about the spirit of the liturgy, which I had had in mind since the beginning of the eighties but had never been able to get down on paper. This work was finally put together in the course of three summer holidays and appeared at the beginning of this year [2000]. So at last I had time free for the second conversation with Seewald, for which he had suggested we meet in the richly symbolic abbey of Monte Cassino, motherhouse of the Benedictine order. There, strengthened by the Benedictine hospitality, we held our new interchange, which

Mr. Seewald had prepared with great care. I had to rely on the inspiration of the moment.

The quiet of the monastery, the friendliness of the monks and of their abbot, the atmosphere of prayer, and the reverent celebration of the liturgy helped us a great deal; and, as it turned out, we were able to celebrate with appropriate splendor the feast of Saint Scholastica, the sister of Saint Benedict. So the monks of Monte Cassino have the thanks of both authors, who experienced this venerable site as a place of inspiration.

I probably do not need to point out that each of the two writers speaks for himself and makes his own contribution. Just as in *Salt of the Earth*, so too here—it seems to me—a real dialogue developed from the differing backgrounds and ways of thinking, in which the unsparing directness of the questions and answers proved fruitful. Mr. Seewald, who tape-recorded my answers, undertook the work of transcription and any necessary editing. For my part, I read through my answers with a critical eye and although, where this seemed necessary, I have smoothed out the language or here and there made minor additions, as a whole I have left the spoken word as it stood, just as the challenge of the moment called forth. I hope this second book of dialogue will find just as friendly a reception as *Salt of the Earth* and that it will be of some help to many of those people who are seeking to understand the Christian faith.

Rome, August 22, 2000

Preface

By Peter Seewald

Monte Cassino, early in the year. The road snaking up to the Abbey of Saint Benedict was steep and narrow, and the higher we climbed, the colder the air became. No one said anything, not even Alfredo, the Cardinal's chauffeur. I don't know—winter was definitely past, but somehow we seemed to be worrying about the cold nights that were still to come.

When, together with Cardinal Ratzinger, I published the book-length interview *Salt of the Earth*, many people took the opportunity to go into a subject they had hitherto found inaccessible. The name of God was indeed more current than it had ever been, but actually people no longer knew what they were talking about when they talked about religion. I experienced this when talking with friends or among the staff of the magazine for which I worked. Within a short period of time, something like a spiritual nuclear attack had befallen large sections of society, a sort of Big Bang of the Christian culture that was our foundation. Even if people did not deny the existence of God, no one still counted on the fact that he had any power in the world or could actually do anything.

At this period I used to visit a church every now and then. Although I had doubts and mistrusted messages of salvation, it still seemed to me beyond contradiction that the world was no accident nor the result of an explosion or something like that, as Marx and others maintained. And certainly not the creation of man, who can neither cure the common cold nor stop a dam from breaking. I became aware that behind the web of worship, prayer, and commandments there had to be some truth. "We have not followed some cleverly concocted story", it says in one of the Letters of the apostles. But it would have seemed stupid to me to start making the sign of the cross or some gesture of humility such as people usually make during Mass. And whenever I looked around inside a church, I could no longer read the meaning of all that was there. The essential thing, the meaning of it all, seemed to be hidden as if behind a veil of fog.

Leaving the Church, which for many years seemed to me hollow and reactionary, had not been exactly easy; returning to her, however, is much more difficult. You do not want only to believe what you know; you want to know what you believe. Great mountains of insoluble questions bar the way. Is Christ truly the Son of God, who brought us salvation? And if he is, then what kind of a God is that? A good God, who helps us? A cynical, bored God, writing on, line by line, in his Book of Life? What does he want with people who are liable to fall prey to the power of evil? What are we here for at all? What about the Commandments? Are they still valid? And what do the seven sacraments mean? Is the master plan for the whole of existence hidden within them, as we are told? Can believing and living still be combined at all, in the twenty-first century, so as to enable us to make some use in the modern world of the basic knowledge drawn from man's heritage?

Well, you cannot answer very many questions or put the answers in a form easily grasped in just a short time. There is much that can never be fully expressed in words. But when Cardinal Joseph Ratzinger sat there opposite me in the Abbey, one of the Church's great wise men, and patiently recounted the Gospel to me, the belief of Christendom from the beginning of the world to its end, then, day by day, something of the mystery that holds the world together from within became more tangible. And fundamentally it is perhaps quite simple. "Creation", said the scholar, "bears within itself an order. We can work out from this the ideas of God—and even the right way for us to live."

Munich, August 15, 2000

Prologue

FAITH, HOPE, AND LOVE

Your Eminence, do you ever feel afraid of God?

I wouldn't exactly say "afraid". We know from Christ who God is and that he loves us. And he knows what we are like. He knows we are flesh. We are dust. Because of that he accepts us in our weakness.

In any case, again and again I am keenly aware of how I fail to live up to my calling. To live up to the idea that God has of me, of what I could and should give.

Do you have the feeling, at such times, that God sometimes criticizes you or disapproves of some of your decisions?

God is not like a policeman or a prosecuting counsel, who tells you off and hands out a punishment. But in the mirror of faith and of the charge I have received, I have to consider every day what is right and when something is wrong. Naturally I then likewise feel that, with regard to myself, something is not as it should be. And that is what the sacrament of confession is for.

People always say that Catholics are full of guilt feelings toward God.

I believe that Catholics are animated above all by a great sense of God's forgiveness. Take baroque or rococo art. There you can see a great joyfulness. Thus, typically Catholic nations like Italy or Spain have a reputation, and with good reason, for being light-hearted.

Perhaps there have been, in particular areas of Christianity, certain forms of education, distortions, in which frightening, burdensome, rigorously strict elements have predominated, but this is not Catholicism properly speaking. My own feeling is that, in those very people whose lives draw upon the faith of the Church, a sense of redemption prevails: God will not abandon us!

Is there some particular language that God uses sometimes to say to us, in quite a concrete way, "Yes, do that." Or, again: "Hold on, there—last warning! Just leave it alone!"

God speaks quietly. But he gives us all kinds of signs. In retrospect, especially, we can see that he has given us a little nudge through a friend, through a book, or through what we see as a failure—even through "accidents". Life is actually full of these silent indications. If I remain alert, then slowly they piece together a consistent whole, and I begin to feel how God is guiding me.

When you yourself talk with God, is that something that has become as easy and obvious as making a phone call?

In some respects one can make the comparison. I know that he is always there. And he knows in any case who I am and what I am. Which is all the more reason for me to feel the need to call on him, to share my feelings with him, to talk with him. With him I can exchange views on the simplest and most intimate things, as well as on those that are weightiest and of great moment. It seems, somehow, normal for me to have occasion to talk to him all the time in everyday life.

On these occasions, does God always behave respectfully, or does he let you see he has a sense of humor?

I believe he has a great sense of humor. Sometimes he gives you something like a nudge and says, Don't take yourself so seriously! Humor is in fact an essential element in the mirth of creation. We can see how, in many matters in our lives, God wants to prod us into taking things a bit more lightly; to see the funny side of it; to get down off our pedestal and not to forget our sense of fun.

Do you also get cross with God?

Naturally I, too, think, from time to time: Why doesn't he give me more help? And sometimes he remains puzzling to me. In those cases that annoy me I can also feel the presence somewhere of his mystery, his strangeness. But getting really angry with God would mean that we had dragged God too far down to our level. Very often, quite superficial things give rise to this anger. And in those cases where anger is really justified I have to ask myself whether there isn't something important being communicated to me in the things that annoy me and the people who annoy me. I never get cross with God himself.

How do you begin your day?

Before I get up, I first say a short prayer. The day looks different if you don't just stumble straight into it. Then come all the things you do first thing in the morning, washing, breakfast. After that there is the Holy Mass and the breviary. Both of these, for me, lay the foundations of the day: Mass is the entirely real meeting with the presence of the risen Christ, and the breviary is a way into the great prayer of the whole history of salvation. The Psalms stand at the heart of it. Here we pray together with the millennia, and we hear the voice of the Fathers. All of this opens a door onto the day for us. Then comes ordinary work.

How often do you pray?

Fixed prayer times are at noon, when in accordance with Catholic tradition we pray the Angelus. In the afternoon there is Vespers, and in the evening Compline, the Church's evening prayer. And in between times, whenever I feel I need help, I can fit in a quick prayer.

Does the prayer before you get up always vary?

No, that is a fixed prayer—in fact, it's a collection of various little prayers, but as a whole a fixed form of prayer.

Have you anything to recommend?

Each of us can surely find something for ourselves out of the Church's treasury.

At night, when one cannot settle down . . .

. . . I would recommend the Rosary. That is a form of prayer that, besides its spiritual meaning, has the power to calm the inner self. If we hold fast here to the actual words, then we are gradually freed from the thoughts that so torment us.

How do you personally deal with problems—that is, supposing you have any problems at all?

How could I not have problems? In the first place, I always try to bring my problems into my prayer and to find for myself there a firm interior foothold. And then, I try to do something challenging, really to give myself entirely to some task that is demanding and at the same time gives me satisfaction. Finally, through meeting with friends I can to some extent distance myself from everything else. These three elements are important.

I believe that everyone, at some time or another, is tired and shattered and drained of energy, and despairing and raging, too, over what seems their quite twisted and unfair fate. Bringing problems into one's prayer, as you were saying—how can that be done?

Perhaps one must start as Job did. One must, I would say, first of all cry out to God, inwardly, putting it quite plainly, and say to him: What are you doing with me?! The voice of Job remains an authentic voice, which also tells us that we may do the same—and perhaps even should do the same. Although Job stood before God truly complaining, God admits in the end that he is right. God says he has acted rightly, and the others, who have explained everything, have not spoken truly of me.

Job enters into a struggle and unfolds his complaint before him. Gradually, then, he hears God speaking; things turn around; they move into a different perspective. That way I emerge from the position of simply being tortured and know that although I cannot at that moment comprehend the Love, which is what he is, yet nonetheless I can rely on it; that whatever it is really like, it is good.

Perhaps we should, simply, deal more strictly with our problems, not allow them to arise in the first place.

Problems just do arise. Certain decisions, failure, human inadequacies, disappointments, all these get to us—and indeed should get to us. Problems are meant in fact to teach us how to work through things like that. If we became steel-hard, impenetrable, that would mean a loss of humanity and sensibility in dealing with other people. Seneca the stoic said: Sympathy is abhorrent. If, on the other hand, we look at Christ, he is all sympathy, and that makes him precious to us. Being sympathetic, being vulnerable, is part of being a Christian. One must learn to accept injuries, to live with wounds, and in the end to find therein a deeper healing.

Many people were able to pray as children, but at some time or other they lost this ability. Do you have to learn to talk with God?

The organ of sensitivity to God can atrophy to such an extent that the words of faith become quite meaningless. And whoever no longer possesses a faculty of hearing can no longer speak, because being deaf goes together with being mute. It's as if one had deliberately to learn one's own mother tongue. Slowly one learns to spell out God's letters, to speak this language, and—if still inadequately—to understand God. Gradually, then, one will become able to pray for oneself and to talk with God, at first in a very childlike way—in a certain sense we always remain like that—but then more and more in one's own words.

You once said: If a person believes only what he can see with his own eyes, then really he is blind . . .

. . . because in that case he is limiting his horizon in such a fashion that the essential things escape him. He cannot after all see his own understanding. Precisely those things that are of real moment are what he does not see with the mere physical eye, and to that extent he cannot properly see if he cannot see beyond his immediate sensory perceptions.

Someone once said to me that having faith is like leaping out of an aquarium into the ocean. Can you recall your first great experience of faith?

I would say that in my case it was more like a silent growth. Naturally there have been high points, when something opened up for me in the liturgy, in theology, in first formulating a theological insight—points at which faith became broad and momentous and no longer merely passed on from someone else. The great leap that you were talking about, a particular event, is something I would be unable to point to in my own life. It was rather as if one were to venture out, slowly and cautiously, a little farther each time, out of the very shallow water, and slowly begin to feel a little of the ocean that is coming in toward us.

I also think that one has never achieved complete faith. Faith has to be lived again and again in life and in suffering, as well as in the great joys that God sends us. It is never something that I can put in my pocket like a coin.

An Image of God

My little boy asks me sometimes: Tell me, Daddy, what does God really look like?

I would answer him that we can think of God as being as we know him through Jesus Christ. Christ says in one place, "Whoever sees me, sees the Father."

And then, when we look at the whole story of Jesus—beginning with the manger, then carrying on through his public ministry, his great and moving words, right up to the Last Supper, to the Cross, the Resurrection, and his sending out the apostles—then we can see something of God's face.

On the one hand, this face is great and serious. It stretches far beyond our vision. But its characteristic trait, in the end, is benevolence, acceptance, goodwill toward us.

Is it not said that we should not make any image of God?

This commandment has been transformed, insofar as God himself has given us his image. The Letter to the Ephesians says of Christ: "He is the image of God." And what is said about man in the creation story is fully realized in him.

Christ is the prototype of man. We cannot see in him the image of God in his eternal infinity, but we can see the image in which he chose to portray himself. From that point, we are no longer *making* an image, but God himself has *shown* us an image. Here he looks at us and speaks to us.

The image of Christ is of course not just a photo of God. In this picture of him who was crucified we see the whole life story of Jesus, above all the story of his inner life. That leads us into a way of seeing him in which our senses are opened up and then surpassed.

How could one give an outline of Jesus in a few words?

This always makes our words seem inadequate. Basically, Jesus is the Son of God, who comes from God and is at the same time true man. In him we meet not merely human genius and human heroism, but God, who becomes visible through him. One might say that in the body of Jesus, torn open on the Cross, we can see what God is like, that is, one who opens himself to us to this extent.

Was Jesus a Catholic?

We can't talk about him in that way, since he stands above us. Today people use the opposite way of speaking, when they say that Jesus was not a Christian but a Jew. That is true only in a limited sense. He was one of the Jewish people. He was a Jew, in that he accepted and lived out the Law, and indeed, in spite of all criticism, he was a pious Jew who observed the Temple regulations. And nonetheless he broke out of the Old Testament mold and went beyond it—on his authority as Son.

Jesus understood himself as being the new and greater Moses, who thus does not merely interpret but actually renews the Law. In that sense he went beyond what already existed and created something new, expanding the Old Testament dispensation into the universality of a people who cover the earth and who will grow and grow forever. He is the one, then, who gives the starting point for faith, whose will, as the Catholic Church knows well, brought it into existence; but who is not simply one of us.

How and when did you personally know just what God wanted from you?

I think one always has to learn that anew. God always wants something more. At any rate, if you are referring to my original vocation, to the basic direction I was meant to take and wanted to take—that was an intensive process of maturing, which in my time as a student was also in part a complicated process. This path led me to turn toward the Church, to priestly guides and companions, and of course to Holy Scripture. A whole tangle of relationships was gradually sorted out.

You once said, anyway, that in your decision for the priesthood there was "a real meeting" between you and God. How should one picture this meeting between God and Cardinal Ratzinger?

Not, at any rate, as you would picture an appointment between two human beings. Perhaps one might describe it as something that gets right past your guard and burns its way into your inmost being. You feel that that just has to be, that it's the right path. It was not a meeting in the sense of a mystical illumination. I cannot claim to have any experience of that type. But I can say that the whole struggle led to a clear and demanding perception, so that the will of God presented itself to my inner vision.

"God loved you first!" it says, in the teaching of Christ. And he loves you without respect for your origin or standing. What does that mean?

One should take this sentence as literally as can be, and I try to do that. For it is truly the great power in our lives and the consolation that we need. And it's not seldom that we need it.

He loved me first, before I myself could love at all. It was only because he knew me and loved me that I was made. So I was not thrown into the world by some operation of chance, as Heidegger says, and now have to do my best to swim around in this ocean of life, but I am preceded by a perception of me, an idea and a love of me. They are present in the ground of my being.

What is important for all people, what makes their life significant, is the knowledge they are loved. The person in a difficult situation will hold on if he knows, Someone is waiting for me, someone wants me and needs me. God is there first and loves me. And that is the trustworthy ground on which my life is standing and on which I myself can construct it.

The Crisis of Faith

Cardinal, people are interested in the Christian faith, on most continents of the earth, as never before. In the last fifty years alone, the number of Catholics worldwide has doubled to over a billion. In many countries of the so-called "Old World" we are experiencing a widespread secularization. It seems as if large sections of European society want to cut themselves off entirely from their own roots. Opponents of the faith talk of a "flight from Christianity", from which we must finally set ourselves free.

In our first book, Salt of the Earth, *we dealt with this subject at length. Many people are ready to accept the antichristian or antichurch stereotypes without further thought. The reason for this is often quite simply that we have lost hold of the signs and the content of the faith. We no longer know what they mean. Has the Church no more to say about this?*

There is no doubt that we live in a historical situation in which the temptation to do without God has become very great. Our culture of technology and welfare rests on the belief that basically we can do anything. Naturally, if we think like that, then life is restricted to what we can make and manufacture and demonstrate. The question about God leaves the stage.

If this attitude becomes generalized—and the temptation to do this is very great, because being on the lookout for God means in fact moving out onto another level of life, which seems in the past to have been more easily accessible—then the obvious thing is to say: What we have not made ourselves does not exist.

There have been enough attempts, meanwhile, to construct an ethic without God.

Certainly, and the calculus here is to find what is said to be most appropriate for man. On the other hand, we have attempts to manufacture man's inner fulfillment, his happiness, as a kind of product. Or, again, there are deviant, esoteric forms of religion on offer that seem to do without faith, that are often no more than techniques to achieve happiness.

All these ways of wanting the world to be measurable and to make do with one's own life are very closely related to the pattern of life and of existence in our time. The Word of the Church, on the other hand, seems to be coming from the past, whether because it is from long ago and no longer belongs to our time, or because it springs from a quite different kind of life that no longer seems to exist in our day. Certainly, the Church has not yet quite achieved the leap forward into the present day. The great task before us is so to fill with living experience the old, truly valid and great sayings that they become intelligible for people. We have a great deal to do there.

An image of God that draws on esotericism suggests a quite different God, who in these new "gospels" appears farther and farther from what is taught by Jews and Christians. Its message is not based, so we are told, on what is said by rabbis or priests or even by the Bible. Rather than on these sources, people are supposed to rely on their feelings for guidance. They are supposed to rid themselves finally of the oppression of these outdated and indeed absurd religions and their priestly castes, so obsessed with power, and are supposed to become once more whole and happy, just as people were meant to be from the beginning. Much of this sounds very promising.

It corresponds to the need we feel nowadays for religion and likewise to our need for simplification. To that extent, there is something obvious about this option, something that seems promising. One must of course ask this: Who or what authorizes this message? Does it carry sufficient authority simply because it sounds plausible to us? Is plausibility a sufficient criterion by which to accept a message about God? Or could it not be that this very plausibility is a flattering temptation? It shows the easier way forward, but at the same time prevents our getting onto the track of the truth.

In the end, we are making our feelings the measure for knowing who God is and how we should live. But feelings are changeable, and quite soon we come to realize for ourselves that we are building on treacherous foundations. However obvious as a way forward that may seem at first —there, again, I come across mere human ideas, which in the end remain dubious. The essence of faith, however, is that I do not meet with something that has been thought up, but that here something meets me that is greater than anything we can think of for ourselves.

Objection: That's what the Church says!

It is substantiated by the history that has grown out of it, in which God both has repeatedly verified his identity and will continue to do so. I think we will discover a great deal about that in this book.

But ultimately it is not enough for man that God is supposed to have said this or that to us, or that we can imagine this or that about him. Only if he has *done* something and is something for us, then what we need has come about upon which we can base our life.

In that case, we can recognize that there are not only words about God, but that the reality *of* God exists. That not only have people thought something up, but something has happened; something has happened to someone [*passiert*] in the literal sense, in the Passion. This reality is greater than any words, even if it is less easily accessible.

For many people, of course, it is not just incredible but presumptuous, a monstrous provocation, to believe that one single person, who was executed around the year 30 in Palestine, should be the Chosen and Anointed One of God, the "Christos", or Christ. That a single being should stand in the center of history.

In Asia there are hundreds of theologians who say that God is far too great and too inclusive to have incarnated himself in a single person. And is not faith in fact lessened thereby if the salvation of the whole world is supposed to be built upon one small point?

This religious experience in Asia regards God as being so immeasurable, on one hand, and, on the other, our ability to conceive him as being so limited that in this view God is only able to represent himself to us in ever-changing aspects, in an unending myriad of reflections. Christ is then perhaps a more conspicuous symbol of God, but still just a reflection, which certainly does not comprehend the whole.

This is apparently an expression of the humility of man toward God. It is held to be quite impossible for God to enter into a single human being. And, thinking about it purely from the human point of view, we could perhaps expect nothing more than that we should only ever be able to see a little spark, a small section of God himself.

Sounds not unreasonable.

Yes. Being reasonable, one would have to say that God is far too great to enter into the littleness of a man. God is far too great for one idea or a single book to comprehend his whole word; only in many experiences, even contradictory experiences, can he give us reflections of himself. On the other hand, the humility would turn to pride if we were to deny God the freedom and the power and the love to make himself as small as that.

The Christian faith brings us exactly that consolation, that God is so great that he can become small. And that is actually for me the unexpected and previously inconceivable greatness of God, that he is able to bow down so low. That he himself really enters into a man, no longer merely disguises himself in him so that he can later put him aside and put on another garment, but that *he* becomes this man. It is just in this that we actually see the truly infinite nature of God, for this is more powerful, more inconceivable than anything else, and at the same time more saving.

If we took the other view, then we would necessarily have to live always with a mass of untruth. The contradictory fragments that are there in Buddhism, and likewise in Hinduism, suggest the solution of negative mysticism. But then God himself becomes a negation—and has in the end nothing positive or constructive to say to this world.

On the other hand, this very God, who has the power to realize Love in such a way that he himself is present in a man, that he is there and introduces himself to us, that he associates himself with us, is exactly what we need in order to escape from having to live to the end with fragments and half-truths.

That does not mean that we have nothing more to learn from other religions. Or that the canon of what is "Christian" is so firmly fixed that we cannot be led any farther. The adventure of Christian faith is ever new, and it is when we admit that God is capable of this that its immeasurable openness is unlocked for us.

Is faith, in principle, always present in man?

So far as we can learn about the history of mankind, through excavations right back into prehistory, we can see that there has always been an idea of God. The Marxists had predicted the end of religion. With the end of oppression we would no longer need the medicine of God, we were told. But even they have had to recognize that religion never comes to an end, because it is present in man as such.

This inner sensor does not, in any case, work automatically, like some piece of technology, but is a living thing that can either develop with the person or, on the other hand, become desensitized and almost dead. With a progressive inner fulfillment the sensor becomes ever more acute, more alive and interactive. In the opposite case, it becomes dull and, as it were, anaesthetized. Nonetheless, even in an unbelieving person there remains somehow a vestigial question of whether there is after all something there. Without taking this inner sensitivity into account we just cannot understand the history of mankind.

There are, on the other hand, whole libraries of books and powerful theories that aim at confuting this faith. A belief against belief seems likewise to be present in principle, and even to have a missionary character. The greatest social experiments of history thus far, National Socialism and Communism, were concerned to show that belief in God was absurd and to root it out from men's hearts. And that will not be the last attempt.

That's why faith in God is not a form of knowledge that can be learned like chemistry or mathematics, but remains a belief. That is, it has a perfectly rational structure—we will come to that. It is not just some dark mystery or other with which I have dealings. It gives me insight. And there are perfectly comprehensible reasons for accepting it. But it is never simply knowledge.

Since faith demands our whole existence, our will, our love, since it requires letting go of ourselves, it necessarily always goes beyond a mere knowledge, beyond what is demonstrable. And because that is so, then I can always turn my life away from faith and find arguments that seem to refute it.

And there are, as you know, whole rafts of counterarguments. We only have to look at the monstrous suffering in the world. This alone seems to prove there is no God. Or let's take the incidental matter of God's invisibility. For those able to see with the eyes of faith, that is his very greatness; but for anyone who cannot or will not make the leap, it makes God somehow refutable. One can also lose the whole in a mass of details. One can read Holy Scripture, the New Testament, in such a way as to see in it no more than a kaleidoscope of fragments, so that some learned man can say that the Resurrection story was made up later, that everything was added afterward, that none of it holds together.

That is all possible. Simply because history and faith are human. To that extent, disputes about faith will never end.

This dispute is always at the same time a man's struggle with himself and a struggle with God, which will last until the end of history dawns.

In modern society people question whether there is such a thing as truth. That is turned against the Church, which still holds fast to this concept. You once said that the deep crisis of Christianity in Europe essentially originates in the crisis concerning its claim to truth. Why?

Because no one any longer trusts himself to say that what faith asserts is true. People are afraid they might be acting intolerantly toward other religions or creeds. And Christians say among themselves that we have become afraid of the absolute quality of a claim to truth.

On one hand, that is in a way healthy. For if we lash out too readily, too casually with a claim to truth, or if we rest too comfortably upon it, we run the risk not only of becoming authoritarian, but also of elevating some secondary and temporary factor to the status of absolute truth.

A certain circumspection with regard to any claim to truth is entirely appropriate. But it ought not to lead us as far as dropping all claims to truth. That leaves us merely blundering about among various types of tradition.

At any rate, boundaries are becoming genuinely less clear. Many people dream of a kind of casserole religion, with the most palatable ingredients carefully selected. People increasingly differentiate between "good" and "bad" religion.

What is interesting is that the concept of tradition has to a great extent made redundant that of religion, and that of confession or denomination—and, thereby, that of truth. Particular religions are regarded as traditions. They are then valued as being "venerable", as "beautiful", and people say that whoever stands in one tradition should respect that one; another person, his own tradition; and everyone should respect each other's. At any rate, if traditions are all we have, then truth has been lost. And sooner or later we will ask what in fact traditions are for. And in that case a revolt against tradition is well founded.

I always recall the saying of Tertullian, that Christ never said "I am the custom", but "I am the truth". Christ does not just lend his weight to custom or tradition; on the contrary, he leads us right out of the customary way. He wants us to depart; he urges us to seek out what is true, whatever will bring us into the reality of the One who is the Creator and Redeemer of our own being. To that extent, we must regard circumspection as a serious obligation with respect to any claim to truth, but we must also have the courage not to lose hold of the truth, to stretch toward it and to accept it humbly and thankfully, whenever it is given to us.

Doubt

You once recounted a story told by Martin Buber about a Jewish rabbi. In this story the rabbi is visited one day by a man who believes in enlightenment. The bringer of enlightenment is a learned man. He wants to prove to the rabbi that there is no such thing as a truth of faith, that indeed faith itself is obsolete, the relic of a past age. As the learned man enters the rabbi's room, he sees him walking up and down, a book in his hand, meditating. The rabbi takes no notice of the champion of enlightenment. But after a while he stands still for a moment, glances at him, and says only: "But perhaps it is true." That was enough. The learned man's knees were shaking, and he practically fled from the house. A nice story, but even so: again and again, even priests leave their Church; monks leave their abbeys. You yourself spoke once of the "oppressive power of unbelief".

Belief is never simply there, in a way that would enable me to say at a certain point in time: I have it, and others do not have it. We have already talked about that. It is something living, which is inclusive of the whole person in all his dimensions—understanding, will, and feelings. It can then fasten its roots ever deeper into my life, so that my life becomes more and more nearly identical with my faith; but for all that it is never just a possession. A man can always still give way to this other tendency within himself and thus fall away.

Faith is always a path. As long as we live we are on the way, and on that account faith is always under pressure and under threat. And it is healthy that it can never turn into a convenient ideology. That it does not make me hardened and unable to follow the thoughts of my doubting brother and to sympathize with him. Faith can only mature by suffering anew, at every stage in life, the oppression and the power of unbelief, by admitting its reality and then finally going right through it, so that it again finds the path opening ahead for a while.

How is it for you? Are you personally acquainted with this "oppressive power of unbelief"?

Of course. If one is trying to share the faith with others in the spiritual situation of our century, as a professor or a teacher of the faith, then one must take particular care to be open oneself to the questions that make faith hard. And then, obviously, one encounters the various life-styles that are offered to us with the promise that they can replace faith, or make faith unnecessary. To that extent, accepting the impact of everything that speaks against faith today, its inner strength, and feeling myself oppressed by it is all an essential part of my work.

But even if I did not wish to, one encounters it anyway in news bulletins, in current affairs, and in every kind of life experience that opens up to us. All that, on the one hand, makes the path of faith laborious to tread. But then when you come out into the light again, you can also see that you have climbed higher, that it is in this way that we get nearer to the Lord.

Is that ever a thing of the past?

Never quite past.

Can one imagine that even a pope might be attacked by doubt or indeed unbelief?

Not by unbelief, but we can and should picture him as likewise suffering under the questions that make faith hard. I shall never forget a meeting I had in Munich when I was a curate. My vicar at that time, Father Blumscheid, was friends with the pastor of the neighboring Lutheran parish. One day Romano Guardini came to give a talk, and the two vicars had a chance to chat with him. I don't know the actual course of the conversation, but Blumscheid told me—he was deeply shocked—that Guardini had said that as you grow older faith does not get easier, but harder. Guardini may have been between sixty-five and seventy at the time. That, of course, is the specific experience of one man, who was in any case of a melancholy cast of mind and had suffered greatly. But, as I was saying, this business is never entirely settled. On the other hand, it does get easier in a way, because the flame of life is burning less fiercely. But so long as we are on the journey, we are traveling.

Does the Catholic Church know with absolute certainty, then, what God is really like, what he is really saying, and also what he really wants from us?

The Catholic Church knows in faith all that God has said to us in the history of revelation. Our understanding of it, of course—even the understanding of it that the Church enjoys—remains greatly inferior to the magnitude of what God has spoken. On that account there is a development of faith. Each generation, from the point of view of its own circumstances, is able to discover new dimensions of faith that even the Church did not know before. The Lord predicts this in the Gospel of John: "The Holy Spirit will lead you into all truth, so that you will come to know those things which would be too much for you now." That means there is always a surplus, something anticipatory in revelation—not only with respect to what any individual may hitherto have understood, but also with respect to what the Church knows. This surplus provides each generation with a new adventure of faith.

What does that mean?

It is never the case that we can say, Now we know everything; now the knowledge of Christianity is complete. There are unfathomable depths both in God and in human life, so that there are always new dimensions to faith. What has at least been vouchsafed to the Church is a certitude about what can *not* be reconciled with the gospel. She has formulated her most essential perceptions of this in her creed and her dogmas. They are all conceived in negative terms. She points out the borderline beyond which one would stray into error. The area within the borders, so to speak, remains both wide and open. On this account, the Church can give the general directions for human life and can say what direction I certainly should *not* take, if I want to avoid a fall. It remains for each person to discover the manifold possibilities on his own path and to explore them.

Many people say, in any case, that Christianity is less a practical religion and more something for the next life, that is to say, a way of collecting good marks for a register kept in the next world.

It is true that a life beyond this one is part of the Christian way of looking at things. If you were to take that away, then it dwindles to a perspective that is still remarkable but fragmentary and incomplete. If one were to look at human life merely within the dimensions of the seventy or eighty years permitted us to live here, then it would appear brutally truncated. In this way there arises this remarkable greed for life. If this present life is the only one there can be, then naturally I must look to it to grab and get as much out of it as I can. I cannot afford to consider other people.

The life beyond gives me the criteria and gives this life the importance and seriousness that I need in order to live, not just for the moment, but in such a way that in the end my life means something, has some value—and not only for me, but more generally. The God who grants our prayers does not take away our responsibility but in fact teaches us to be responsible. He leads us to live out what is set before us in responsible fashion and thereby to become worthy in the end to stand before him.

Christ says, "Ask, and it will be given unto you. Seek, and you shall find. Knock, and the door will be opened to you." On the other hand, when my son for instance is about to do a piece of schoolwork, he asks God for help. But, to be quite honest, it doesn't always help.

We ask, for instance, for good health; a mother does that for her child, a man for his wife; we ask that a people as a whole may not fall into great error—and we know that what we ask is by no means always granted us. In the case of someone for whom it is a matter of life and death, this can become a serious problem. Why has he had no answer, or at least nothing like the answer he had asked for? Why is God silent? Why does he withdraw? Why is it that just the opposite of what I wanted is happening?

This distance between what Jesus promised and what we experience in our own lives makes you think, every time—it has that effect in each generation, for each single person, and even for me. Each one of us has to struggle to work out an answer for himself, so that in the end he comes to understand why God has spoken to him precisely like that.

And what answer is there?

Augustine and other great Christians say that God gives us what is best for us—even when we do not recognize this at first. Often, we think that exactly the opposite of what he does would really be best for us. We have to learn to accept this path, which, on the basis of our experience and our suffering, is difficult for us, and to see it as the way in which God is guiding us. God's way is often a path that enormously reshapes and remolds our life, a path in which we are truly changed and straightened out.

To that extent, we have to say that this "Ask, and you will receive" certainly cannot mean that I can call God in as a handyman who will make my life easy every time I want something. Or who will take away suffering and questioning. On the contrary, it means that God definitely hears me and that what he grants me is, in the way known only to him, what is right for me.

To come back to the particular case in question: It may also be beneficial for your son to learn that God isn't simply going to jump in when he has not learned his vocabulary properly, but that he has to do that for himself. It may sometimes mean that he is not spared the little discipline that lies in failure. For perhaps he really needs precisely this discipline in order to find the way he should go.

Lamenting like Job?

The writer Joseph Roth, in line with ancient Jewish tradition, well and truly disputes with his God. "In your meaningless fecundity you have given life to millions of others like me", he wrote, under the impact of the horror of the First World War. "I don't want your grace!" he cries to heaven in desperation, "Send me to hell!"

Perhaps in Jewish tradition that is more strongly pronounced, if only because Christ, the God who enters into misery, who suffers with us and who saves souls, has not yet made his appearance: a God who comes face-to-face with us, no longer merely as the great Unknowable Being, as he appears to Job in the end, but as someone who has been down to the uttermost depth, so that he can say of himself, in the words of the psalm, "I am a worm, and no man", someone who has been trampled underfoot.

At just those times when we are in trouble the question always comes, "Why are you doing this?" We talked at the beginning about how in many circumstances this telling God quite openly that we do not understand can already be the starting point for personal prayer and for overcoming trouble. We say that with an underlying certainty that I will get the right answer, because he who was crucified, whose experience was just as miserable and just as dreadful, is always there before me.

Perhaps I am mistaken, but Christians have a more reverent attitude to God. Augustine says, "Lord, I do not dispute with you, for you are truth . . . I do not call you to account . . . But in your mercy permit me to speak, I who am dust and ashes."

This question greatly troubled Augustine, who was always a suffering and struggling man. To start with, he thought that once one had converted one was on the high road to heaven. Later on he noticed that even this high road can be terribly difficult and that there are some very dark valleys. He was of the opinion that even Saint Paul, to the end of his life, suffered temptation, which is certainly something he read into Paul's story from his own experience. But precisely because Augustine was so oppressed, it was essential for him to be able to talk to God as the merciful One, to seek refuge in him, to see his loving face and not to have to dispute with him.

In that sense I believe that in fact the figure of Christ takes something of the bitterness out of our conflict. The answer that only begins to be suggested in the Book of Job with the appearance of the Creator has in the meantime been developed a good bit further.

Once again, it is in times of trouble that many people look to their faith for help. Sometimes it works, but sometimes we have the feel-

ing, My God, where are you? Why aren't you giving me more help when I need you?

The Book of Job is the classic cry of the man who experiences all the misery of existence and a silent God. And an even apparently unjust God. Job is despairing and angry, so that he really pours out before God everything that has brought him down and makes him doubt that life is worth living.

There are the questions: Is it good to be alive? Is God good, and is he really there, and does he really help? We are not spared these dark nights. They are clearly necessary, so that we can learn through suffering, so that we can acquire freedom and maturity and above all else a capacity for sympathy with others. There is no final or rational answer, no formula of life in which we could explain these things. For in those instances when it gets under our skin and goes to our heart there are other factors in play that can't be explained by a universal formula but in the end can only be worked through by undergoing personal suffering.

"I have assigned to me", says Job, "nothing for my own but nights of grief. Lying in bed, I wonder 'When will it be day?' Restlessly I fret till twilight falls. . . . My eyes will never again see joy." If a person is not even spared this bitterness of the soul, then what is faith actually doing for him?

It's quite proper to put this question, since if I am doing something, then it should have some point, some meaning. One wants to know: is this really right? Does it mean something, or is it really just self-deception? The question is only wrong if you look at everything there is solely from the point of view of *self*, on the principle of "What do I get out of it?" You are then seeing things from the perspective of a greed in relation to life as a whole, a perspective closed up within oneself, which prevents one understanding anything any more and will eventually ruin one's life.

Christ once said: Anyone who wants to save his life will lose it. And only the person who loses his life, who is ready to give it up, can manage to see things in true perspective and will thus find his life. That means that in the end I just have to drop the question as to what I get out of it. I have to learn to recognize that it is important to just let myself go. I have to be ready to give myself.

That's easy to say.

But a part of every human love is that it is only truly great and enriching if I am ready to deny myself for this other person, to come out of myself, to give of myself. And that is certainly true of our relationship with God, out of which, in the end, all our other relationships must grow.

I must begin by no longer looking at *myself*, but by asking what *he* wants. I must begin by learning to love. That consists precisely in turning my gaze away from myself and toward him. With this attitude I no longer ask, What can I get for myself, but I simply let myself be guided by him, truly lose myself in Christ; when I abandon myself, let go of myself, then I see, yes, life is right at last, because otherwise I am far too narrow for myself. When, so to speak, I go outside, then it truly begins, then life attains its greatness.

Now it will no doubt be said that this business can take a long time.

Well, of course it isn't a journey you can make from one day to the next. If you're interested in quick happiness, then faith doesn't work. And perhaps that is one of the reasons for the crisis in faith nowadays, that we want our pleasure and our happiness at once, and not to take the risk of a life-long venture—a venture made in the trust that this leap will not end in nothingness, but that it is by its nature that act of love for which we were created. And which alone gives me what I want: loving and being loved and thereby finding true happiness.

Moving Mountains

But Jesus himself says, "If you have faith, even no greater than a mustard seed, then you will be able to say to this mountain, 'move over there!' And it will move. Nothing will be impossible for you."

That is indeed, for me at any rate, one of the most mysterious sayings in the New Testament. Even the Fathers, the great theologians, the saints, have struggled with this saying. We cannot here—any more than with the saying, "Ask, and you will receive"—tie ourselves down to a prosaic understanding that says, Right, now I really and truly believe, so I ought to be able to say to the mountain of Monte Cassino, Go away. What is actually meant are those mountains that obstruct our lives. And they are usually far more massive than the mountains you can point to on the map. Those mountains I can in fact overcome if I let myself go toward God.

Is that a kind of auto-suggestion?

The act of believing is not about talking oneself into some notion, or about ascribing some active power to faith. The act of believing consists in trusting that God is there, that I can put myself in his hands. And then even the mountain will go away.

In this connection the Lord uses the image of the mustard seed, as being the smallest of all grains or seeds, out of which in the end a tree will grow in which all the birds of the air will be able to nest. The mustard seed comprises, on the one hand, smallness—wherein I am wretched—but at the same time the potential for growth. In that way there is in this mustard seed a profound depiction of faith. Faith is seen thereby not as the mere acceptance of certain propositions, but is the seed of life within me. I am only a true believer if faith is present within me as a living seed, from which something is growing and which then truly changes my world and, in doing so, brings something new into the world as a whole.

Jesus made us a great promise. He said, "What I teach I do not have from myself, but from the One who sent me. Whoever does the will of God will come to know whether this teaching is from God or whether I teach from what I know myself." And even the Pharisees cried out then, "Never has any man taught like this man."

That corresponds exactly to what we have been reflecting on. The truth of Jesus' word cannot be tested in terms of theory. It is like a technical proposition: it is shown to be correct only by testing it. The truth of what God says here involves the whole person, the experiment of life. It can only become clear for me if I truly give myself up to the will of God, so far as he has made it known to me. This will of the Creator is not something foreign to me, something external, but is the basis of my own being. And in this experiment of life it does in fact become clear how life can be put right. It will not be comfortable, but it will be right. It will not be superficial or pleasant, but it will in a profound sense be filled with joy.

That is indeed the real meaning of the saints for us, that they are people who have ventured upon this experiment of the will of God. To a certain extent they are lights for mankind, signposts who show us what happens, how life can be put right. I believe that is fundamental for the whole question about the truth of Christianity.

God and Reason

The Church and her saints emphasize that one can grasp the truth of Christianity by reason, that one can demonstrate its reasonableness and give reasonable arguments in its favor. Is that true?

Yes, but within limits. It is true that the faith is not just a kaleidoscope of images, so that we could arrange it this way, or perhaps that. Faith speaks to our reason, our understanding, because it expresses truth—and because reason was created for the sake of truth. To that extent, faith without understanding is no true Christian faith.

Faith demands to be understood. We, in this conversation, are seeking to find the way in which all of this—from the idea of creation to Christian hope—can be seen as a meaningful whole that embodies something reasonable. To that extent one can show that faith is appropriate material for understanding.

Again and again, scientists have taken God and faith as their theme. I have brought a few quotations with me. Isaac Newton, for instance, the founder of theoretical physics, says: "The wonderful arrangement and harmony of the universe can only have come into being in accordance with the plans of an omniscient and all-powerful Being. That is, and remains, my most important finding." Augustin-Louis Cauchy, the French mathematician, remarked: "I am a Christian, that is, I believe in the divinity of Christ just as Tycho Brahe, Copernicus, Descartes, Newton, Leibniz, Pascal did . . . like all great astronomers and mathematicians of the past." And the Italian Guglielmo Marconi, the Nobel prize winner whom we have to thank for wireless telephones and thereby for a mobile culture, expresses it thus: "I declare with pride that I am a believer. I believe in the power of prayer. I believe in it not only as a believing Catholic but also as a scientist."

Certainly, we are not plunging ourselves into a superstitious venture when we become Christians. But I would only bring two reservations: faith cannot be understood in the same sense that a mathematical formula might be for me entirely comprehensible, but reaches into ever deeper levels of being, into the eternal nature of God, into the mystery of love. In this area there is a limit to what one can understand by merely thinking it out. Above all, to what, as a limited man, one can understand and work through with complete clarity.

We are unable even to understand another man, because his person reaches down into depths more profound than our ability to conceptualize. We cannot, in the end, understand the structure of matter, but can only conceive of it up to a certain point. It is thus the more obvious that what meets us in God, and in God's Word, cannot in the end be made subject to our understanding, because it far surpasses it.

In this sense faith cannot be rationally demonstrated. I cannot say, Whoever does not accept this is just stupid. Faith has its own way of life, in which what we believe is gradually substantiated by experience and is shown to be meaningful as a whole. There are therefore convergences, from the point of view of reason, that make it right for me to enter into it. They give me the certainty that I am not merely handing myself over to some superstition. But an exhaustive demonstration, such as can be given for natural laws, does not exist.

Can we say that it is necessary to broaden one's mind in order to come to know God better?

Even a simple person can know God quite well. It is not necessarily the case that a broad acquaintance with the scientific and historical knowledge we now have will make someone capable of understanding God better.

You can drown understanding in facts. Anyone who fails to perceive the *mystery* at work within the facts of nature or of history is just stuffing his head and his heart with a lot of things that may even make him incapable of any breadth or depth of perception.

A great amount of scientific knowledge can, on the one hand, lead to someone's being no longer able to see beyond the facts, so that he is hemmed in by facts. Because he knows so much, he is now only capable of thinking on a factual level and can no longer bring himself to make the leap into mystery. He sees only what is tangible. And, from a metaphysical point of view, in this way a person becomes more stupid. The other side of it is that sometimes, precisely by the breadth of our vision, in that we can see so many glimpses of divine reason in reality, this really does add breadth and scope to our image of God, and we stand before him with greater reverence and even with humility and awe.

A particular example of the way our image of God may change: the earlier idea that God sees each person, that he knows exactly what everyone is doing each second of the day, was at one time abandoned. It was said to be a childish fantasy, if not a threatening gesture intended by the Church to instill fear. Today, through the advance of technology, this image has in a strange way returned to us. In the meantime we have not only put satellites into space, which broadcast television images to us all, but likewise navigation systems, which can locate any single car anywhere in the world and can guide us to our destination. Furthermore, computer technology and the Internet show us that by means of certain stimuli, millions upon millions of corresponding impulses and motions can be controlled and distributed worldwide, whether in Oslo or in Kapstadt. At any rate, by means of this expansion of man's ability to conceptualize, an image of God that had already been banished to cold storage because it seemed too naïve now returns, looking quite new and interesting.

Yes, that is something we should be grateful for, that this helps us to new ways of seeing things. In this way doors are opened that had previously been shut. As we understand more about the world, so our image of God looks greater and more intelligible. But that does not happen automatically.

A Contradiction

On one side, we find the commandments of God—on the other side, our own human nature. Both are created by God. Nevertheless, anyone can see that the two are often very badly mismatched. Thinking wrong things and doing wrong things are both obviously quite human. Through this paradox we often find ourselves in a situation that seems beyond us.

The Christian faith holds that the creation has been damaged. Human existence is no longer what was produced at the hands of the Creator. It is burdened with another element that produces, besides the innate tendency *toward God*, the opposite tendency *away from God*. In this way man is torn between the original impulse of creation and his own historical inheritance.

The possibility of this is already built into the nature of finite creatures, but has only developed in history. On one hand, man is created to love. He is there in order to lose himself, to give himself. But it is also easy for him to withhold himself, to want to be just himself. This tendency is built up to the point where, on one hand, he can love God and, on the other, can be angry with him and say, I want to be independent, I just want to be myself.

If we observe ourselves carefully, we can see this paradox, this inner tension of our existence. On one hand, we recognize that what the Ten Commandments say is right. That's what we want and what we like doing. That is to say, being good to other people, being grateful, respecting other people's property, finding great love in a sexual relationship so that this becomes a lifelong mutual responsibility, telling the truth, not lying. In some sense that is indeed a trend that is not merely *contrary* to our nature and lying on our shoulders like a yoke.

On the other hand, we forever feel an itch to get out from underneath it.

That is the love of contradiction, the convenience of lying, the temptation to mistrust—all this is present in man because of an impulse toward destruction, a wish to say No.

This paradox points to a certain inner disturbance in man, so that he can no longer simply be the person he wants to be. I see what is good and approve it, said Ovid, a Roman poet, and then still do the other thing. And Paul, in the seventh chapter of the Letter to the Romans, insisted, likewise: The good that I wish to do, I do not do; and the evil that I do not wish to do, that is what I do. In Paul's case, this gives rise to the cry: Who will release me from this inner contradiction? And that is the point at which Paul truly understood Christ —and the point from which he then carried Christ, as the answer that releases us, out into the contemporary pagan world.

There is, though, an external contradiction, too. It is the contradiction between the good news of this supposedly good and "loving" God and the actual condition of the world. The result is a disappointment with God. Many people can see nothing of the alleged healing at work. And sometimes I, too, think that faith can perhaps no longer hold its ground against our more advanced ideas. It can not bear scrutiny in the full light of the facts.

Here the inner contradiction of which we were speaking a moment ago is reinforced by collective momentum. There is a collective consciousness that sharpens the contradiction —that agrees with the selfish tendencies, the turning away from God, and always prefers the momentarily easier choice in life. Each person doesn't merely live for himself, he is lived, he is shaped, or even led astray and distorted, along with others.

There are various stages in the rise or decay of societies. Communities may be supportive and help me along the road, so that the inner contradiction is gradually weakened and dissolved. But, on the other hand, there is a collective unity of being average, where one says, Well, the others are doing the same. Those are societies in which theft has become normal, bribery is no longer seen as improper, and lying is the normal way of carrying on.

Societies can either drag a man down—or help him farther up. In the first instance, material things are dominant and habits of thought are so tied to material considerations that any ideas that reach out beyond this are seen as antiquated, as foolish and inappropriate for man. In the second case God is truly present in some visible manner, and it is easier to move toward him.

But why should life not be just easy and pleasant and fun?

Of course it is easier for the moment to take pleasure in material things, in what is tangible, in things that bring us happiness and can be directly bought and accessed. I can go into a pleasure shop; for the price of entry I can experience a sort of ecstasy and thereby buy release from all cares, from the difficult path of self-development and of self-transcendence. This is a dreadfully strong temptation. In this way happiness becomes a commodity that can be bought and sold. That's easier; it's quicker; we seem to have bypassed the inner contradiction—because the question concerning God now seems quite unnecessary.

One might regard it, however, as the civilized way of life, the sophisticated way, and the one absolutely suited to our modern world.

But we also know that this quickly turns out to be a disappointment. The individual notices that, in the end I am still empty, burned-out, and when I come back down to earth after the ecstasy I can no longer stand myself or the world. And at this point at least I know I have been cheated.

It is true that we are never alone with our inner world but are always collectively on stage. This collective identity can make things either harder or easier. Because of this, in the early Church the catechumenate was developed. The aim was to create a kind of alternative society in which each person could be oriented toward God and through living together with others could eventually come to the point of learning to see him. In the time leading up to baptism, which indeed was called *illumination*, the moment arrived when this perception came to life within each one, and along with it, autonomy of faith.

I think this has once more become necessary in societies based on atheistic or agnostic materialism. Earlier, it seemed as though Church and society were largely identified one with the other. Now the Church must once more make an effort to create social spaces in which people find on offer not only that burdensome collective identity that drags us down, but also a collective identity that opens up possibilities, that supports the individual and brings him into the process of learning to see.

The question is whether faith really makes us so much better, more merciful, more caring toward our neighbor, less covetous, less vain. Let's take those people whom God himself has called to faith, those people who, from the point of view of their whole purpose in life, should have nothing else in their minds but to please God and to become, as it were, perfect people. Why is it that among clergy, among monks and nuns, we meet so much bearing of grudges, so much envy and jealousy, so many lies and such a lack of willingness to help? Why was their faith not able to make them better persons?

That is indeed a most pressing question. There we can see once again that faith is not just there, but that it either withers or grows, that it either rises or falls on the graph. It is not just a ready-made guarantee, something one can regard as accumulated capital that can only grow. Faith is always given only in the context of a fragile freedom. We may wish it were otherwise. But just therein lies God's great gamble, which we find so hard to understand, that he has not given us stronger medicine.

Even if we are bound to notice inadequate patterns of behavior (behind which, of course, there is always a weakening of faith) within the world of those who believe, we cannot ignore the positive side of the account. In the stories of so many simple, kindly folk whom faith has made good, we see after all that faith has a very positive effect. I'm thinking especially of elderly people in quite ordinary parishes, who through their faith have matured to great goodness. When we meet them we feel something warm, a kind of inner light.

And, conversely, we must note that, with the dimming of the light of faith, society has become harder, more violent, and more corrosive. Even a theologian so committed to the critical stance as Vorgrimler has said that the climate has become not better, but more noxious and inflamed.

Mystery

The Christian world is one in which invisible things are as much taken for granted as visible ones. Christians are surrounded by angels and guardian angels. They can call on the help of the Holy Spirit. They can, if they wish, call on the Virgin Mary for aid and consolation. The great Catholic scholar Romano Guardini talks about making spiritual mysteries visible*. The method he suggests is to fix your attention on some holy thing or practice, and then to concentrate all your thoughts and all your heart in this symbol. Then you would be able to feel right away how it sets you in order and sanctifies you. For non-Catholics that sounds strange, of course, or even downright naïve.*

Once again, we should not understand this in a superficial way, which could, in the end, even be superstitious. As if we were to see ourselves in a universe full of friendly powers that take care of half our lives for us. But it is right that we should be aware in faith of a reality that goes beyond tangible things. The great saints are indeed still living. This great family is here, and noticing their presence means that I am loved and cared for.

In order truly to appropriate these things, as Guardini has it, I must of course make myself familiar with this whole matter *from the inside out* and take them to myself through understanding them—and then I can recognize the way they point out for me. This is not just a means to make myself comfortable by offloading half my life, but a direction.

Recently on the news here in Italy a woman told what had happened to her. She was expecting a baby, and the heart operation she was going to have was high-risk. She told the reporter quite serenely that she had simply said to Padre Pio, "Padre Pio, help me and my baby", and then she knew that nothing would happen. Perhaps that is very childish and simple, but it reflects something of a basic trust that we enjoy when we know that we have brothers and sisters in the other world. They are close; they can help me; I can call on them in all trust.

In any case, fewer and fewer people seem to be aware of the mysteries of faith. How can this be?

Perhaps our faith had in some ways become too mechanical. Perhaps there was also too much outward show, too little inner reality, in Guardini's terms.

Faith has to be rediscovered and relived in every generation. On the other hand, we see how a generation that is no longer aware of the Christian faith and its saving powers turns elsewhere to look for such things in esoteric forms, turning to stones and heaven knows what else for help. That is to say, they look for new forms by which to call on the help of unseen powers, because man feels that he could or should have some other help. To that extent, we Catholics, and above all those in positions of responsibility in the Church, must ask ourselves why we have been unable to proclaim our faith in such a way as to offer answers to today's questions. So that people would once again see and feel that there is something in this faith that is just what they are after.

Is Everything Already Written?

In Arabic there is an expression that is meant to express one of the great mysteries of this world: Maktub. *Translated, it is something like: "It is written". Perhaps everything has already been written down, the whole history of the world, the story of my birth and my death. I once heard in the course of a Mass, Blessed are they whose names are already written by God, that is to say, in the great* Book of Life. *Does God show us the way we have to go, so that I have only to recognize what is signposted for me?*

I believe—though I am no specialist in Islam—that in this matter there is an opposition, or at least a clear distinction, between Islam and the Christian faith. Islam seems to proceed from a strict notion of predestination; everything is predestined, and I live in a ready-woven web. As against that, Christian faith always reckons with the freedom factor. That is to say, on one hand, God embraces everything. He knows everything. He guides the course of history. Nonetheless he has so arranged it that freedom has its place. That I can deviate, so to speak, from what he had planned for me.

Can you explain that further?

It is very mysterious and difficult. In Christianity, too, the so-called teaching on predestination was developed. According to this teaching, it is already settled that those for whom it is planned will go to hell, and the others to heaven; it has been decided from all eternity. The faith of the Church has always rejected this. For the idea that as an individual I can do nothing one way or the other—that if I am bound for hell, then I just am, and if I am going to heaven, then that's the way it is—is certainly not consistent with the faith.

God has created true freedom and allows his own plans to be confounded (even if he does so in such a way that he can then make something new out of them). History shows this. First the sin of Adam upsets God's plans. And God answers this by giving himself more powerfully, by giving himself in Christ.

That is, so to say, the one great example. There are many other lesser ones. Let's take the people of Israel. They were supposed to live in a theocracy, an arrangement whereby there were no human rulers, but only judges who applied the divine Law. But the Israelites wanted a king. They wanted to be like other people. And they wrecked the plan. God gave way. He gave them Saul, then David, and from that point he built the road to Christ again, to the King who overthrew all monarchy by dying on the Cross.

We have here models by which Scripture would have us understand that God fully accepts freedom, on the one hand—and, on the other, is greater than we and is able to make a new beginning out of failure, out of destruction, a new beginning that in some way improves on the original and appears greater and better. How that can be—that God knows everything but that other plans are still possible—the greatest theologians and philosophers have racked their brains over it. At some point it is beyond us, simply because we are not God and because our horizons are in the end extremely limited.

But I think we can understand what is obvious: God holds history in his hand, holds me in his hand, but leaves me the freedom to become a loving person for myself—or to refuse love. God has not absolutely programmed me but has built in those possibilities for variation that we call freedom.

Are Miracles Real?

Faith sees miracles as being always possible, and within their own lifetimes the apostles were offered a lot of money for the secret of their miraculous powers.

There are plenty of provocative accounts of inexplicable events, which move some people to mockery and others to awe. In the great basilica of Padua, for instance, you can see in a shrine the tongue of Saint Anthony, who is said to have been a great preacher. In Nevers the body of Bernadette is preserved, and in Ars that of Saint John Vianney; both are incorrupt. And they are not embalmed, as was the case with the Communists' saint, Lenin. How can that be? If we could ask God himself, what would he say about these miracles?

I certainly don't feel qualified to tell you what God would say. But the question of miracles is there, and a part of what Christians believe is that God has power in the world and really can do things.

To what extent natural laws are broken in this, or whether these laws already have implicit within them a degree of variation that God can make use of, is not the primary question. We can see nowadays, with increasing clarity, that we know the laws of nature only as rules of thumb. What nature is, how universally applicable the laws of nature are, in the end we cannot say with certainty. What is important is to notice that God, after he made creation, did not retire. Retire, in the sense of: Now the machine can go on running in the way it's been set up. No, God can do things. He is still the Creator and is still able to intervene.

Is every intervention a miracle?

We can't twist that into a superstitious view of miracles, as if we could have miracles available on order. We can't make cheap miracle recipes. But we cannot, either, in a rationalistic way know better than God and presume to tell God what he can and cannot do.

I read a very interesting remark on this point. It comes from a book about the Protestant theologian Adolf Schlatter, who was a very firm believer. Schlatter was given an appointment in Berlin, at the time when Adolf Harnack, the great liberal theologian, was teaching there. The Lutheran church intended thereby to balance the liberalism of Harnack to some extent.

Harnack was a truly noble man. Although this appointment was a move against him, he welcomed Schlatter in a most positive manner and said, This is quite right, we will be able to understand each other. And indeed they worked well together. On one occasion, at some session or discussion, when someone alluded to the points of opposition between the two theologians, Harnack said, The two of us, Herr Schlatter and I, are divided only on the question of miracles. Upon which Schlatter called out, No, on the question of God! for the question of miracles poses the question of God. Anyone who does not recognize miracles has a different idea of God.

I think that hits the nail right on the head. It's not a matter of whether or not we recognize this or that unusual event as a miracle. It's whether God remains God. And whether he is still able to make himself known in the world as Creator and Lord.

John Paul II said once: "If you concern yourself with God, then you can receive some of his light, light that shows you the way of the Lord and reveals a little of God's plan." Does that mean that with faith we can even see into the future?

We can indeed recognize something of God's plan. This knowledge goes beyond that of my personal fate and my individual path. By its light we can look back on history as a whole and see that this is not a random process but a road that leads to a particular goal. We can come to know an inner logic, the logic of God, within apparently chance happenings.

Even if this does not enable us to predict what is going to happen at this or that point, nonetheless we may develop a certain sensitivity for the dangers contained in certain things —and for the hopes that are in others. A sense of the future develops, in that I see what destroys the future—because it is contrary to the inner logic of the road—and what, on the other hand, leads onward—because it opens the positive doors and corresponds to the inner design of the whole. To that extent the ability to diagnose the future can develop.

It's the same with the prophets. They are not to be understood as seers, but as voices who understand time from God's point of view and can therefore warn us against what is destructive—and, on the other hand, show us the right road forward.

If Jesus Christ is the Son of God and God himself, almighty and omniscient, then we would perhaps also have to say: Yes, at that hour, two thousand years ago, when he hung in agony on the Cross, he knew me. Through his divine foreknowledge, he already knew my name.

In the Letter to the Galatians, Paul says: "He knew me and gave himself up for me." From a purely empirical standpoint, of course, he did not know Paul. But Paul knew that he had been called by the risen Christ, that the eyes of the Lord had sought him out.

We ought not to try to imagine how Christ could, as a man, run his eye over all the infinite number of persons in history; but that when all is said and done, in that moment of agony in the garden, in the moment of his Yes to the Cross, he had us in mind, that he knew me as well, we can say that. This action comprehends the decision of love that was made in eternity and that is formative and determinative in the temporal life of Christ. Thus I know that I am not just someone born later, standing outside the circle of light, but that there is a personal relationship with me, whose vital root is in Christ's very act of self-giving.

God, Yes—Church, No?

The original meaning of the Greek word Church *is: "Those belonging to the Lord". Does that mean that the Church belongs to God himself?*

Exactly. *Ekklesia* means *called out*, those who are called out. The word in its technical sense refers to the "assembly", and in the Greek-speaking area people thought of the democratic assemblies of that time. But in Christian usage its reference was to the assembly at Sinai, the assembly of the people of Israel. In that way it refers to "those called together by God", those who have gathered together with him, who belong to God and who know that he is in their midst.

The underlying notion is, as you said, that the Church has been appropriated by God to be his particular possession in the world, something that especially belongs to him, the living temple. The Christians took quite seriously the idea that God does not live in stone but is alive. Those people in whom he is alive and who belong to him, accordingly, form his true temple. The expression *people of God* also signifies belonging to God in a special way—and living on the basis of being owned by him.

In the course of two thousand years of Christian history, the Church has divided time and again. In the meantime, there are around three hundred distinguishable Protestant, Orthodox, or other churches. There are way over a thousand Baptist groups in the United States.

Over against these there is still the Roman Catholic Church with the pope at her head, which claims to be the only true Church. She remains at any rate, and despite every crisis, indeed the most universal, historically significant, and successful Church in the world, with more members today than at any time in her history.

I think that in the spirit of Vatican II we ought not to see that as a triumph for our prowess as Catholics and ought not to make much of the institutional and numerical strength we continue to enjoy. If we were to reckon that as our achievement and as our right, then we would step outside the role of a people belonging to God and set ourselves up as an association in our own right. And that can very quickly go wrong. A Church may have great institutional power in a country, but as soon as faith is no longer there to back it up, the institution will break down.

Perhaps you know the mediaeval story of a Jew who traveled to the papal court and who became a Catholic. On his return, someone who knew the papal court well asked him: "Did you realize what sort of things are going on there?" "Yes," he said, "of course, quite scandalous things, I saw it all." "And you still became a Catholic", remarked the other man. "That's completely perverse!" Then the Jew said, "It is because of all that that I have become a Catholic. For if the Church continues to exist in spite of it all, then truly there must be someone upholding her." And there is another story, to the effect that Napoleon once declared that he would destroy the Church. Whereupon one of the cardinals replied, "Not even we have managed that!"

I believe that we see something important in these paradoxical tales. There have in fact always been plenty of human monstrosities in the Catholic Church. That she still holds together, even if she groans and creaks, that she is still in existence, that she produces great martyrs and great believers, people who put their whole lives at her service, as missionaries, as nurses, as teachers, that really does show that there is someone there upholding her.

We cannot, then, reckon the Church's success as our own reward, but we may still say, with Vatican II—even if the Lord has given a great deal of life to other churches and communities—that the Church herself, as an active agent, has survived and is present in *this* agent. And that can only be explained by the fact that *he* grants what men cannot achieve.

Guardini once described the purpose of the Church thus: "She must steadily hold out to man the final verities, the ultimate image of perfection, the most fundamental principles of value, and must not permit herself to be confused by any passion, by any alteration of sentiment, by any trick of self-seeking." A difficult requirement.

Yes, but one that is right. Even if in this case it is expressed with strictness. Guardini, who was such a very understanding man, loved to set out requirements uncompromisingly, and that is also important. We must not drown the requirements in compromise until they gradually disappear from view. The Church cannot act according to the motto: What is going to be possible; what is not? She is not there in order to discover the most acceptable form of compromise, but to hold out to people, without distortion, the whole magnitude of God's Word and his will—even if this speaks against herself and against her own spokesmen.

I am always impressed by what Paul says in his farewell speech to the presbyters at Ephesus (he already knew that he would be made prisoner when he reached Jerusalem). I have told you, he said, about the *whole* will of God. I have not kept anything back from you, nor have I sought to make it easier for you. Nor have I given you my own version, but have proclaimed to you the whole will of God! And that is what the Church is for.

Presumably it has never occurred to you to leave the Church. Isn't there anything about the Church that annoys or irritates you?

Leaving the Church would indeed never have entered my head. I feel so much at home in her, my life has been bound up with her from my birth, that leaving her would maim or even destroy me.

Of course there are things about her, big and little, that are annoying. From the local Church, right up to the Church's overall leadership, within which I now have to work. People are always involved, and this always gives rise to annoyance. But you don't leave your family because you're annoyed; and certainly not if the love that binds you together is stronger, if that is what upholds you in life.

And so it is with the Church. Here too, I know that I am not here on account of this or that; I know that there have been so many mistakes in history, that there may be concrete irritations. But I know also that none of these things can take away the essential quality of the Church. Simply because that comes from a quite different source—and will always reassert itself.

Joseph Roth writes in his novel, The Radetzky March*: "In this decaying world the Roman Church is the only thing left to give shape to life, to help life to keep its shape. Yes, we could even say, that she dispenses shape. . . . In instituting sin, she is already forgiving it. She does not allow the existence of any faultless human beings: this is the really human thing about her. . . . Thereby the*

Roman Church demonstrates her most eminent characteristic, that of pardoning, of forgiving." Is the Church in essence a Church of sinners?

Quite obviously! We have just seen how the Church is upheld by God in spite of sinners. This quotation articulates a particular way of looking at the Church, which sees her as being good and useful on purely secular grounds. One quite essential aspect of the Church is that she gives shape to life, that she upholds a certain shape, that she is not blurred in a mist of uncertainties, that she can say what God's will is. If we understand her purely as a historical entity, then we put God at the service of human ends. In that case we begin to see people wanting to have some kind of religion, but regarding God himself merely as a useful construct for the purpose of keeping people together and bringing them close to you.

On the other hand, I would criticize what was said about the Catholic Church having instituted sin and then forgiven it straightaway. The Church does not invent sins but recognizes the will of God and has to declare it. Of course, the great thing in this quotation is that upon the Church, which has to declare the will of God in its full magnitude, in its unconditional rigor, so that man should know his true measure, is bestowed as a gift, at the same time, the task of forgiving.

In practice, the Church can say to people: Whoever tries to be in the right on the basis of his own resources, whoever believes he can live in such a way as to need no forgiveness, commits an offense. There is an arrogance in that, a pride in one's own achievement and in being self-made, which in the end is inhuman.

The point really is that we should not have this kind of

vanity at all. And I should never reach the point of not needing to be forgiven. On the contrary, if I am trying to live more and more according to the will of God, to identify his will with my own, then I know, too, that I shall always be forgiven. I am a being who has the humility to accept the fact that I need forgiveness. In this respect, humility and trust are what make a man truly human.

"Yes to God, No to the Church" has become a popular slogan. Saint Cyprian, bishop of Carthage (200–258), said on this point: "Outside the Church there is no salvation", since "Whoever does not have the Church for his Mother, does not have God for his Father." Is that still true today?

It is not true in the sense that implies that all non-Christians are destined for hell. But it does mean that we need our mother, even if we don't know her; the community, which brings us to birth in the faith and which presents us to God.

Cyprian is talking about the relationship between God and the Church in the context of persecution. He is thinking of people who leave the Church because of their fear of being martyred and who think that they will, of course, still keep on with Christ and God. He is telling them that whoever leaves the living community, the living body, is climbing out of Noah's ark and will drown in the flood. It is in this sense that he is showing them how the Church and faith in Christ are indivisible.

I cannot just make Christ my private possession and try to keep him for myself. To a certain extent, the discomfort of belonging to his family goes along with Christ himself. Faith has been bestowed on us in this community context; it is not otherwise available. Cyprian did not invent any theory concerning what God will do about those who did not know the Church. Even Saint Paul, who so insists on the importance of the Church, tells us that we must behave as we should *within* the Church; *God* will do whatever he is going to do about those outside; *he* will judge them. Thus Paul, too, does not evolve any theory about how God will settle the business about those others. But he does tell us that whoever has come face-to-face with Christ cannot separate him from the Church; it is within her that he must live the life of Christ.

This has remained a pressing question for two thousand years.

Perhaps I may add one more thing: Nowadays the situation has changed a little further. Johann Baptist Metz once said that the formula today is: No to God, Yes to religion. People want to have some kind of religion, esoteric or whatever it may be. But a personal God, who speaks to me, who knows me personally, who has said something quite specific and who has met me with a specific demand, and who will also judge me—people don't want him. What we see is religion being separated from God. People don't want to do without this sensation of the Wholly Other, this special religious feeling, entirely; they want it available in many shapes and forms. But there is in the end no guarantee of its continuing to be there, unless the will of God and God himself are also present. In that sense we are not so much in the middle of a religious crisis—religions are springing up all over the place—as in the middle of a God crisis.

This morning I wanted to go to the Mass of the Benedictine community in the church here at Monte Cassino. I was late getting there, and I was in a real hurry. But to my misfortune there was no one to be seen anywhere who might have helped me. I wandered around like a blind man in this monastery, which is as big as a town, almost swearing, but I could not find the blooming way to get there. There were innumerable doors, and I knocked on them, but they all led nowhere in particular, at any rate not to the place I was so desperately searching for. Is it ever possible to find one's way to God, to the Church, alone?

Certainly not completely alone. Part of the essence of Christianity—and this is included in the concept of the Church—is that our relationship to God is not just an inner one, one made up of my "I" and his "Thou", but is also a matter of being spoken to, of being led. A meeting is part of every path to conversion. The Church is there so that people who have searched for the door and found it can be in her. Among all the variety of temperaments, there will always be someone who suits me and who has the right word to say to me.

As human beings we are there so that God can come to people by way of other people. He always comes to people through people. So we, too, always come to him through other people who are being led by him, in whom he himself meets us and opens us up to him. If we could lift ourselves up to the ultimate degree simply by reading Holy Scripture, then this would be just another philosophical movement, without this element of community that is such a vital element in faith.

The emperor demanded of Saint Lawrence in Rome that he should hand over the treasures of the Church. A little while later Lawrence, who was to die as a martyr on this account, came into the presence of the emperor and showed him the great army of poor people in the city, with these words: "This is the greatest treasure of the Church."

Holy Scripture tells us, indeed, that Christ came from among the poor of Israel. On the fortieth day after his birth, his Mother brought the gift of the poor and showed us thereby that among these simple people the inner vision had remained clear. They had not lost sight of the whole by splitting it with a thousand distinctions, but had conserved an inner simplicity, a purity, truthfulness, and goodness that can see clearly.

Of course, the Church needs intellectuals too, absolutely. She needs people who will put their spiritual powers at her disposal. She also needs generous wealthy people, who want to place the power of wealth at the service of what is good. But she still lives also on the enormous strength of those people who are humble believers. In this sense the great host of those who need love and who give love is indeed her true treasure: simple people who are capable of truth because, as the Lord says, they have remained children. Through all the changes of history they have retained their perception of what is essential and have kept alive in the Church the spirit of humility and of love.

With the coming of Christ, so we are taught, the "end time" has already begun. Along with it, the "Age of the Church" has dawned, which will last until the Lord comes again. What does that mean? In other words, is the fortune or misfortune of the earth, and of all its people, inseparable from the fortune or misfortune of the Catholic Church? Or, to put it even more pointedly: If it hadn't been for the prayer and the activity of the Church, would God quite possibly have long since allowed the world to perish?

Let us leave what God would have done, and what he could have done, an open question. But even by purely empirical criteria it is quite evident, it seems to me, that the Catholic Church has a quite fundamental part to play in the movement of history. If her faith collapsed and she were to declare herself, so to speak, spiritually bankrupt and say, We have been mistaken, then a fracture would run through the whole of history and of mankind, the implications of which would be quite unimaginable.

We have already seen how the postconciliar crisis, if it did not trigger the crisis of '68, without doubt enormously reinforced it. In any case, one cannot conceive that particular drama without it. And that is merely what we can, so to speak, comprehend and see. You have quite rightly spoken of deeper things, the power of prayer, of faith, of love. God is brought into this world by those means, so that something of his light can spread abroad among mankind. If this power were to disappear, that would be a historical catastrophe.

Part I

GOD

Cardinal, even though the progress of modern science uncovers more and more of the secrets of creation, in the end it will for us probably remain forever an enigma. Why has God never just stood up and said: Right now, everyone listen! I'm going to tell you just how it was done and how everything in your little world works.

The creation is indeed a mystery, and the more we know about it, the more physics is able to see into the delicate structure of matter, the more mysterious it appears. The history of mankind, with all its imponderables and its impenetrable elements, just adds another entire world of mystery.

To the question, "Why did God make it like that?" we cannot, of course, give any final answer. Why does he keep so quiet? Why is he so powerless in the world? That is a question the believer in particular must always be asking himself. Or, Why is he not more unambiguous and unmistakable? On the other hand, we have to recognize that our standpoint has a necessarily limited perspective. It would not help us if we were suddenly offered a complete explanation for the world and able to see its workings, as this would transcend all our capacities. We can only hope to accept God as he is and thereby to make sense of it.

What sense should we make of it?

I believe that by setting forth on the adventure of a history that is not ultimately comprehensible, but which is, surely, guided and carried forward by his Love, we shall bit by bit begin to see. In this way we are set a task that is appropriate for us humans. It's not a matter of having a demonstration set before us, as a finished article, but always just enough for us to follow a path and thereby ourselves contribute something to the mystery and the greatness of the world. I would say that we are given enough to live by. And the limit of our knowledge is not only a challenge but also a gift. It leads us into the adventure of going on, of learning, in which our measures of reality expand. The presupposition for this is in fact always the act of humility, of bowing our heads before the God we cannot comprehend.

1. Man

The theologian Hans Urs von Balthasar—what a marvelous name for a theologian!—said that everything can be seen in two ways, that is to say: as a fact and as a mystery. Regarded as a fact, man is a marginal phenomenon in the universe, produced by chance. But seen as a mystery, he was produced, for his own sake, by the will of God. Is that part of the basic understanding that is essential for any approach to the Christian view of the world and of man?

Yes, I would certainly say so. To start with, we become aware of facts, what is the case. That is also true of history, in which everything, basically, might have been different. No one, of course, can be satisfied with mere facts. If only for the reason that we ourselves are mere facts, and yet we know that we can and should be more than just something that exists by chance.

For this reason it is essential to look beyond sheer factual reality and to recognize that man was not just thrown up into the world by some quirk of evolution. The underlying truth is that each person is meant to exist. Each person is God's own idea. Within everything that just for the moment exists factually, a plan and an idea are at work, and this gives meaning to my search for my own ideal self and to my coexistence with the world and with the onward path of history.

Each person is God's idea? What does that mean?

Yes, that is the basic Christian belief. When Holy Scripture presents an image of the creation of man—with God as the potter, who shapes him and who then breathes the spirit of life into him—that is meant as being archetypical for each and every one of us. In the psalms, man says with respect to himself: YOU have shaped me with clay; YOU have breathed into me the breath of life. What is thereby portrayed is the fact that each person stands in direct relationship with God. And each has thus in the great web of world history a significant place and role that have been assigned to him and by means of which he can make an irreplaceable contribution to history as a whole.

The Breath of God

In the beginning the earth was bare and empty; God had not yet made it rain, is what it says in Genesis. Then God fashioned man, and for this purpose he took "dust from the field and blew into his nostrils the breath of life; thus the man became a living creature". The breath of life—is that the answer to the question of where we come from?

I think we have here a most important image, which presents a significant understanding of what man is. It suggests that man is one who springs from the earth and its possibilities. We can even read into this representation something like evolution. But that's not all. There is something more, which does not come from the earth and which has not simply been developed, but which is completely new: and that is God's own breath.

The essential point in this picture is the double nature of man. It shows both the way he belongs to the universe and also his direct relation to God. The Christian faith says that what we learn here about the first man is true of every man. That each and every human being has, on the one hand, a biological origin and yet, on the other, is more than just a product of the available genes and DNA, but comes directly from God.

Man has within him the breath of God. He is capable of relating to God; he can pass beyond material creation. He is unique. He stands in the sight of God and is in a special sense directed toward God. There is indeed a new breath within him, the divine factor that has been introduced into creation. It is most important to see this special creation by God in order to perceive the uniqueness and value of man and, thereby, the basis of all human rights. This gives man a reverence for himself and for others. God's breath is within him. He sees that he is not just a combination of biological building blocks, but a personal conception of God.

The first man, into whom God breathes his breath, is called Adam. This name is, on one hand, the Hebrew word for a human being, but at the same time is a play of words on Adama, *clay. The Lord planted a garden for this man, so it says, in Eden. Does this picture tell us clearly what we are meant for?*

At any rate it gives us some glimmer of an idea. The garden is an image for the undamaged creation and for the secure existence within it. Here creation is neither destroyed nor abused, but nourished and protected—and its development shaped by the Spirit. All in all, this image presents the breadth, the joy, and the safe existence within creation. It tells us that God intended us to live in inner harmony with creation, as well as in the security represented by life with him. In that sense these two conditions, being guardian of creation and being in direct contact with God, so as to carry on the work of creation together with him, really are suggested in this image.

Genesis shows us that creation is a process. Everything takes place step by step. "It is not good", God saw in the course of this process, "that man should be alone. I will make him a helpmate for a partner." So next God made from the earth all the different animals of the field and all the birds of the air and brought them to the man to see what he would call them.

A good opportunity, actually, to talk about animals, our closest companions. Adam gave each of them a name. Are we allowed to make use of animals, and even to eat them?

That is a very serious question. At any rate, we can see that they are given into our care, that we cannot just do whatever we want with them. Animals, too, are God's creatures, and even if they do not have the same direct relation to God that man has, they are still creatures of his will, creatures we must respect as companions in creation and as important elements in the creation.

As far as whether we are allowed to kill and to eat animals, there is a remarkable ordering of matters in Holy Scripture. We can read how, at first, only plants are mentioned as providing food for man. Only after the flood, that is to say, after a new breach has opened between God and man, are we told that man eats flesh. That is to say, a secondary way of ordering life is introduced, and it comes in second place in the story as we are told it. Nonetheless, and even if someone feels hurt by our using animals in this way, we should not proceed from this to a kind of sectarian cult of animals.

For this, too, is permitted to man. He should always maintain his respect for these creatures, but he knows at the same time that he is not forbidden to take food from them. Certainly, a sort of industrial use of creatures, so that geese are fed in such a way as to produce as large a liver as possible, or hens live so packed together that they become just caricatures of birds, this degrading of living creatures to a commodity seems to me in fact to contradict the relationship of mutuality that comes across in the Bible.

Certainly, the animal world itself presents a strikingly brutal aspect of creation. We all know how dear little kittens may, from one moment to the next, hunt down, torment, and kill others of their own kind. The one that survives is the one that obviously has the greatest capability of destroying others.

It is in fact one of the great riddles of creation that there seems to be a law of brutality. The Catholic writer Reinhold Schneider, who himself was inclined to suffer from depression, exposed all the horrific elements in nature and in the animal world with the truly microscopic vision of someone who suffers himself. He let himself be brought by this to the point of despairing of God and of creation.

In her faith, the Church has always seen it in this way: that the destructive effect of the Fall works itself out in the whole of creation. Creation no longer simply reflects the will of God; the whole thing is somehow distorted. We are confronted there by riddles. The dangers to which man is exposed are already made visible in the animal world.

Men and Women

Now comes the moment, in Genesis, that perhaps first turns the world into our world of men. The principle of partnership is now unfolded, and the Bible clothes this event in a very lovely picture: "But the man found no helpmate to be a partner for him", it says. God made the man fall into a deep slumber; then he took one of the ribs from his side and closed the place over with flesh. The Lord God fashioned the rib into a woman and brought her to Adam.

Then the man said, "Now at last this is bone of my bone and flesh of my flesh." Henceforward, a man would leave his father and his mother and be joined to his wife, and the two would become one flesh.

Adam, that is, literally, "the man", called his wife Eve. *"Eve" means life, and so Eve became the mother of all living creatures. Perhaps men have never yet quite got over this gift of a bone; in this figure there seems to be a great mystery concealed.*

This, too, is one of the great archetypal images the Bible gives us, so that through them we can glimpse things that we can scarcely bring into conceptual form. In the first place, the common nature of man and woman is expressed there. They are *one* being and have *one and the same* human dignity. At any rate, their equal dignity is depicted here in the most splendid fashion. The other point is their being turned toward each other. This is shown in the wound, which is present in all of us and which leads us to turn to each other.

The image we meet here in Scripture runs in different variants through the entire history of religions. Plato, too, tells the myth of how man was divided in two and how the two halves became man and woman. Each of them, seen in this light, is only a half—and hence, each is forever seeking its other half. The translation as "rib" is, anyway, uncertain. Perhaps the same picture is being presented here, of how man is divided and each part is thus made to fit the other. The man for the woman, the woman for the man. They are searching for each other so as to find their wholeness together.

And this wholeness cannot otherwise be achieved?

Man is created with a need for others, so that he may pass beyond his own limits. He needs to be completed. He is not made to be alone—that is not good for him—but is made to turn toward someone else. He must look for himself in the other person and find himself in him.

In this text from Genesis there follows the prophetic declaration that the man will on this account leave his father and his mother and will become one flesh with the woman. They will be one flesh with each other, one united human being. The entire drama of the two sexes' need for each other, of their being turned toward each other, is contained within this declaration. In addition it is also said that they are there in order to give themselves each to the other, so as to make the gift of new life in doing so, and then finally to devote themselves to this new life. In this sense, the mystery of marriage is contained within it, and basically the family is likewise envisaged.

We might sometimes think that women, representing as it were a second attempt, are an improved version of creation, more successful than men. They seem to be not only more beautiful but also maybe more fully developed as persons.

I wouldn't want to get into that argument. It is indisputable that women have particular gifts, that in many ways they are stronger and have a greater capacity for suffering. That, by virtue of the particular way that has been given them to express their love, they are able to carry within them another person and can themselves give flesh and blood to that person, all of this gives woman a particular distinction and her own special status. For the rest, we should each of us, man or woman, give ourselves into God's hands and try to realize the wholeness of human existence in our life together.

The question is whether men and women are not, in reality, two fundamentally different kinds of being?

Yes, but we will not agree to that. There is one kind of human being. And because the body is not just an exterior addition to man, then these physical differences naturally affect the person as a whole, and the difference represents two distinct ways of being human. I think we should be equally opposed to false theories of equality and to false theories of difference.

It is false when people want men and women to be cut to the same measure and say that this tiny biological difference has absolutely no significance. That tendency is dominant nowadays. Personally it still horrifies me when people want women to be soldiers just like men, when they, who have always been the keepers of the peace and in whom we have always seen a counter-impulse working against the male impulse to stand up and fight, now likewise run around with submachine guns, showing that they can be just as warlike as the men. Or that women now have the "right" to work as garbage collectors or miners, to do all those things that, out of respect for their status, for their different nature, their own dignity, we ought not to inflict on them and that are now imposed on them in the name of equality. That, in my opinion, is a Manichaean ideology that is opposed to the body.

But it is far from being a new, contemporary invention.

Plato said that men and women should be put in the same barracks, that they should do all the same things, because biology didn't count. The only thing that counts in man is the spirit, and if children arrive, then they should be put into a state nursery. Basically this ideology of equality is a kind of "spiritualism", a way of despising the body that refuses to recognize that the body itself is the person. Because of this, it seems to me, this kind of egalitarianism does not exalt women but diminishes their status. By being treated as male, they are dragged down to being undistinguished and ordinary.

There is also of course a false ideology of difference. Through that it became customary to regard women as lower beings, who are only there to do the cooking and the cleaning, while the lords of creation talk and make war and regard themselves as a superior caste with a superior field of activities. From that standpoint, women were regarded as being physical, sensual, not open to spiritual things, not creative, and so on and so forth. Thus the ideology of difference developed into a caste system. This way of looking at things overlooks the particular quality of God's creation, in which differentiation exists as complementarity within unity.

It's not infrequent for partnerships to end in a dispute between the sexes.

Man and woman belong to each other. They both have their gifts, which they have to develop so as to realize and to bring to fruition the whole breadth of what it means to be human. That this diversity in unity includes tensions and can lead to attempts to break apart is something we well know. That is the case in every friendship. The closer you are, the easier it is to get in each other's hair.

Love makes a demand that cannot leave me untouched. In love I cannot simply remain *myself*, but I always have to lose myself by having my rough edges taken off, by being hurt. And it is just this—that it hurts me so as to bring out more of my potential—it seems to me, that constitutes the greatness of love, that is part of its healing power. To that extent we should not think of love just as romantic love, so that, so to speak, heaven comes down to earth for the two lovers when they find each other, and they then live happily ever after.

We must think of love as suffering. Only if we are ready to endure it as suffering and thus ever again to accept each other and once again to take the other to ourselves, only then can a lifelong partnership develop. If, on the contrary, we say when we get to the critical point, I want to avoid that, and we separate, then what we are really renouncing is the true opportunity that is to be found in man and woman being turned toward each other and in the reality of love.

Beyond Eden—The Fall

We have already spoken of a certain derangement of the created order. This perception is at the basis of the doctrine of original sin, which was developed by Augustine. This teaching has been, and still is, the subject of dispute even within the Church. The story is that through the sin of Adam, who turned away from God and who, being tempted by Eve, ate of the fruit of the tree of knowledge, death and sin came into the world. In Genesis it even says that man and woman suddenly felt afraid of God. Can the Fall be reckoned as the universal characteristic of man as such?

Not as *the* universal characteristic of man, but as a reality whose presence we can perceive—even if we can recognize its origin only in images. A friend of mine, who is now dead, a very independent, critical person, once said: Well, I have difficulty with many doctrines. But there is one doctrine I don't need to believe at all, because I experience it every day, and that is original sin.

In our reflections about man there is a fault line that will always become visible to us, a certain disorder within man, in that he is not the person he ought to be able to be. This disorder is presented to us in Genesis as, so to speak, a starting point for history. The Old Testament does not draw the logical conclusion, the doctrine of original sin, but an awareness certainly developed with increasing clarity that men always incline toward evil. And the biblical God himself says, both before and after the flood, "I see that they are but flesh; they are weak; they incline toward evil."

It was Augustine who set out the doctrine of original sin systematically, that is true, but its essence is already to be found in Saint Paul's Letter to the Romans. Paul rereads the Genesis story in the light of Christ. And he recognizes that this story of the beginning is already telling what happens in the *whole* of history. This pride has been present in man from the very beginning, this desire to have for himself the key to all knowledge, to be able to do without God and to have the key to life itself, the desire never to die, and so on. Withdrawal from God leads inevitably to hiding from God. The confidence of love turns suddenly into fear of the dangerous and frighteningly powerful God.

Does that mean that man was dominated from the beginning by his obsession with knowledge and that therein lies his whole misfortune?

For Paul the Genesis story is at any rate an image of the way that this disorder has been present in a mysterious way from the very beginning. It is a condition of the whole of human history, and we have to reckon with it. Certainly, we were unable to put a name to this condition, or to form a clear idea of it, until the power that is able to overcome it had made its appearance. Only after Christ had come, and had taken steps against it, did we find this condition bearable and were able, so to speak, to admit its existence.

Besides Paul's Letter to the Romans there is the second chapter of the Letter to the Philippians, a primitive Christian hymn, which was known before Paul came to write. Adam's impulse, according to this, was to try to seize the key to all knowledge and thus to possess what God had reserved to himself. Thus he wanted to set himself up as high as God and to be able to do without him.

God for his part initiates a contrary movement by giving Christ down into the poverty of human existence, right as far as the death on the Cross. In that way he opens up the door for us again, through which we can come to God once more, and shows us how pride lies at the heart of all sins. At the same time he shares our suffering, so as to draw us again into the relationship of the family of God. I believe that we should therefore never read the Genesis story without keeping in mind at the same time the story of Christ.

But original sin was not banished from the world by the death of Christ on the Cross.

No, we can all see that; it's still here. But what was before just a baffling barrier and disorder that we could not overcome or get beyond has now found its remedy in the forgiving power of God. This means that our actions, our life, our behavior are not unimportant, but they are set in a new context, while at the same time we are given a pattern of the life of faith that, as we walk in the company of Jesus, also offers a way to overcome these disorders.

In any case, it was not only Adam and Eve who were shut out from sanctifying grace by God, but the whole of mankind. Why? What could those born afterward do about it?

The great question really is exactly how we are to understand this word "original" and the continuing presence of this disorder. We certainly get stuck here, in trying to formulate an answer. But let us take up the cue you gave with *sanctifying grace.*

The loss of this grace means the breaking off of a certain relationship. The original trusting, living relationship with God, which at the same time strengthens and heals the relationships of human beings with each other, is torn asunder; the relation between them is disturbed; God is hidden from us. We hide ourselves from him, and because we have so thoroughly concealed ourselves from him, we cannot see him either.

It is this disordered relationship, this world of disordered relationships, into which we are born. And we can then see that this is portrayed in the Bible in a way that is marvelous from the psychological viewpoint, how in their conversation after the Fall Adam and Eve blame each other and each unloads his guilt onto the other. The disruption of the relationship with God, then, immediately sets them at odds with each other. For anyone who has turned against God has by the same token turned against others.

What is meant by the idea that the loss of sanctifying grace lies at the heart of original sin is that a certain disruption of relationships has become a part of the texture of human history. Precisely because we are not, as individuals, directly responsible for this, but encounter it as part of the existing situation, we stand in need of the one who straightens the relationship out. And because God has no intention of simply torturing or tormenting or straightforwardly punishing people, he turns himself into the one who restores this relationship and thus overcomes the disruption. As soon as we speak of *original sin*, a disrupted relationship, into whose distortions we find ourselves thrust, then we must always go on to say that God set to work at once to rebuild the relationship and to make it right. If we ever talk about the concept of original sin without mentioning God's response, then we pass into the realm of the absurd.

Then the eyes of them both were opened, it goes on in the Bible story, "And they realized that they were naked. They wove fig leaves together and made themselves aprons." I think we can scarcely accept that such an ancient and elemental myth has anything to do with a prudish morality?

No, of course not. This demonstrates how man, who is no longer standing in the splendor of God, and of course no longer sees the other in the light of that splendor, now stands as it were naked before others, and it is no longer possible for each simply to accept the other as he is. Here, too, damage has been inflicted on normal relationships. We hide from each other in clothing—or we feel compelled to provide ourselves with a social identity, so to speak, in this way. The garment is thus a symbolic representation of the attempt to be ourselves, whereby we attempt an external restoration of the personal dignity that has suffered intimate damage.

Through a theology or a philosophy of clothing, which is implied here, we touch on a profound anthropological insight that I believe we need to consider in more detail. But certainly it is not just a matter of setting up moral prudery as the main consequence of original sin.

The Soul

What kind of creatures are we *remains one of the fundamental questions for man, as well as that of* where *we come from. Saint Augustine put into words this longing for an answer. Long before Sigmund Freud, he was always and everywhere interested in just two things, as he himself says: "I want to know God and know the soul, nothing else at all."*

In this respect, the story of creation distinguishes between two great realms. The realm of bodily, physical things and the realm of the spirit. Man stands in the middle and, consequently, shares in both realms. He is made up of body and soul, as both a physical and a spiritual being. And his soul is a spiritual being. Is that something like a fair summary of our basic makeup?

To some extent. Man is indeed a kind of bridge. He is the point at which the material world and the spiritual world meet and mingle and thus occupies a special place in the matrix of the created order.

Through man, the material world is lifted up into the spiritual realm, and through their combination in man we see that the two are compatible, each with the other. Material being is not a thing along side of which the spirit leads an unconnected and indivisible existence. The unity of creation is demonstrated at the point where the two are united in man. That gives him a quite special function: that is to say, sharing the responsibility for the unity of creation, incarnating spirit in himself and, conversely, lifting material being up to God—and thereby, all in all, making a contribution to the great symphony of creation.

Man's genetic code is now reckoned to be almost unlocked. But there is one thing that scientists will probably always be left wondering about: Where is the seat of our soul? Does faith have the answer?

Just as we cannot assign a geographical location to God, let's say up above Mars or wherever, in the same way we cannot pin down the soul geographically, either in the heart or in the brain, as did the two great anthropological theories of antiquity. The soul is not like that. It has no corporal location, but occupies the whole of man. The Old Testament presents us with a whole range of symbolism for the soul. It talks about the liver, about the nerves, about the womb, about the heart; it mentions the most various organs of the body. The whole body plays its part in spiritual as well as physical life. The different organs give symbolic expression to different aspects of human existence and to different aspects of the human soul, but at the same time they show us how the whole of the body is inhabited by the soul and gives expression to the soul in various and specific ways. To some extent we can say that there are places where the soul is especially present, but there is no geography of the soul.

Is the conscience, which sometimes torments us so terribly, a part of the soul? Or is the conscience, as some people believe, only a product of our upbringing?

The actual workings of the conscience are, of course, those of a living organism. It can, accordingly, either develop and grow in a person or wither and be stunted. One cannot deny that the way in which the conscience actually operates is determined by the social realities around one. Both the helpful factors that awaken and develop the conscience and also those that threaten it, that stunt its development or distort it —by which it develops in the wrong direction and becomes a false conscience, whether lax or over-scrupulous—these factors are all to be found in the social environment.

Are there people without a conscience?

I would venture to assert that no human being can just kill off other people without knowing that that is wrong; in some corner of his mind, he knows it is wrong. It is impossible for someone to see another person in desperate need without feeling that he really ought to do something about it. There is, so to say, a primitive reaction within every human being, a basic instinct for good and evil.

And even though they tried to train SS members to believe that they had to kill for the sake of the German race and that that was something good to do, and though Göring said that Adolf Hitler is our conscience and that he was the only standard of right and wrong, these people still knew that that was not right. And in that way, in such situations of quite basic attacks upon human existence, it repeatedly becomes clear that man has a deep and inner consciousness of such things. To that extent, morality is not just something instilled in him from without, by education, but is, in the form of a basic capacity to choose between good and evil, a part of his spiritual makeup.

In the rite of the Holy Mass it says at one point, "but only say the word, and my soul shall be healed." Is God the only one who can heal our soul?

Only he can, in the end. But in order to heal it, he has set up healing powers all around us. Here again, it is the fact that our relationship with God develops by the agency of other people. God willed it thus, so that he comes to us through other people—and through these other people, in the sacrament of penance, he gives the word that basically only he can give. In the end only God can say, Your sins are forgiven, because these sins are in the last analysis an offense against him.

Any healing certainly requires the participation of other people, requires their pardon, their acceptance, their kindness. Only through such a process of companionship and sharing, illuminated by God, will God bring about the healing we need.

Critics of the faith, who talk about Christianity having had, on balance, a catastrophic effect on civilization point to concepts such as that of original sin as being one of the "inborn defects" of a "world religion in a state of decay". They allege that such concepts are pure inventions and that in addition they convey an attitude of contempt for human beings, because they supposedly implant the notion that we should regard ourselves as "corrupt".

And one modern philosophy of life says, You can do anything, if you want to; don't worry about things; get on with living. The basic Christian teaching about the misery of the state of sin and about penitence seems pretty faint here. Very few notice its absence.

That is what Nietzsche said above all, that Christianity is a religion of resentment, of those who fail and who take their revenge by explaining how true greatness consists in being small and who stand the natural order of things on its head by praising not the strong but those who suffer. In that sense, he said, it is the philosophy of slaves, who thus take their revenge by burdening mankind with sin.

The notion that Christianity reduces us to servitude and that the Church holds sway over us by, first, persuading us of the existence of sin and, then, presenting herself as the agent of forgiveness is very widely held. It is true that wherever the idea of God disappears from people's view of life, the concept of sin loses its meaning as a matter of course. For if God has nothing to do with me, if he takes no interest in me, then there cannot be any distortion in my relationship with him—because I haven't got one. At first sight, sin seems then to have been cleared out of the way. And at first one might think that life then becomes merry and easy again; it takes on, so to speak, the dimensions of an operetta.

But it has rapidly become apparent that the operetta phase of existence is of very brief duration. Even if man wants to know nothing more about sin and has apparently got rid of whatever torments his consciousness, he soon notices that he still feels guilty. In the end he cannot deny that there are always accounts to be settled between "Thou" and "I", and debts of guilt to be paid. Nowadays there is even collective guilt coming into consideration.

Let us look at the whole panorama of the present day. Here, where sin against God has been widely banished from people's consciousness, we can make that much more impressive a reckoning of the guilt from history—the German people are continually ruminating, so to speak, on their debit account, and are suffering from it—so that we can see that it is not such a simple matter to solve this problem. By denying the existence of God, and of the will of God, you can get rid of the concept of sin, but not of the particular problem of human existence that was thereby represented and expressed.

Freedom

According to Christian teaching, gifts *are what God makes available to us for our life. So that things will go well for us. Now, is freedom another gift—or, is it rather an instance of God's* grace*?*

By grace, we understand God's turning toward man with benevolent intent. God then concerns himself in a new and specific way with man and gives him something that is not, so to speak, already to be found within the created order. Freedom, on the other hand, belongs to the *basic structure* of creation, to the spiritual existence of man. We are not just laid out and determined according to a particular model. Freedom is there so that each one of us can shape his own life and, along with his own inner self, can in the end follow the path that best corresponds to his essential being. Accordingly, I would not refer to freedom as a grace from God but rather as a *gift* inherent in creation.

In any case, it is questionable what this freedom really amounts to. If you put your stake on that, and use your freedom to do something that God doesn't want, then you get punished for it for all eternity.

Now, what do we really mean by *punishment*, when we are talking about God? Is that something he inflicts on you because he just wants to have his own way? No, punishment is the situation in which man finds himself if he has alienated himself from his own essential being. If, to take one example, he kills someone. Or if he does not consider the dignity of someone else as a person, if he lives in a way that denies the truth, and so on. Man has then made use of his freedom, but he has at the same time misused it. He has ruined and trampled upon the projected outline of his life, the purpose for which he was brought into existence—and he is also thereby bringing himself to ruin.

Freedom means that of my own free will I take upon myself the potential of my being. It is certainly not the case that it is then only a matter of Yes or No. For even beyond the No, there opens up an infinite interplay of creative possibilities for good. Basically, then, our idea that unless I say No to evil, my freedom has already been taken from me is itself a perversion of freedom. Freedom really finds its creative space in the realm of what is good. Love is creative; truth is creative—it is under these conditions that my eyes are truly opened, and I can recognize things for what they are.

If we look at the lives of the great men, the saints, we can see how, in the course of history, they bring to light in creative fashion quite new human potentialities, which inwardly blind or stunted people have hitherto been quite unable to perceive. In other words, freedom comes into its own in revealing and developing those things in the realm of good that as yet lie waiting to be discovered and in extending thereby the potentialities of the created order. Freedom is lost whenever it holds that it can only assert its own will in saying No. For in that case I have exercised my freedom but have thereby at the same time distorted it.

2. God

Let us come to the essential matter, as you call it, to the origin and the goal of life, to God. The Christian Creed begins with the words, "I believe". In any case, Christians do not just believe, in a general way, in some kind of higher power or higher level of nature.*

This saying "I believe" is a conscious act of the self. An act in which the will and the understanding, the teaching and the guidance I have been given, are all cooperatively involved. This act comprehends the trusting or, if you like, reaching out, transcending my own limits, turning toward God. And this act is not just a matter of relating to some higher power or other, but to the God who knows me and who speaks to me. Who is truly an "I"—even if in a far higher sense—toward whom I can move and who is moving toward me.

What do you mean by saying that God is an "I"?

I mean it in the sense that he is a person. God is not just a universal mathematical formula. He is not just an omni-

* The Apostles' Creed: "I believe in God, the Father almighty, creator of heaven and earth. I believe in Jesus Christ, his only Son, our Lord. He was conceived by the power of the Holy Spirit and born of the Virgin Mary. He suffered under Pontius Pilate, was crucified, died, and was buried. He descended into hell. On the third day he rose again. He ascended into heaven and is seated at the right hand of the Father. He will come again to judge the living and the dead. I believe in the Holy Spirit, the holy catholic Church, the communion of saints, the forgiveness of sins, the resurrection of the body, and the life everlasting. Amen."

present spirit of the world. He is not an indeterminate harmony of nature, or an "infinity" that cannot be named, but is the Creator of nature, the Origin of all harmony, the Living One, the Lord.

Just a minute; you believe that God is a person? He can listen and see and feel . . . ?

Yes, God has all the essential characteristics of what we mean by a "person", in particular conscious awareness, the ability to recognize, and the ability to love. In that sense he is someone who can speak and who can listen. That, I think, is what is essential about God.

Nature can be marvelous. The starry heaven is stupendous. But my reaction to that remains no more than an impersonal wonder, because that, in the end, means that I am myself no more than a tiny part of an enormous machine.

The real God, however, is more than that. He is not just nature, but the One who came before it and who sustains it. And the whole of God, so faith tells us, is the act of relating. That is what we mean when we say that he is a Trinity, that he is threefold. Because he is in himself a complex of relationships, he can also make other beings who are grounded in relationships and who may relate to him, because he has related them to himself.

"Whoever accepts this creed", you once said, "is actually renouncing the laws of the world in which he lives."

What that means is that the mystery of the Resurrection of Christ lifts us up beyond death. Of course, living as men in this world, we are still under the sway of the laws of nature. In nature it is a matter of growing and dying. In Christ, however, we can see that man is an end in himself. He is not just one element in the great process of growing-and-dying, but is, and remains, a separate end product of creation. In that way he has been plucked up out of the mere turbulence of the eternal rise-and-decline and has been brought within the unending and creative love of God.

Why is God symbolized by a triangle, from the midst of which an eye gazes piercingly out at us?

The triangle is an attempt to portray the trinitarian mystery of unity. In this way man is trying to express the way in which this threefold entity becomes one single reality, thus welding the threefold relationship of love into the highest possible unity. The symbol of the eye is an archaic symbol for perception as such and is common cultural property throughout the history of religions. It means that God is the all-seeing God and that man is the one who is seen but who through the agency of God himself becomes in his turn able to see.

There is of course a certain danger in this picture. At the time of the Enlightenment it played a great part in turning people away from God. For a God who gazes down upon me, despite my pleas, always and everywhere, who leaves me nothing to keep to myself—no "privacy", we would say today—that is the kind of God people want to get away from. If, therefore, seeing appears to be something threatening, a dangerous seeing that takes my freedom away, then it has been misinterpreted and is the opposite of a true image of God. The eye has been correctly understood as an image when it is seen as an expression of eternal attentiveness, if it says to me, I am never alone; there is always someone there who likes me, who accepts me and supports me.

In Jewish tradition there is a story that God, before he created the world, had only a latent existence. His features had not yet been realized. God, according to this idea, needed the world in order to become what he now is. For how could there be a king without any people? How could God love when there was no one there for him to love? The question is, What was there before *the beginning? Who made God?*

This idea comes from one Jewish tradition among many. Similar thoughts occurred later in Christian mysticism, for instance, in the writings of Meister Eckhart. In any case, in speaking as if God only became himself through the act of creation, they do not correspond to the original story in the Bible. No, the Christian God, the God who reveals himself to us, is God. "I am who I am", he says. Thus an ever further questioning—along the lines: Who made him, who made the one who made him, and so on—becomes superfluous. Or, equally, this question: Is the Spirit of creation truly the fullness of being, the one who stands beyond all coming into being and decay?

I think that you can put it this way: Reality is in itself creative. God has no need of the world. That is something the Christian faith, and likewise the faith of the Old Testament, always emphasized. In contrast to the *gods*, who need mankind in order to be maintained and nourished by them, *God* does not strictly speaking need them. He is the One, the Eternal, the Fullness of Being. Trinitarian belief tells us that he is the one who is in himself loving, the one who portrays in this eternal cycle of love at the same time the highest unity, and yet both a face-to-face encounter and a life companionship.

On the other hand, the idea "God is love" does indeed also bring the question: Who is being loved? This is resolved in God the Trinity, who gives himself and thereby becomes Son and gives himself back again and is then Holy Spirit. In this sense, the creation is an act of total freedom, and that too is something the Christian tradition (and along with it, a substantial part of the Jewish tradition) has always emphasized, that God did not have to undertake creation, but did so quite freely.

But why ever should God take on himself the risk of this venture of creating the world and man?

Romano Guardini, who saw all that was painful in creation and who said, Why does he do it this way, if it would still be possible without? was dreadfully tormented by this question. We can give no answer. We can only accept that he did want to do it this way, in spite of everything; that he wished for a creature who could stand face-to-face with him, who could recognize him, and who could thus, so to speak, enlarge the circle of his love.

The ancients tried to express this by means of a philosophical idea: All good carries within it an impulse to share. And that would be the reason why he, who is goodness itself, is overflowing. Even this is not the final answer. But an essential part of the answer is that creation is an act of free self-giving and is not, so to speak, something God needed to do because he would otherwise not be completely God and would thus be able to offer only half a hope.

Is God Male or Female?

Is God in fact male or female?

God is God. He is neither male nor female, but over and beyond those he is God. He is the Wholly Other. I believe it is important always to remember that for biblical belief it has always been perfectly clear that God is neither male nor female, but is, precisely, God, and that both man *and* woman are in his image. They are both derived from him, and their potentiality in both cases is contained within him.

The difficulty, at any rate, is that the Bible addresses God as Father and thus portrays him in terms of a male image.

First of all we have to say that the Bible does indeed, when addressing God in prayer, use the image of him as Father, and not as Mother, but that in images used in talking *about* God it always equally attributes feminine characteristics to him. When, for instance, it is talking about God's sympathy, the Old Testament does not refer to that with the abstract word "sympathy", but uses a term with a corporal reference, *rachamin*, the "motherly body" of God, which represents sympathy. This term demonstrates the motherly characteristics of God, albeit in the spiritual dimension. With the whole range of metaphorical terms it uses with reference to God, the Bible makes it clear through this mosaic of images that both man and woman come from God. He made them both. Both of them, consequently, have their being in him, while he nonetheless stands above them both.

There remains the question of why this is not made explicit in the way God is addressed in prayer.

Yes, why is this strictly limited to calling God *Father*? And the next question, which puts the matter much more pointedly, is: Why did God come to us as "Son"? Why did God become incarnate as a man? And why did this Son of God, in his turn, teach us to join with him in saying *Father* to God, so that this business of saying Father did not remain just an image, which might have become obsolete in the course of the history of our faith, but is now the very word that is put into our mouths by the Son?

Do you know?

I would in the first place hold on to the fact that the word "Father" naturally remains an image. It remains true that God is neither male nor female, but is simply God. Yet at the same time we are talking about an image that was given to us authentically by Christ himself, as an expression to use in prayer, and is thus non-exchangeable: an image in which he tried to convey to us something concerning the way God sees things.

But why? At the moment we are in a new phase of reflection on this question, but I think that in the end we cannot provide an answer. What we can say is perhaps two things. First: in the religions that existed in the world all around Israel there were god-couples, with a god and a goddess. Monotheism, in contrast to that, excluded the idea of a god-couple and, instead of that, regarded mankind, or alternatively Israel, as the chosen partner, the bride, in relation to God. In this history of election we find the fulfillment of the mystery of how God loves his people as a bride is loved. In that way, the female image is given forever to Israel, and likewise to the Church, and finally it is made personal and concrete yet again, in a special way, in Mary.

The second point is that wherever images of the mother-goddess have been used in worship, they have so altered people's thinking about creation that creation has been transformed into emanation and birth, and thus, almost of necessity, pantheistic models of divinity have been developed. The God who is portrayed in the image of the Father, on the contrary, makes things by means of the *Word*—and that is the point at which the specific distinction between the act of creation and the creature becomes quite clear.

What Is God Like?

Even if God is neither man nor woman—can we say what he is like*? The Old Testament tells us of great outbreaks of wrath and subsequent acts of judgment. "For I, the Lord your God," he says then, "am a jealous God: and to those who hate me, I punish the guilt of the fathers in the sons, as far as the third and fourth generation." Is God still as wrathful as he used to be, or has he changed?*

The very first thing I would like to do is to complete the quotation. In fact, it says: "I extend the punishment to the third or fourth generation, but my mercy lasts for *a thousand* generations." We can see how this oracle portrays an unequal balance between wrath and mercy. Mercy is a thousand times greater, as compared with wrath, and in this sense the oracle means that although I may have merited punishment and thus have fallen out of God's love, I can always be sure that God's mercy is a thousand times greater.

But this Judaeo-Christian God does show himself to be wrathful.

The wrath of God is a way of saying that I have been living in a way that is contrary to the love that is God. Anyone who begins to live and grow away from God, who lives away from what is good, is turning his life toward wrath. Whoever falls away from love is moving into negativity. So that is not something that some dictator with a lust for power inflicts on you, but is simply a way of expressing the inner logic of a certain action. If I move outside the area of what is compatible with the ideal model by which I am created, if I move beyond the love that sustains me, well then, I just fall into the void, into darkness. I am then no longer in the realm of love, so to speak, but in a realm that can be seen as the realm of wrath.

When God inflicts punishment, this is not punishment in the sense that God has, as it were, drawn up a system of fines and penalties and is wanting to pin one on you. "The punishment of God" is in fact an expression for having missed the right road and then experiencing the consequences that follow from taking the wrong track and wandering away from the right way of living.

But does one not necessarily have a feeling of dependence, even of being led by the hand like a child, when it says: "It is God who brings into being within you both the will and the action." What kind of a God is that, who always has to be showing us how we are nothing without him? Doesn't he, for his part, bear some responsibility for us? For who can do anything about the fact that he is living here on earth? There are plenty of people who are not exactly overjoyed about it.

It is important that the Church should draw a large enough image of God and not decorate it with artificial dreadful threats. In the past that did happen in part of catechetic teaching, and perhaps it still happens here and there. In contrast to this, we must present a picture of God, in all his greatness, as seen through Christ, a God who gives us a great deal of free play. Sometimes one would almost rather he spoke to us somewhat more clearly. We would be more inclined to ask: Why does he let us have so much room to maneuver? Why does he let evil have so much freedom and so much power? Why doesn't he intervene more positively?

Where Is God?

Let us stay with God, with the question of where and how we can find him. There's a little story about this: Once, a mother brought her son to the rabbi. Then the rabbi asked the boy something: "I will give you a guilder if you can tell me where God lives." The boy didn't need to think about it very long; he answered: "And I will give you two guilders if you can tell me where he doesn't live." In the Book of Wisdom, it says that God "lets himself be found by those who do not tempt him and shows himself to those who do not mistrust him". But where exactly is God?

Let us start with the Book of Wisdom. There we find a saying that seems to me to speak to us today: "God does not let himself be found by those who put him to the test", that is to say, he does not allow himself to be found by those who wish to conduct experiments on him. This truth was already known in the Hellenistic world, and it hits its mark right up to today. If we want to, so to speak, test God—are you there or not?—and undertake certain things to which we think he must either react or not react, if we make him the object, so to speak, of our experiment, then we have set off in a direction that will not lead us to find him. God is not prepared to submit to experiments. He is not a thing we can hold in our hand.

One of my friends says, I don't feel anything, even if I go to church on a Sunday. I merely see there's nothing there.

God is just not something we could ever force to call out at given moments: "Oh, here I am." God is found precisely when we do not subject him to the criteria of falsification used by modern experiments and existential proof, but when we regard him as God. And to look on him as being God means to stand in a quite different relation to him.

I can actively and methodically investigate material things; I can subject them to my control, because they are inferior to me. But even another person is beyond my understanding if I treat him in this way. On the contrary, I only come to know something of him when I begin to put myself in his place, to get inside him, by some kind of sympathy.

This is more than ever true of God. I can only begin to seek God by setting aside this attitude of domination. In its place I have to develop an attitude of availability, of opening myself, of searching. I must be ready to wait in all humility—and to allow him to show himself in the manner he chooses, not as I would like him to do it.

But just where is God exactly?

As your rabbinic story shows us quite beautifully, he is not in any particular place. To put it more positively: There is nowhere where he is not, because he is in everything. Or to put it negatively: He is never where sin is. Whenever contradiction exalts nonbeing to a position of power—he is not there.

God is everywhere, and yet there are various stages in his proximity, because each higher level of being is a little closer to him. But wherever understanding and love grow, we reach a new kind of closeness, a new form of his presence.

God is present, then, wherever faith and hope and love are, because they, contrary to what happens with sin, constitute the personal space within which we move into the dimensions of God. Thus God is present in a quite specific sense in every place where something good is happening, a sense that goes beyond his general omnipresence and his comprehension of all being. He may be encountered as a more profound presence wherever we approach those dimensions of existence that most closely correspond to his inner being—namely, those of truth and love, of goodness of any kind.

This more profound presence—*does that mean that God is not somewhere or other far away out in space, but is right here in our midst? He is within each individual person.*

Yes, that is what Paul said in his speech to the Athenians on the Areopagus. In that speech he quotes a Greek poet: In God we live and move and have our being.

That we exist and move within the atmosphere of God the Creator, that is obviously true, first of all, purely from the point of view of our biological existence. And it becomes ever more true, the more we penetrate into the quite specific essence of God. We can put it this way: Wherever one person does something good for another, there God is especially near. Whenever someone opens himself for God in prayer, then he enters into his special closeness.

God is not an entity who can be located in accordance with physical or spatial categories. He is not so many thousands of miles up or at a distance of so many light years. The closeness of God is instead a closeness in terms of categories of being. Wherever there is something that best reflects him and makes him present, where there is truth and goodness, in those cases we are in contact with him, the Omnipresent, in a special way.

But that also means that God is not automatically there; he is not always present.

He is always present in the sense that without him I should be cut off from the aggregate stream of existent being, if you like to put it like that. In this sense, there is a certain presence of God, a simply existent presence, everywhere. But the more profound presence of God, the presence that is a gift to man, can fade or even disappear altogether—or, on the contrary, it can become really strong.

In someone in whom God is present through and through, there is naturally a much stronger presence of God, a greater inner closeness, than in the case of someone who has completely distanced himself from God. Let's consider the Annunciation to Mary. God wishes Mary to become his temple, a living temple, and not merely by physical occupation of her body. But it only becomes possible for God truly to dwell in her because she opens herself to him inwardly; because she develops her inner being to become entirely compatible with him.

But might it not equally be the case that God withdraws himself, at least temporarily. Einstein, for example, revered God as architect of the universe but also in the end held the opinion that God took no further interest in his creation or in the fate of man.

This idea of God as the master builder, as the great architect of the universe, comes from entertaining too narrow an image of God. Here, God is only the marginal hypothesis, the theory we still find necessary in order to explain the origin of the universe. He puts it all together, so to speak, and then it starts working. But since, in relation to the world, he was nothing more than the final cause in a system of physics, quite naturally, therefore, he left the stage after that. And now nature is a complete working system, but God is unable to move, and his relationship to the human heart, to this other dimension of existence, is what this kind of picture of creation is, from the start, quite unable to envisage. In this perspective, he is no longer "the living God", but really a kind of hypothesis, and this hypothesis is intended, in the end, to be likewise redundant.

But still, theologians sometimes talk about an "absence of God".

That is something quite different. We already find in the Holy Scriptures this business of God hiding. God hides from disobedient people. He is silent. He does not send any prophets. And in the lives of saints, too, there is this dark night. They are, so to speak, thrust into a kind of absence, the silence of God, as for instance happened to Thérèse of Lisieux, and they then have to share in the darkness of the unbeliever.

That certainly does not mean that God does not exist. Equally, it does not mean that he has become powerless or that he is no longer loving. Here it is a matter of situations in the history of mankind, or in certain people's lives, in which their inability to perceive God brings about a kind of "darkness" of God, as Martin Buber expressed it. In this inability or unwillingness to perceive God or to relate to him, God then appears to have withdrawn.

What Does God Want?

Clement of Alexandria, one of the great Church Fathers, once said: "Man was made by God because he desired him for his own sake." Well, then, if God is all unselfish love, why should he then insist on being worshipped and glorified?

The Holy Father has picked up the expression "made for his own sake" in various ways in his encyclicals. He borrowed it from Immanuel Kant and has taken it on farther in a new way. Kant said that man was the only being who constitutes an end in himself and is not just the means to some other end. The Pope is now saying: Yes, indeed, man as a being is an end in himself and does not exist merely to further some other end.

That is at the same time the great principle that protects each individual. For from within this Creator God derives the principle that no one has the right to use some other person, however poor or weak he may be, simply as the means to God knows what end, however high it may be. With reference to experiments on humans—and also precisely to experiments on embryos—that has now become a really significant truth, a truly important safeguard of human dignity. The basic law of human rights is just this, that no human being may become the means to any end but must retain his own inalienable dignity.

This state of affairs does not, however, mean that it is right for man to withdraw into himself, to transform himself as an individual into a final purpose for his own life. It is inherent in man to be a relational being.

What does that mean?

In the first place, that the inclination to love, to form a relationship with someone else, is inbuilt in him. He is not an autarchic, self-sufficient being who develops alone, in isolation, not an island unto himself, but essentially created for relationship. Without relationship, in an unrelated state, he would destroy himself. And it is precisely this basic structure of his being that reflects God. For this is a God whose essential being, in just the same way, rests on relationships, as we learn from the doctrine of the Trinity.

Man's capacity to relate is directed in the first instance to other human beings, but it is also structured in such a way as to turn toward infinity, toward truth, toward love itself.

Is that an imperative for man?

This in no way degrades him. This relationship does not make man an end in himself, but establishes his greatness, because he himself stands in direct relationship with God and is the direct product of God's will. One should not, therefore, regard the worship of God as an external occupation for man, as if God wanted to be praised or as if he needed to be flattered. That would of course be childish and, as a matter of fact, irritating and ridiculous.

Well, what, then?

Worship, understood in the correct sense, means that I am truly myself only when I form relationships, that only then am I true to the *inner ideal* of my being. And my life is then tending toward the will of God, that is to say, toward a life more closely in agreement with truth and with love. It's not a matter of doing something to please God. Worship means accepting that our life is like an arrow in flight. Accepting that nothing finite can be my goal or determine the direction of my life, but that I myself must pass beyond all possible goals. That is, pass beyond them into being inwardly at one with him who wished me to exist as a partner in a relationship with him and who has given me freedom precisely in this.

And that is what God really wants with us?

Yes.

3. Creation

In the Beginning Was the Word

"In the beginning God made the heavens and the earth," it says in the Book of Genesis, "and the earth was bare and waste, and darkness lay upon the face of the deep, and the Spirit of God moved above the waters. Then God said: 'Let there be light!' And there was light."

None of us was there when the earth came into being. According to an old Jewish tradition, God is supposed to have made the world more or less exactly in accordance with the biblical account: God looked at what it said in the Torah, we are told, and constructed the world according to that design. And John also begins his Gospel with the sentence: "In the beginning was the Word."

Yes, and indeed these accounts are related; each of them explains the other. In early Judaism, that is, in the period when Jesus was living, they developed the idea that the Torah came into being before the creation of the material world. With the creation of the earth, so to speak, a workshop was provided for the Torah. That may seem to us somewhat naïve, but there is an important notion enshrined here, namely, that the world has a spiritual significance.

The world is created in order to provide a setting for the Covenant by which God binds himself to man. It is created, so to say, in accordance with the inner structure of the Covenant, and the Torah is the official document that sets out both the Covenant and the marriage. This first sentence of the Torah—"In the beginning God made the heavens and the earth"—is taken up quite deliberately in John's Gospel, indeed the entire account of creation is to some extent summarized in a single sentence: "In the beginning was the Word."

What does that mean, exactly?

The sentence in John serves also as a key to the interpretation of the account in Genesis. It makes it clear to us that the individual elements in this account of creation are to be seen as images.

God divided the day from the night; he made the heavens and the earth; he made birds and sea-creatures . . .

These images express the basic content of the account, that the world was created and that it derives from the *Logos*, which means "significance" as well as "word". Logos, that is to say, the "dynamic of reason", was one of the great fundamental terms in the Greek and Hebrew world of that time, and what was important about it was that Logos means not just idea but also at the same time speech. In other words: This God is not just thought; he is also speech; he is action. "In the beginning was the Word", that is to say, the spiritual meaning, the idea of the world, comes before the world itself. The world is, so to speak, the physical embodiment of the idea, of the original thought God carried within him and which through this embodiment has been made into a historical setting for the relationship between God and his creation.

In the meantime science has brought us knowledge that puts the statements of the Bible in quite a new light. As a a professor explained to me with respect to the discoveries of genetic research, thousands of millions of years ago, a kind of book was written, or, rather, a scroll. It contains all the information required to enable life to develop, in no matter what form, as an animal, as man, as a primitive cell, or as a herpes virus. Scientists have assigned letters of the alphabet to these chemical chains, to be exact, A, C, G, and T. It is in fact quite astounding, since all the words on this scroll are made up just from these four letters. The sum total of human genes, the genome, is quite genuinely a book: a book with countless sentences in it. This book containing the whole story of life, so the professor told me, "was written thousands of millions of years ago, just once for all—and it was all written in the same consistent style."

That certainly is one of the new ways of looking at things that modern science makes available to us. By such means we can, so to speak, look at the alphabet of the story of creation. The ancients talked about the mathematical structure of the world, and now we are able to verify this new version. Truly, then, the Word is the generative principle, and creation is thus to a certain extent the development and making concrete of an primordial document.

The Crown of Creation

To enable us to visualize the temporal dimension of creation, someone once suggested thinking of the entire history of the earth in terms of one single year. In this model, the first of January is the day on which the earth came into being. Then on the first of April—in real terms, that is, about 3.4 billion years ago—life first appeared on this planet in the shape of single cells. But the first fish did not appear until November 27, and the dinosaurs not even until December 12. God must in any case have been very fond of them. They dominated the earth certainly for 150 million years, and without causing devastation.

Mammals finally appear on December 27, and Man not until December 31, that is, fifteen to twenty million years ago. The story of Homo Sapiens himself begins only about 150,000 years ago. Thus it was pretty late when the Crown of Creation first saw the light.

First of all, these figures are of course only estimates. They are made on quite reasonable grounds, but we should not regard them as absolute. Nonetheless, I find this chronological scheme quite important, because it agrees with what the Bible and the Fathers tell us, that it is at the end of history that the goal of history appears.

It is specifically said about Christ, who is the fulfillment of man's potential, that he has come at the end of time. The Holy Scriptures give us a picture in which there is a whole prehistory, concerning which we cannot enter into detailed reflections. This prehistory is not merely a preparation for what was coming later. For there is much that has disappeared or that turned out to be merely a transitional phase. But it does become clear that it is an immeasurably long path, and the adventure of human existence appears as a kind of finale.

If I may intervene: How much longer have we to go?

We can form no judgment on that point. We only know that the essence of this finale was always latent in the developing process but comes to fruition only later on and, to a certain extent, will incorporate in itself the entire development.

If God is a loving God, and if he loves all men equally, why has he made us so differently equipped for life? Some of us are handsome and much courted; others rather lonely. Some are clever and quick to grasp things; others have to struggle hard for every little achievement. That's not to mention those people who come into the world severely handicapped. It surely can't be true that each individual soul is responsible for its own state—or, is it?

Of course not, for that would presuppose that each of us had, earlier, made the preparations for his own life that was still to come. On the other hand, this theory of the transmigration of souls would empty human existence of its once-for-all character and undermine human responsibility. No, we don't know. We can only say one thing: God has made a very varied world, even in the prehuman realm, and humans, too, offer a spectacle of great variety. That is not necessarily a bad thing. Someone who has no gift for mathematics may be very talented artistically; someone who is no good at anything intellectual may have real creative powers in working with his hands.

I believe that we may have constructed too one-sided a picture of man's potential. People are often measured according to a so-called intelligence test, which again only measures a certain kind of intelligence. We perceive people according to certain standards of ability or success and are no longer able to see the whole wealth of varied gifts, all of which have their own purpose, their own value, their own significance.

Naturally there are extreme cases, people who are seriously disadvantaged, educationally subnormal people, others who grow up in deprivation, those who cannot find any way to realize their potential. Here we come up against the problem, yet again, of why there is so much suffering in the world. But without supposing we can ever find an answer to this, we need to hold on to the fact that even the mentally handicapped are not people who ought not to exist. The mentally handicapped person has his own dignity precisely in his handicapped state. And Christ, who allows them to put a crown of thorns on his head and who says of himself, I am a worm and no man, has placed himself among the great tribe of handicapped people, who bear a message for mankind. As people who are suffering, who demand our love and who also return our love, they are in a special way able to have a special mission in life—if only we become aware of this.

There are quite sufficient reasons for calling man the Crown of Creation. We have invented nineteen thousand languages. We sing opera, and we play musical instruments we have made ourselves. We measure immense distances—but, on the other hand, this Crown of Creation often shows himself to be a bloodthirsty creature who again and again turns his own home into a kind of slaughterhouse. And hardly is one sorrow at an end before we are busy preparing the next. We have hardly survived one war, and we start getting ready for the next. And even those who yesterday were victims will tomorrow be active participants.

Here you have sketched out the essential tension, and the whole drama, of human existence. Man's greatness is quite undeniable. This little creature, which biologically is among the more deprived creatures, with diminished sensual sensitivities (here, too, we see greatness in what is inferior), has developed faculties that open up space to him. Man can look out into space with his human eye and can turn again from outer space to gaze upon the tiniest details of his own life. Again, he has in this way penetrated into the chambers of the wellsprings of life itself, so that he can now attempt either to change it or, alternatively, to make good use of it and help its development.

I think that the greatness of man is more obvious to us nowadays than ever before—and, of course, also the danger of falling from greatness. For the greater a creature is, the greater the danger it runs. And the greater its potential, its powers, and its capacities are, so much the greater are the dangers that arise from them. A gnat can do what is in it to do, no more and no less. Man, however, with all humanity, holds in his hands the entire sum of hidden human potential. He can in the end develop methods of destruction that are beyond the capability of any other living thing.

That is the inner paradox of human existence. He is called to greatness, but his freedom can allow the contrary temptation, that of wanting to be great over against God and thus to become a kind of anti-God, to develop into a serious threat. This is always liable to be his fall from greatness, so that he turns into a demon of destruction.

Sometimes we even feel like saying to God, If you had only made man a little less great, then he would be less dangerous. If you hadn't given him his freedom, then he would not be able to fall so far. And yet, we don't quite dare to say it in the end, because at the same time we are grateful that God did put greatness into man. And if he takes upon himself the risk inherent in man's freedom and all the falls from greatness it involves, then we feel horrified by the thought of what that might mean, and we have to try to summon up all the positive forces at our command, but we also have to share in God's fundamental attitude of putting trust in man. And only by holding fast to this fundamental trust are we able to set ourselves to oppose the dangers that threaten man and to find them bearable.

When God created the earth, he made it a part of a solar system that, in its turn, belongs to the system of the Milky Way, with its hundred million stars, within a whole sea of similar galaxies that all spin around in the universe. The system that is closest to our own hangs in space two million light years away from us. Is it then so inconceivable that somewhere beyond our own tiny world, in this immeasurable universe, there may exist other creatures of God, perhaps even humans similar to ourselves?

It seems somehow obvious to suppose that we cannot be alone in this great immeasurable ocean of stars. We cannot absolutely exclude this hypothesis, because we have no cognizance of the whole breadth of God's thought and his creative work. Yet it is a fact that thus far all attempts to discover anything of this kind have failed. Meanwhile, one strand of thought, scientifically well grounded, tends to regard extraterrestrial life as being extremely improbable. Jacques Monod, for instance, who was certainly not a Christian, says that in view of everything we are able to discover about the world from a biological standpoint, the possibility of the existence of extraterrestrial beings is so small as to be verging on the impossible.

What we can say is simply: We do not know. But thus far there are no serious grounds for thinking that similar beings exist elsewhere.

On the other hand, we do know in any case that God took man, on this little speck of dust that is earth, so seriously that he came and lived here himself and has bound himself to this earth for all eternity.

That corresponds to the model of divine action that is known to us. God always takes up exactly what seems unimportant and shows himself to man in what seems like a speck of dust, or, as in Nazareth, in a little place that is next to nowhere. Thus God always corrects our standards of judgment. It shows that what is quantitatively immeasurable belongs to a quite different order of reality from the immeasurability of the heart, as Pascal has already remarked. What is quantitative has its own indisputable status, but it is also important to see this quantitative value, for instance the infinite size of the universe, in relative terms. One single understanding and loving heart has quite another immeasurable greatness. It corresponds to a quite different order from any quantitative entity, in all its great power, but it is no less great.

Would it be shown in revelation if we had relatives somewhere in space?

Not necessarily, because God had no intention of recounting everything to us. Revelation was not there to give us a complete knowledge of God's ideas and of all space, with no gaps in it. One of the Wisdom books, often quoted by the Fathers, says about this in one place: God has given us the world to argue about. Scientific knowledge is, so to speak, the adventure he has left to *us ourselves*. In revelation, on the other hand, he tells us only as much about himself as is needed for life and death.

Christian teaching has divided the world into two realms, a visible realm and an invisible realm. It talks about "above" and "below". What does this mean?

Above and below is of course an image to help us understand, a natural development from our own way of looking at things. This symbolism certainly can turn into a naïve way of looking at things, a physical scheme, in which case you miss the main point. But as an archaic symbol, with its own force, it remains valuable. It teaches us to distinguish high and low, to see that there are levels of existence, greater and lesser, that there is one high above all, the living God.

The distinction between visible and invisible is something we also experience quite directly. There are forces we cannot see and that are nonetheless quite real. Let's take above all the essential things, matters of the spirit and the heart. I can indeed see something of the inner person in someone's eye, in his expression and in other ways, but only as a kind of reflection of what lies deeper within. Looked at in this way, what is invisible shows through material things for a little way, so that we become certain of what is invisible and are motivated to action by this invisible reality. At any rate, the forces we cannot see, but whose effects are clear in practice, signify to us that the world has depths that eyesight and visible phenomena just cannot fathom.

In connection with "above" and "below", with "visible" and "invisible", mysterious entities make their appearance in the Old Testament. They appear as God's messengers or as an "angel of the Lord". Three of these angels, the archangels, are actually named in the Bible. There we have Michael (in translation, the name means "Who is like God?"); then Raphael ("God has healed") and Gabriel ("God has made her strong"). In the past, we used to learn in school that angels are pure spirit endowed with will and understanding. Is that still right?

Yes, that's still as true as ever. Scripture tells us that, and there is a primitive knowledge in man, somehow, that we are not the only spiritual beings. God has filled the world with other spiritual entities who are close to us because his whole world is in the end one single place. They are also an expression of his fullness, of his greatness, of his goodness.

In this way angels are indeed part of the Christian conception of the world, part of the breadth of God's creation, which is equally represented in other spiritual beings who are immaterial. They also constitute an immediate and living environment for God, into which we are meant to be drawn.

According to the teaching of the Church, there are in the angelic realm not only archangels and cherubim and seraphim and just ordinary angels, but also the guardian angels. It is scarcely believable that each one of us really has his own guardian angel, with whom we can even cooperate.

That is a belief that has developed in the Church and that is well-founded. No one is obliged to believe it. It does not have the same degree of certainty as the declarations about Christ or about Mary. But it is one of the inner convictions that have grown up in Christian experience, that God somehow gives me a companion who is especially attentive to me and to whom I should turn for help. Of course, it will not be equally easy for everyone to be inwardly aware of this.

Do you know your guardian angel personally?

No. For my own part, I feel able to relate to God so directly that I am indeed thankful there is a guardian angel, but I converse directly with God. That depends on one's temperament. It is given to other people, and for them it is a most comforting certainty. But it is important that we not stop at this, but that we allow ourselves really to be led onward to God and that ultimately the relationship always remain directed to God himself.

So-Called Evil

The myth tells us that the spirits in heaven were originally splendid with grace and glory. They were able to look upon God and to bow down before him and enjoyed complete bliss. But one of these angels in God's presence, Lucifer, fell victim to the temptation of pride and rebelled against the Lord. For that, he and his companions had to suffer the fall down to hell.

Even today men argue about the phenomenon of evil, which the biblical myth is meant to explain. Meanwhile, scientists are investigating an observable "increase in empirically quantifiable cruelty and irrational spite" in our society. "I come up against the rule", Saint Paul wrote long ago, "that evil is present within me, even though I want to do good." And we are told that Luther saw the evil one, Satan, in bodily form and threw an inkwell at his head. The underlying question remains: Why did God create Satan? Why should the King of Heaven make an opponent for himself?

The story of the fall of the angels is not as such related in the Bible but has been developed from various texts in the course of time. Certainly, evil spirits make their appearance in the Bible. Less in the beginning, but gradually it becomes clear that there are not only good angels but also spiritual entities that are evil and that enter into the world and into man, that threaten him and, so to speak, try to drag him down with them.

But we can never say that God created Satan. The very point of the story of the fall of Lucifer, which gradually developed in Christian consciousness, is that such evil powers—which become clearly visible in the world around Jesus when he drives out devils—are not as such created by God. God created only what is good. And evil is not an independent reality but is only ever conceivable as the negation of some entity that is itself good. Only thus can it maintain its existence, because pure negation can have no independent existence.

What is temptation like, then?

I say it once more: God did not create a god of evil; he did not make an alternative counter-god. What he did create was freedom and the state of affairs that our judgment is often unable to hold firm under the pressure of that freedom.

The perception of evil spiritual powers is explained in the Bible to this extent, that it is a matter of created powers who, as it were, hold a mirror up to us. We can to some extent recognize in them a kind of model of what this threat within freedom looks like. And the threat always develops in this way: the greater a being is, the more it wants to determine its own life. It wants to be less and less dependent and, thus, more and more itself a kind of god, needing no one else at all. This is how the desire arises to become free of all need, what we call pride.

There is always a certain temptation intrinsic in all spiritual being. It consists in a kind of perversion by which love is seen as dependence and no longer as the only gift that can truly bring me alive. So that one sees this relationship no longer as life-giving, but as a limitation of one's own independence.

Is it possible somehow to recognize evil?

I would say that no one can demonstrate the existence of the devil. But the realization that above and beyond human malice there are disorders and disturbances in creation, a kind of power of envy, which drags us along and tries to drag us down, this is real for us and is explained by the Bible and by the Christian faith in this way. Certainly, we must never allow the idea to develop of the devil as a counter-god, who could stand face-to-face with God and challenge him to combat. What is negative has no power in the end. Evil is indeed a constant threat and temptation but is in the end not a comparable alternative to God. We must always be aware that only God is God and that whoever builds on him, therefore, need never fear satanic powers.

What about Hitler? Was he, as many people think, "Satan incarnate"? Sartre once said, "The devil is Hitler, that is, Nazi Germany." And the Jewish philosopher Hannah Arendt, referring to the horrible deeds of Fascism, uttered that famous phrase about "the banality of evil".

That a person who had made his way up from the lowest level of society—he had loafed around not doing much of anything and had no real education—that he could set a century in motion, that he could make political decisions with demonic insight and could make people listen to him, even educated people, that is terrifying.

On the one hand, Hitler was a demonic figure. One only need read the history of the German generals, who time and again made up their minds, just for once, to tell him to his face what they really thought and who were then yet again so overcome by his power of fascination that they did not dare to. But then when you look at him from up close, this same person who has a demonic fascination about him is really just a quite banal hoodlum. And finally the fact that the power of evil makes itself at home precisely in what is banal shows us something of the character traits of evil: the greater it is, the more pitiful, the smaller the element of true greatness.

In a similar way, Hitler was able to foresee demonic situations. For instance, I once read an account of how the preparations were made for Il Duce's visit to Berlin. Those who were responsible for various aspects of it made their suggestions, and after a long time he said: "No, none of that is right. I can see how it ought to go." And in a kind of ecstasy he delivered a lecture about it, and it was all done like that. That is to say, there is some kind of demonic power that takes possession somehow, that makes what is banal great—and makes what is great appear banal—and above all makes it dangerous and destructive.

One certainly cannot say that Hitler was the devil; he was a man. But there are reliable reports by eyewitnesses that suggest he had some kind of demonic encounters, that he would say, trembling: "He was there again", and other such things. We cannot get to the bottom of it. I believe one can see that he was taken into the demonic realm in some profound way, by the way in which he was able to wield power and by the terror, the harm, that his power inflicted.

Can we then altogether exclude the possibility that there might be some unfathomable abyss within God himself? A dark side to him? Much as in the human saying "Two souls, alas, sleep in my breast"?

Of course, this question has come up time and again in the history of religions, even in the so-called gnostic movements in the history of Christianity. In his own way, Carl Gustav Jung reframed the question and ventured to ask whether the ultimate reality must not also have two sides to it. And furthermore: Is this God not perhaps at the same time also a demon? Doesn't evil have its origin in God himself? For if evil really exists, is it not necessarily something that comes from him?

Christ has, so to speak, taken the wind out of the sails of this question, which makes the world seem truly terrifying because it makes God seem terrifying. He did this by dying for our sake and thereby showing us the *unfathomable depth of God's love.* Thus, the Letter of James can say, "There is no darkness in him" (that is, in God); the darkness comes from elsewhere; we can, on the contrary, rely completely on God; the demonic element, evil, can find no place in him, and therefore the ultimate end of things, when God will be all in all, will truly mean liberation from the oppression of evil.

The question then arises, of course, of where evil comes from, if it does not originate from within God. How can it have any existence at all? If evil came into existence without him, then is he in fact the creator of everything? We find ourselves yet again faced with a fathomless pit of difficulty. The Christian and the biblical answer says: It comes from freedom.

It is in this sense that evil is not some new kind of creature, possessing its own reality, which could lead its own existence, for it essentially consists of negation, eating away at the substance of creation. It is not a kind of being—for being can indeed originate only from the wellspring of being—but a negative. That the negative can be so powerful is bound to shock us. But I believe it is also comforting to know that evil is not a kind of creature but is more like a parasitic plant. It lives on what it takes out of the other being, and in the end it kills itself off, just as surely as a parasitic plant does when it completely dominates its host and kills it.

Evil is not something with its own nature, its own being, but is simply negation. And when I take a step into evil,

I leave the realm of the positive development of being in favor of the status of parasite, of the corrosion of being and the negation of being.

Heaven and Hell

One of the most important elements in the faith, which is also among those we find increasingly strange and somehow suspect, is the idea of heaven and hell and, beyond that, of purgatory.

What that means is that death is not the end. That is the fundamental certainty which is the starting point for the Christian faith. In one form or another, it is in any case common to the whole of humanity. Somehow, man knows that there is something more, something else. It means that we have a responsibility before God, that there is a judgment, that human life can either turn out right or come to disaster.

With regard to turning out right, which is what we all hope for despite all our failures, purgatory plays an important part here. There will be few people whose lives are pure and fulfilled in all respects. And, we would hope, there will be few people whose lives have become an irredeemable and total No. For the most part, the longing for good has remained, despite many breakdowns, in some sense determinative. God can pick up the broken pieces and make something of them. In any case, we need a final cleansing, a cleansing by fire, to be exact, in which the gaze of Christ, so to say, burns us free from everything, and only under this purifying gaze are we, as it were, fit to be with God and able, then, to make our home with him.

That sounds provocatively old-fashioned.

I think it is something very human. I would go so far as to say that if there was no purgatory, then we would have to invent it, for who would dare say of himself that he was able to stand directly before God. And yet we don't want to be, to use an image from Scripture, "a pot that turned out wrong", that has to be thrown away; we want to be able to be put right. Purgatory basically means that God can put the pieces back together again. That he can cleanse us in such a way that we are able to be with him and can stand there in the fullness of life.

And what will Buddhists do in the next world, or the Protestants? In an old Bavarian tale it says that there is a separate heaven for Prussians, since otherwise heaven would no longer be a paradise for the Bavarians.

I would say that from the human point of view one of the functions of purgatory is to get rid of these particularist attitudes. It strips off from one person what is unbearable and from another the inability to bear certain things, so that in each of them a pure heart is revealed, and we can see that we all belong together in one enormous symphony of being.

As far as the Buddhists are concerned, what they want, because everything that exists basically involves suffering, is to break free from this wheel of mortality and suffering and pass out into pure nothingness, which, on the other hand, is still not the same as nothing at all. In that sense even here—though in a quite different way of looking at things—is to be found something like a hope for an ultimate rightness of being.

With our Protestant friends we share the hope that there is a heaven and a hell. The fact that they are unable to accept belief in purgatory derives in part from the teaching on justification. And perhaps we ought not to argue nearly so much about it. When it comes down to it, we are all glad that God himself can still put right what we cannot.

Prayer for the dead is obviously based on this.

There is a fundamental urge in man to do something more for the dead and to perform additional acts of love, above all if he realizes that he still owes them something. We believe that it must be possible, even beyond this great threshold, to send something after them, so to speak, to make a gesture. But if heaven and hell are all there is, that becomes meaningless.

In that sense, implicit in prayer for the dead is a profound awareness that we can still do something for them. And I think that it is just this very human aspect that shows what is meant by purgatory. Those who have died are still in a state in which our prayers can be of help to them.

Augustine once made a distinction between "creation" (creatio prima) *and "continuing creation"* (creatio continua). *The Church talks about "God's great plan of salvation". Does this mean, to use the same image, that God is sitting in front of his great book and still writing the story of life, chapter by chapter?*

At any rate, Christ also says at one point in the Gospel of John: "My Father has been working, and is still working." He even uses the word "working", because he himself is addressed as a worker, and he says: God has been working and is still working. It is exactly the same as what we understand by the term "living God". God has not withdrawn himself. In him, on the one hand, everything is already there as a whole in a single moment—and yet it is never the unloving progress of a clockwork mechanism, but always a matter of his continual living presence. In this sense it is true that God is always working with us in history. In every step of its progress, it comprehends and includes the once-for-all essence of his idea, of his Word, in short, the full presence of God.

Certainly, you could easily hit upon the idea that it is man himself who is writing the new chapters in creation. For steps that previously took nature millions of years nowadays workers in gene research and bio-design can put together in what, from the point of view of history, is the wink of an eye.

This artificial reassembling of genes naturally poses a serious problem. On the one hand, it is a great opportunity. We have come so far in our exploration of the basic structure of life that we can read its code and can therefore combine genes or, alternatively, separate them. As long as this is done for the purpose of healing, and with due reverence for creation, it is good. To the extent that man believes himself to be able to be a demiurge, a co-creator, however, an engineer of the world, he can in just this way become a destroyer of life.

It is important to be completely clear about this: great reverence toward those things we should not touch must become a fundamental rule of all human conduct. We must be quite aware that man cannot and must not be seen as being secondary to our projects for genetic development. We must realize quite clearly that even the beginning of genetic manipulation is liable to develop into an assumption of domination over the world, which will then carry within it the seeds of destruction.

Man is incapable of creating anything; he can only reassemble things. With this capacity, provided that in all humility and reverence he serves the ideas already implicit in creation, he can become an assistant and keeper in God's garden. But wherever he puts himself forward as maker of things himself, then creation is threatened.

The Tree of Life

If the attempt to pluck the fruit of the tree of knowledge *was a crime that altered the state of natural being, the Creator, in the Bible story, utters the strictest possible warning against a further, still greater transgression, which is indeed the one absolute taboo, to wit, the attempt to pick the fruit of the* tree of life.

In Genesis it says that God posted heavenly guardians to the east of Eden—the cherubim with their flaming swords—in order to guard the way to this tree until the end of the world. "Now, man has become like one of us", says God in the text of Holy Scripture, "since he has knowledge of good and evil. He must not be allowed to stretch his hand out next and pick from the tree of life also and eat some and live forever!" Does this mark out a final boundary without ambiguity? Beyond that, does our own destruction begin to operate with absolute certainty?

These great images from Genesis will remain in the last analysis inexhaustible, and their meaning never exactly delimited. Beyond each and every perception of ours are further hidden dimensions.

First I would like to unfold the classic view of this image, as it was developed in the writings of the Fathers of the faith. The teachers of the Church point to the fact that man was not shut out from the tree of life until after he had maneuvered himself into a position that was not appropriate to him by eating from the tree of knowledge. He seized something that, if he lays claim to it of his own will, can only become his doom. The answer God gives to this new situation is that man may not now also pick from the tree of life, since to be immortal in this condition would indeed be perdition.

In that sense being barred from the tree of life, which is bound up with being destined to die, is a grace. If, in the form in which we now live, we had to live eternally, it really would not be a situation worth working toward. In a life that is characterized by so much confusion, death is still indeed a contradiction and, for some, a tragic event—and yet at the same time a grace, because otherwise this kind of life would become eternal and the world become quite unlivable.

Must not the message of this image be taken even more seriously today than ever before?

One can of course always uncover new levels of meaning in such images. When we see now how people, with genetic codes available to them, are really starting to pick from the tree of life and make themselves lords of life and death, to reassemble life, then precisely what man was supposed to be protected from is now actually happening: he is crossing the final boundary.

With this kind of manipulation, man makes other men his own artifacts. Man no longer originates in the mystery of love, by means of the process of conception and birth, which remains in the end mysterious, but is produced industrially, like any other product. He is made by other men. He is robbed thereby of his proper status and of his true splendor as a created being.

We do not know all that may happen in this realm in the future, but we can still be certain of this: God will take action to counter an ultimate crime, an ultimate act of self-destruction, on the part of man. He will take action against the attempt to demean mankind by the production of slave-beings. There are indeed final boundaries we cannot cross without turning into the agents of the destruction of creation itself, without going far beyond the original sin and the first Fall and all its negative consequences.

The problem of the manipulation of human life has become acute.

Here, there is no getting around this: the life of man must never become something that we can manipulate. We must preserve the barrier that stands here as a boundary to everything we see as possible to do, everything we can do, everything we regard as permissible, and all our experimentation. Man is not just an object for us; rather, each and every single person represents God's own presence in the world.

It seems sometimes as though this boundary were no longer in front of us, but as if we had already crossed it. With gene technology another tool has come into being that makes available to us the entire biological inheritance of the planet.

We began some time ago to change life by that means. There are already many thousands, maybe hundreds of thousands, of people whose life is absolutely unconnected with what used to be the act of conception, but who began life as ova and sperm outside the body of the mother. There are children who have three mothers: one from whom the ovum comes, one who carried the embryo, and one who wants to bring the child up. Many children have fathers who died many years before their birth.

Whether it will be choosing the child you want, put together according to sex, color of eyes, height and weight, or whether it may be the prolongation of life in another body—many things will become possible in the future. When, at the end of 1999, a group of scientists succeeded for the first time in completely deciphering one of the twenty-four human chromosomes (one of the smaller chromosomes, but still a great reservoir of around thirty million items of genetic information), one of the ladies concerned said to a reporter: Well, yes, it was a "really devilish piece of work". Can it be that this researcher was quite right?

Yes, unfortunately, she may have been right. In any case, we must first of all distinguish between what people have made and what people are. Whoever has come into being as a person in that way is a person and should be recognized and loved by us as such. The fact that we reject this way of producing human beings should not result in stigmatizing those people who are brought into life in this way. We recognize in them, despite this, the mystery of human identity, and we accept them as such—that, I think, is most important.

With the step you have just described, people have set their foot on a path of doom. The Catholic Church has warned against this reconstruction of humanity, right from the start. This work presented itself at first in apparently innocent forms, just in the way that many things start out looking innocent. First of all, it was help for childless married couples. Here the problem is still relatively small, if these are genuine married couples with good intentions who can conceive their child in this way. Even so, this is already a step down a slippery slope, if one believes he can get a child under any circumstances whatever, can consider it an absolute right. In this way, the child becomes a mere possession. It is no longer a free gift on the part of the Creator, presented in the context of the unpredictable freedom of nature.

I think there is today in general terms a danger of seeing

children as a right, as a possession. Parents not only want to represent themselves in their child, but to achieve whatever they failed to do in their own lives—in order to make a second attempt at their lives and thereby validate themselves. In these circumstances the children necessarily rebel against the parents. This is a rebellion in defense of being oneself, of having a right to one's own life.

Every person comes, of himself, out of the freedom of God and stands in that freedom as of his own right. The upbringing by his parents must be a matter of leading the child to what is his own, and not of laying a claim on their own behalf, for that is the true heart of authoritarian programming. It is wrong, though, to reject all education with the argument that one's freedom is being more or less manipulated thereby. Freedom needs help initially, needs accompaniment. And a really understanding education does not manipulate the child into my life, but tries to leave him free to be himself and to help him make his own way.

Coming back to the reconstruction of human beings . . .

As I said, it starts off harmlessly, philanthropically, but if one no longer allows oneself to be given the child as a gift, but insists that it be created, one has already crossed an important threshold. The technological act takes the place of the act of love, which really belongs with in vitro fertilization. From this point onward, various consequent problems necessarily arise. First there is already the question of what happens to the other so-called unnecessary fetuses, that is, to beings who are people but who are treated from the outset as superfluous products.

The practice at the moment is to destroy them by the thousands in mass killings.

And so, little by little, there follow many consequences that ultimately, step by step, will change our relationship to human nature.

What will happen next, at what point this will lead to what kind of catastrophe, we do not know. Thank God, we do not know. But we do know that we must oppose such a domination of human beings, which aims to make it possible to manipulate it and dispose of it as required. It is not a matter of attacking the freedom of science or standing in the way of technological advance, but of defending the freedom of God and the dignity of man, for that is what is at stake. It is incumbent on anyone who has gained this insight from his faith—but there are certainly enough non-Christians who share this particular insight—to be committed to ensuring that this boundary is recognized and acknowledged to be uncrossable.

4. Order in Creation

The Fundamental Evidence of the Universe

Even if God remains opaque to us, perhaps we can, in what follows, see something of the structure of the world and of what man is supposed to be doing here in this divinely originated universe. That is, always supposing there is a God at all. You have repeatedly referred to objective values and talked about "the fundamental evidence of human life", the gospel of the universe. The difficulty of modern man, you said, consisted in having shut himself off from this fundamental evidence. There are principles of behavior, you said, that are absolute and always right, and others that are truly and always wrong because they contradict the nature of being. What does that mean?

The Christian picture of the world is this, that the world in its details is the product of a long process of evolution but that at the most profound level it comes from the *Logos*. Thus it carries rationality within itself, and not just a mathematical rationality—no one can deny that the world is mathematically structured—not, that is to say, just an entirely neutral, objective rationality, but in the form of the Logos also a *moral* rationality.

But how can we know that with such certainty?

Creation itself offers indications as to how it should be understood and upon what terms it should be accepted. This can be obvious even to non-Christians. But faith helps us recognize the clear truth that in the rationality of creation is to be found not only a mathematical but also a moral message.

The first step in recognition comes through what we call the *conscience.* In this is present a primitive awareness of certain things that can never turn out well. To kill an innocent person, for whatever reason, is something that every man, unless seriously distorted by bad education and training, recognizes in his inner heart to be wrong. In a quite general fashion the respect for life is part of this, or, for instance, keeping one's given word, that is to say, veracity and truthfulness.

Of course, these values are very generalized. We know that Hans Küng has tried to amalgamate them into a kind of universal ethos, accessible to all mankind—but we needn't discuss that now. But this attempt does still show that it makes sense to talk about a certain transparency in creation, whereby these directions become perceptible. And although enormous differences become apparent in practice, the constant fundamental values can be traced in all the great religions and throughout the spiritual history of mankind. Let's take lying. There are people who say that it is sometimes right to do it, that sometimes it's necessary. But surely no one would maintain that it is right in itself.

In order for these basic elements of evidence to remain efficacious and clear, we need the help of subsequent education. This help, by means of which very general and somewhat hazy perceptions are sharpened and made applicable, is one part of the path that leads us to Christ. The tradition of the Church calls this path *illumination*, because things we somehow felt, but which were still unclear, become clear.

These elements of the "fundamental evidence of the universe", these "basic principles of life", which obviously we ignore or forget time after time—are they to be found in the primitive myths of the flood, the Tower of Babel, or of Sodom and Gomorrah? Is the message of these stories really a sort of knowledge of how to survive for all mankind?

These stories, which are to be found right across the spectrum in the history of religions, are quite certainly like warnings. The story of the flood occurs in the most varied and widely scattered geographical settings, which were quite certainly not in direct cultural contact. They express in some sense an experience and an insight common to mankind, a racial memory that has survived in man. In these stories, certain quite specific messages are interpreted for us.

Let us consider for instance the Tower of Babel, with which man tries to create a universal civilization by means of technology. He tries to bring about by his own ability and efforts the dream, which in itself is right and good, of *one world*, of unified humanity, and by means of a tower reaching up to heaven, he tries to seize power and make himself like God. Basically this is the same as the dream of modern technology: possessing divine power, being able to get at the controls of the world itself. In this way, these images truly embody warnings from a primitive knowledge that can still speak to us.

Let's stay with the Tower of Babel. The Bible gives us here a remarkable piece of information: "The Lord said, Behold, they are all one people, and they have one language. But this is only the beginning of what they will do. Nothing in all their plans will be impossible for them. Very well, let us go down! We will confuse their language down there, so that none of them any longer understands what the other is saying." That sounds rather arbitrary.

Yes, almost as if God were envious and didn't want to let man get too big. What we have here is picture language that makes use of the material then available to Israel. It is still not altogether free of certain pagan elements; only as the interpretation developed were these things set aside. Of course it isn't a matter of God being anxious about man becoming too powerful and wanting his throne, but rather that he sees how man, in assigning to himself an inflated importance, damages his true self.

We can perhaps interpret this image in this way: In Babel, both the unity of mankind and the temptation to become like God, and to reach up to his height, are linked solely with technical ability. But unity on this basis, we are being told here, will not hold and leads to confusion.

In the world of today we could well be following the same pattern. Town centers look the same in South Africa as in South America, as in Japan, in North America, and in Europe. The same jeans are worn everywhere; the same hits are sung; people watch the same things on TV and admire the same stars. In that sense, there is a unity of civilization, right down to McDonald's and a single menu for mankind.

While at first sight this growth of uniformity seems right and good, as a power to effect reconciliation—just like the unity of language in the building of the Tower of Babel—at the same time people are being increasingly alienated from one another. They don't really get any closer to one another. Instead of that, we are experiencing an increase of regionalism, a revolt on the part of the various cultures that just want to be themselves or that feel oppressed by others.

Is that a plea against the uniformity of culture?

Yes, because people are losing their true selves and what belongs to them. Any deeper communication between people is being lost now if it cannot be produced and imparted by these superficial outward forms of relationship and by having mastery of the same technical apparatus. Man is far more profound. If he is united with others merely on this superficial level, at the deeper level within, he will rebel against this uniformity, because he unconsciously recognizes that it reduces him to slavery.

We can say that the story of the Tower of Babel takes a critical view of a certain way of uniting the ways in which man arranges his life and his world, a way that achieves only apparent unity and only seems to make man greater. In reality, it robs him of his depth and of his greatness. Besides this, it makes him dangerous, because, on the one hand, he has great power, but, on the other, his moral capacity lags behind his technical capacity. Moral strength has not grown in correspondence with the power to make or destroy things that man now has. That is why God intervenes to oppose this kind of unification and is creating unity of a quite different kind.

What do you mean by that?

For us Christians, the Old Testament and the New always belong together. The texts of the Old Testament are the first step along the way. We are persuaded that they remain incomprehensible unless one takes the next step in reading. We will be able to look at that later with respect to the connection between Adam and Christ and some other examples. The story of Pentecost, in which God sets in motion his model of unity, also belongs here. This story is the counterpart to that of the Tower of Babel and thereby completes the picture and makes it properly comprehensible. The apostles are not speaking some kind of common language in this story, and yet everyone there understands one another. Multiplicity remains, but it is now transformed, by a unity at heart, into an inner unity.

Pentecost shows the opposite pattern to the Tower of Babel: a unity in which all the richness of humanity is preserved. God does wish for unity. It is to that end that his whole activity in history is directed; to that end Christ came into the world; to that end he creates the Church. But he wishes for a unity that is both higher and more profound.

The warning of the Tower of Babel unavoidably reminds us of the electronic revolution of the present moment, which is shaking our world to its foundations and changing it as perhaps no other revolution has ever done before. We seem to be on the point of creating a whole new universe. Virtual realities on the Internet, and e-commerce with its dot-com enterprises have become, not just a game or form of entertainment, but a way of playing for enormous sums of money, for power, for entire national economies, on which the lives of millions of people depend.

And a further development is emerging: most people in the Western world spend more time sitting in front of computers or operating computerized systems than they spend with "normal" reality, that is to say, with other people or with nature. These are substitute realities, and resisting these deceptive illusions in this perfectly unified cyber-world requires ever-greater effort.

Here we can see once more how the course of history reveals certain intuitions embodied in an image that we just could not have conceived earlier. Of course this is not part of the literal meaning of the text. But when we read it in the light of our experience, then we can see that the intuition that is to be found in it has been made concrete for us today. In the light of this image we can see the implications of current developments and why the creation of this kind of unity constitutes a threat.

From one of the other great myths among the images of the Bible, that of the flood, we might draw conclusions about other floods, the flood of stimulation and incentives, of images, slogans, everything that the capitalist market forces bring to bear . . .

That, too, is an image with many dimensions. Water has always been ambivalent in its significance. As a spring and as rain, it is a great gift, the gift of life itself. In the form of oceans and of the flood, on the other hand, it represents a danger that threatens the earth and that can swallow up life. Thus the primal flood became the archetype of destructive powers that overwhelm life, that tear down the limits set by God to preserve life. The dikes burst, and life is covered beneath the resulting flood. In this way the primal flood remains an image deeply graven into human consciousness, an image with far-reaching implications. For today we can see that many kinds of flood may breach the dikes, may ruin life, may destroy culture, may devastate humanity.

5. The Two Testaments

The Old Covenant

The Old Covenant is the story of God's relation with his Chosen People. God himself gives them a name. It was after he had struggled all night with the patriarch Jacob in the river Jabbok. Jacob would not allow himself to be overthrown even by the Lord of the universe, and thenceforth he was to be known as "Israel", he who fights with God.

But why did God choose one special people at all? And why this people in particular?

In the Old Testament the special significance of this choice is emphasized again and again, in Deuteronomy, for instance. God says to the people through Moses: I did not choose you because you were a great and numerous people, an important people, not because you possess this or that quality; but because I love you I have freely chosen you.

We cannot question the motives for this choice by any process of rational thought; it remains God's mystery. But this does imply something: God chooses. Yet he does not make a choice so as to exclude the others, but in order to come to the others by means of the one chosen, and to enter in a concrete fashion into the interplay of history.

Even so, this Chosen People *has had to spend two thousand years of its three-thousand-year history in exile, and even today it has a struggle to make its own state secure. We have to ask ourselves: Why did the Egypt of the Pharaohs become so great and powerful, while the very people with whom God had made his covenant had to face centuries of expulsion, persecution, and suffering—right up to the attempt at absolute extermination in the Holocaust?*

God's way of looking at things is different from ours. Being chosen by God does not mean that he will make you great in worldly terms. He does not turn his people into a great power, but he reveals himself in small things and works through them. Political power is not what counts in God's reckoning, but faith.

A people who were always in danger of being ground down between the great powers of Egypt and Babylon, like corn between millstones, was obviously called to have faith. Thus God creates his own history in something that is far from being a world power. And the lesson we can draw from this for the Church is that she, too, is not important on account of worldly power or influence but simply because she incorporates and represents God's alternative. Her greatest moments are those when she is suffering persecution and not those times when she has at her disposal great wealth and worldly power.

Through this we can learn for ourselves the system of values as to what is, or is not, important in life. But to try to work out God's reasons in detail is not our task. He shows us the way, points the direction, and retains his sovereignty.

It is a remarkable story. Although the Jews have lived two thousand years in exile, have been chased out of one country and then another, their religion has not just evaporated. This is a phenomenon still without parallel in the history of mankind. The question is whether the development of the world as a whole has not some mysterious connection with the development of the Jewish people.

That actually seems to me to be quite obvious. The way that this tiny people, who no longer have any country, no longer any independent existence, but lead their life scattered throughout the world, yet despite this keep their own religion, keep their own identity; they are still Israel, the way the Jews are still Jews and are still a people, even during the two thousand years when they had no country, this is an absolute riddle. This phenomenon in itself shows us that something else is at work here.

God did not make his people into a great power; on the contrary, they became the people who suffered more than any other in the history of the world. But they always kept their identity. Their faith could never die. And likewise it is still like a goad in the very heart of Christianity, which sprang out of the story of Israel and is inseparably bound up with it. You can see, in this way, that there is something more than mere historical chance at work. The great powers of that period have all disappeared. Ancient Egypt and Babylon and Assyria no longer exist. Israel remains—and shows us something of the steadfastness of God, something indeed of his mystery.

Israel was the cradle of the Christian faith, and we can say without exaggeration that these two great world religions have decisively shaped the basic pattern of life over large parts of the earth. Right up to our own times, the contribution of the Jews in developing the culture of various countries has been critical. America is the most striking example of this. Are the Jews still God's Chosen People?

That is, especially just recently, a hotly disputed question. It is quite obvious that the Jews have something to do with God and that God has not abandoned them. And that is how the New Testament sees it, too. Paul says to us in the Letter to the Romans: In the end all of Israel will be brought home. It is another question, how far, with the rise of the Church—the people of God called from all peoples—and with the coming of the New Covenant, life under the Old Covenant, a life that remains closed to the New Covenant that comes from Christ, is still a valid way of life.

Nowadays there is an enormous variety of theories about this. As Christians, we are persuaded that the inner heart of the Old Testament is directed toward Christ and that it receives its proper answer, its whole direction, only when it is read from the standpoint of Christ. Christianity, as compared with the religion of Israel, is not a different religion; it is simply the Old Testament read anew with Christ.

We have already seen, in a whole series of examples, how Old Testament stories and texts are like a beginning that is waiting for something more. They first become complete and comprehensible when we read them from the point of view of the New Testament. So the New Testament is not just something grafted on. And our own relationship with the Old Testament is not that of people who, so to say, appropriate something that really belongs to other people. It is rather a matter of there being a real progression, and the Old Testament remains an unfinished fragment if you stop before you start the New. That is our fundamental belief as Christians.

But hand-in-hand with this belief goes the other, that Israel still has a mission to accomplish today. We are in fact waiting for the moment when Israel, too, will say Yes to

Christ, but we also know that while history still runs its course even this standing at the door fulfills a mission, one that is important for the world. In that way this people still has a special place in God's plans.

God has not, then, retracted his word that Israel is the Chosen People?

No, because he is faithful. Of course, we can see that Israel still has some way to go. As Christians, we believe that they will in the end be together with us in Christ. But they are not simply done with and left out of God's plans; rather, they still stand within the faithful covenant of God.

Does that mean that Jews will have to recognize the Messiah, or ought to do so?

That is what we believe. That does not mean that we have to force Christ upon them but that we should share in the patience of God. We also have to try to live our life together in Christ in such a way that it no longer stands in opposition to them or would be unacceptable to them but so that it facilitates their own approach to it. It is in fact still our belief as Christians that Christ is the Messiah of Israel. It is in God's hands, of course, just in what way, when, and how the reuniting of Jews and Gentiles, the reunification of God's people, will be achieved.

"I, too, am an Israelite, a descendant of Abraham, member of the tribe of Benjamin", says Paul in his Letter to the Romans, although one part of Israel has been afflicted with "hardness of heart". And, further: "From the point of view of the gospel they are enemies of God . . . , from the point of view of their being the Chosen People they are beloved of God." Strong words.

This is another of the paradoxes that the New Testament sets before us. On one hand, their No to Christ brings the Israelites into conflict with the subsequent acts of God, but at the same time we know that they are assured of the faithfulness of God. They are not excluded from salvation, but they serve salvation in a particular way, and thereby they stand within the patience of God, in which we, too, place our trust.

The Book of Books

The Bible, which we have frequently quoted, contains seventy-three books: forty-six in the Old Testament and twenty-seven in the New. The oldest book comes from Moses and is over three thousand years old. And the Holy Spirit is supposed to have shown the writers what they should write and how to write it. He has enlightened them and preserved them from error: "This is written for generations yet to come, so that a people that has not yet come into being may praise the Lord."

But do all the parts of the Bible contain the Word of God? For surely the Holy Spirit ought to have known that the earth is not flat, like a plate, but round like a ball?

Well, yes, you could put that question, jokingly. But then look, you have to think about the special character of the Bible.

Let us compare Holy Scripture with the Koran, for example. Moslems believe that the Koran was directly dictated by God. It is not mediated by any history; no human intermediary was needed; it is a message direct from God. The Bible, on the other hand, is quite different. It is mediated to us by a history, and even as a book it extends over a period of more than a thousand years. The question of whether or not Moses may have been a writer is one we can happily leave to one side. It is still true that the biblical literature grew up over a thousand-year history and thus moves through quite different stages of history and of civilization, which are all reflected in it. In the first three chapters of Genesis, for instance, we meet with a quite different form of culture from what came later, in the exilic literature, or in the wisdom literature, and then finally in the literature of the New Testament. It becomes clear that God did not just dictate these words but rather that they bear the impression of a history that he has been guiding; they have come into being as a witness to that history.

Anyone who starts reading this book will find thrilling stories in it and apt parables for living—but also a great mountain of contradictions.

I can understand the Bible as the Word of God only if I read it in the tension engendered by seeing it as a whole, accepting everything and taking one thing with another—not merely as isolated words or phrases. It is something very real and very dramatic. It is because faith is not set before us as a complete and finished system that the Bible contains contradictory texts, or at least ones that stand in tension to each other.

The Bible is not a textbook about God and divine matters but contains images with perceptions and insights in the course of development, and through these images, slowly and step by step, a historical reality is coming into existence. I can only understand these images as God's Word if I relate one to another and let each correct the other. And in any case, if I isolate them from their living context as God's Word, then I am reading historical sources. Each still has its own particular situation, of course, but they are all merely fragments—and no longer always speak as the Word of God.

Complicated.

It is one thing to regard the Bible strictly as a collection of historical documents, which expose the human element, so to speak, without mercy. It is another thing to see the Bible as a whole as the Word of God, in which everything relates to everything else, and everything is disclosed as you go on. It follows straightaway that neither the criterion of inspiration nor that of infallibility can be applied mechanically. It is quite impossible to pick out one single sentence and say, right, you find this sentence in God's great book, so it must simply be true in itself.

The level on which I perceive the Bible as God's Word is that of the unity of God's history. That is also true of Jewish interpretation. That differentiates between the Torah—which is considered the actual canon of Scripture—and the prophetic and other books, which form a framework, so to say. In our Christian reading of it, we are more than ever convinced, as we said, that the New Testament offers us the key to understanding the Old.

This is the reason why patristic theology and mediaeval theology never referred to the Bible itself as "revelation". Revelation is the greater thing that stands behind the Bible. And inspiration means that the people who wrote the text —and in many cases, this was a process of collective development—speak as members of the people of God and speak out of the history of God's people. The fact that, through many stages of mediation, they bring the history of God's people and of God's guidance to verbal expression means that they, too, are anchored in God the subject.

It is said that the whole history of mankind, from alpha to omega, is written in the Scriptures. All wisdom, every mystery, indeed everything that has ever happened right up to the present day and what has yet to happen. It is said to be hidden in the text, locked up with a secret code. We therefore have to learn the code of the Bible. What do you think of this theory?

If you take that in a superficial, mechanical way, then it is quite wrong. Many people think they've cracked the code and then say that the Apocalypse is talking about atomic war and God knows what other events. Of course, it's possible to discover things that correspond in a quite astonishing way and then think that everything is already set out there. But it is quite certainly wrong to think that all empirical facts and events are already in the Bible in a coded form.

The whole totality of the Bible, as it really is, is quite different. The Bible speaks to the whole of history and gives those lights that are essential to illuminate its path. But God does not do the thinking for us. He does not replace careful learning, does not replace our own spiritual striving. He leaves us the world to argue about, as we said, so that we can come to grips with it ourselves. He does not jump in to plug the gaps in our knowledge, but he does give us wisdom—and naturally the wisdom brings knowledge with it; otherwise it would not be true wisdom. He gives us those directions that man needs so as to live aright. These indications are of course valid for the whole of history, for all places and times, but they do always need to be relearned.

There is a saying of Gregory the Great, which is also quoted in the Catechism, that goes like this: The Word of Scripture grows with the reader. And the reader grows as well, and then the Word really shows its greatness, and at the same time it grows out into history.

Many people think that the Bible is full of cruelty, intolerance, and mercilessness. Someone supposedly found 250 passages in the Bible that talk about destroying enemies. Yet, on the other hand, an old monk once told me that as soon as you begin to read the Holy Scriptures regularly, then everyday life begins to change for you, and change in a very healing way.

Yes, I should say that, too. If I only read the Bible in order to see what horrible bits I can find in it, or to count up the bloodthirsty bits, then of course it won't heal me.

For one thing, the Bible reflects a certain history, but it is also a kind of path that leads us in a quite personal way and sets us in the right light. If, therefore, I read the Bible in the spirit in which it was written, from Christ, in fact, or if I read it as a believing Jew, if I read it from the right starting point, that is, and read in faith, then indeed it has the power to transform me. It leads me into the attitude of Christ; it interprets my life to me and changes me personally.

You once said that it is really the people who own the Bible, not the scholars.

This is a view I share with liberation theology. It is true that the Bible was written by the people of God; the individual authors are inspired, and thus the Church is active in speaking through them, and God is speaking through the Church. Because of this, it is made just as much available for the faith of simple people.

In order to expound the purely historical, technical matters, obviously learned people, specialists, are needed. But the real and essential meaning of the Bible is something the simple believer can grasp just as well. It really is made available to everyone and in its way is comprehensible to everyone. Saint Augustine once said something very fine: Both the little hare and the great wild ass drink from the brook, from the spring, and each has its thirst quenched. And it really is like that: both the hare and the wild ass can drink, and each gets what it needs to quench its thirst.

There are a whole series of obscure writings that were not included in the collection of the New Testament. Today these texts, which are known as apocrypha, *are again being unearthed and are often quoted. Was the canon perhaps closed in too much of a hurry?*

The history of the canon is one of the most difficult areas, even in the Old Testament. Here, too, there are interesting and important apocrypha, on the one hand, but also there are differing canons.

At a very early stage people distinguished between the Alexandrian canon, of the Bible as it was translated into Greek, and the Masoretic canon, which was finally laid down in Judaism in the period after the coming of Christ. Substantial parts of it—the Torah and, for instance, much of the prophetic writings—were already seen as canonical, but the development of the canon as a whole was still underway in the time of Christ.

From the point of view of the New Testament, on the whole, the Alexandrian canon was adopted. The rabbis, on the other hand, chose to have a somewhat narrower canon with the Masorah, because the Alexandrian canon included too much Christian material for them. Then finally Luther decided in favor of the Masoretic canon, which he saw as the only authentic canon, and on that account Protestants have a narrower Old Testament canon than we do.

The history of the New Testament canon is basically very involved and hard to understand. Even though some parts of it were fixed before the end of the second century, the enquiry and discussion dragged on into the fifth century.

Looked at purely as a *historical* process, or from a liberal point of view, as the Lutheran theologian Harnack said, one might come to the conclusion that what is in the canon has been gathered together in somewhat haphazard fashion, but the really important and valuable literature has nonetheless been included in its entirety. Judged from the point of view of *faith*, the canon has certainly not been put together by just any one, such as a group of scholars who might have met together and studied the matter, but by the Church in living out the Scripture, not just growing piece by piece, but above all it had to be truly authenticated through the liturgy. The critical questions were: What can be proclaimed? What is universally applicable? What is recognized not only among Semitic Christians but also among Christians of Greek and of Latin culture? In a difficult process in the interior of the Church, she sorted out, so to say, what could be recognized as a common basis for Church life (and in this process there were some small differences between different regions of the Church).

Today some people are trying to unbind the canon and begin again. In particular, some movements in feminism see themselves as being better validated by the gnostic writings that were not included in the New Testament. For that reason they want a different canon. But that, of course, means disputing the existence of the living Church and putting some academic construction or other in its place. Thus there is a decision of faith at stake. The question is: Do I believe there is a Church, which in shared faith has recognized the basis of this faith—or do I assume that the choice of texts is just a matter of historical chance? If I take the second as my starting point, then of course I want to find a different sort of Christianity, and I am fishing for a new origin for it.

On the other hand, not a single one of the original versions of the Gospels is available. And it is almost unavoidable that mistakes were made in copying and translating them. Have we really still got the authentic Holy Scriptures?

I would answer Yes, without qualification. There will always be some dispute, of course, about particular words or sentences. You only need to look at the new Nestlé-Aland critical edition of the New Testament, and you can see how many variants there are in that enormous critical apparatus. But however interesting it is to study the variant readings, however much one can learn from the manuscript tradition, which reflects movements and experiences in the life of the Church, nonetheless the substance of Holy Scripture remains the same. That does not change, even if I were to choose different manuscripts or other readings. They offer interesting variations and viewpoints. But the text as a whole, its essential substance, is still there, and the very fact that it is transmitted with variations in detail assures us of its faithfulness.

Francis did not just read the Bible; he played a kind of roulette with it. When he was founding his order, we are told, the saint opened a page at random and said: "This is how we'll do it!" And then he opened at another page and said: "This will be our rule!" Saint Augustine, too, once found the Bible open in front of him at a certain page and made that text his own; and that meant that he would have to change his life quite radically.

That's a very old way of doing it. Augustine himself came across it as an older tradition. By this method he finds the message for his conversion, just as Francis found his message of guidance. The King of Belgium, Baudouin, once told me that he used to do that sometimes and that it was incredible how it helped him and amazing how it gave him just the message he needed. In one serious cabinet crisis, when he could hardly see any way he could get another government formed, he went into the chapel, took his Bible in his hand, and found a text that suddenly told him what he had to do. So it does happen.

And is obviously to be recommended when you are forming a government . . .

To a certain extent. But you can't just make it a standard recipe, otherwise we would be turning Scripture into an oracle. What is right and important is for us to read the Bible regularly, to let it keep us company and guide us. In inner conversation with it, we will always find words that especially speak to us and help us on our way in particular situations.

6. The Law

The Four Laws

The Church has developed the teaching of the four laws. These are supposed to show the ordered structure on which life in this world is built up. These laws are: first, natural law; second, the law of desire; third, the Law of the Old Covenant given through Moses; and fourth, lastly, the law of the New Covenant given through Jesus Christ. Have I got that right?

First of all, you have to recognize that these laws are not all on the same footing. *Natural law* expresses the fact that nature itself conveys a moral message. The spiritual content of creation is not merely mathematical and mechanical. That is the dimension which natural science emphasizes in the laws of nature. But there is more spiritual content, more "laws of nature" in creation. It bears within itself an inner order and even shows it to us. We can work out from this the ideas of God and the way we should live.

Second point: the *law of desire* signifies that the message of creation has been obscured. There is a kind of countercurrent to it, which is in the world through sin. It expresses the fact that man kicks against the goad, as we say. Paul puts it like that: Man is aware of a law within him, driving him to do the opposite of what he truly wants to do. This is on another level, then. While the natural law expresses the inner message of creation, the law of desire means that man builds his own world and has thus introduced into the world an opposite trend.

That is the way it was expressed and expounded by Thomas Aquinas, above all.

Yes, in all things Thomas gives us the synthesis and the summing up.

Third point: the *law of the Old Covenant.* This law, too, has several layers of meaning. The heart of it is the Ten Commandments from Sinai. Besides this the whole of the five books of Moses, which make up the legal framework of Israel, are also referred to as "the Law". They present Israel's framework for living, its order of prayer, and at the same time its moral order. Paul then critically questioned the value of this order. He established thereby that this law was a power for bringing order—and it remains so for our Jewish fellow-citizens, and in many respects even for us, and we are certain to talk about this later—but that, on the other hand, it is still not able to set man completely free. And the reason for that is this: the stronger the demand made by the law, the stronger becomes the inclination to fight it.

It is Jesus Christ who is seen by Paul in the end as liberating us from the law into the freedom of faith and love. Thomas Aquinas, linking up with what Paul says, nonetheless talked about another *law*, that is to say, about the *law of Christ*, which, however, is a law of quite a different kind. Thomas says that the new law, the law of Christ, is the Holy Spirit, that is, it is a power that motivates us from within and is not just imposed on us from without.

Thus we have here four different levels: first, the message of creation. Second, the contrary movement of man in human history, when to some extent he tries to build his own world against God. Third, when God speaks to man in the Old Testament, a message that indeed shows him the way but arouses resentment and makes man somehow powerless.

So the Old Testament Law remains provisional; it points to something beyond itself. And then, fourth, finally, Christ, who motivates us from within to go beyond the outer laws and thus offers us the inner direction for our lives.

That's a story that confuses me: Jesus says, "Do not think I have come to abolish the law and the prophets. I have come, not to abolish, but to fulfill them. Amen, I say to you: 'Until heaven and earth pass away, not the least little letter of the law will pass away, until all things have been fulfilled.'"

Christ does not come as a lawbreaker. He does not come in order to declare the Law invalid or meaningless. Moreover Paul does not do so, even if some people think they can see a tension between Paul's position and the saying of Jesus that is transmitted in Matthew. He says that the old Law, in its smallest details, fulfilled an essential educational function. Christ comes in order to complete it. But that also means, in order to lift the Law up onto a higher level. He fulfills the Law in his suffering, in his life, in his message. And now what happens is that the whole Law finds its meaning in him. Everything that was intended by it, everything it aimed for, is truly realized in his person.

That is why we no longer need to fulfill the Law according to the letter, in the way its prescriptions regulate everything down to the last detail. Our fellowship with Christ means that we are in the sphere where the Law is fulfilled; where it has found its true place; where it is quite literally "lifted up" [*aufgehoben*] to a higher level, that is, both preserved and at the same time transformed.

In every nation, there are whole libraries full of legal prescriptions concerning the way people should live together and how they should behave toward each other. In contrast to this, Christ has obviously succeeded in expressing for all *people on earth, comprehensibly and in a way we can put into practice, and concentrated in just a few sentences, the main rule of life in this world.*

When they asked him: Master, which is the most important commandment? he gave the following reply: "You must love the Lord your God with all your heart, with all your soul, and with all your mind. That is the first and most important commandment. The second is of equal importance: You must love your neighbor as yourself." And he says, as if to make it comprehensible for absolutely everyone, "On these two commandments depend all the law and the prophets."

That is indeed the great breakthrough, the great synthesis, which Jesus gave us. Instead of the various points of view and details, he surveys it all and tells us: This twofold commandment really includes everything. God and our neighbor belong together inseparably. Jesus managed a tremendous simplification there, which at the same time does not make it either cheap or banal, but gets to the essence of it. Here we see the true heart of the matter, that carries everything with it, the point around which it all turns, the only point that really matters, as Paul says. If we haven't grasped the fundamental commandment, all our talking is just babbling and sounding brass, nothing real. Pious practices and activism of any kind are all empty unless love is within to give them life. They don't bring man into contact with God and don't even help one's neighbor. Thus this concentration, this simplification, which shows us the simplicity of God and at the same time the magnitude and the beauty of his demand on us, is truly the critical breakthrough.

We should of course add that in ancient Israel the legal framework, the moral ordering of the state, and the ordering of worship, are all interconnected. With the coming of Jesus this network is separated. Religion receives, as it were, its independence. It still informs the state and its law, and presents it with moral standards, but there is a distinction between the law of the state and what morality or faith tells us.

From that point of view, each state will always have to have its own laws and its own legal principles. These would be just hanging in a void unless they had an inner life; unless people could recognize from within the essential demand upon their lives and in this way turn the legal measures from mere outward rules, traffic regulations, into a just manner of living together.

Is that what you meant when you once said that the true natural law is a moral law?

Yes. Nature, as we already said, does not merely have laws according to which it runs, which science can investigate, but carries within itself a more profound message. It gives us signposts. And when the Church talks about natural law, she does not mean laws of nature in the sense used by natural science, but the inner directions that shine forth for us from within creation.

The Ten Commandments

In the wilderness of Sinai Moses drew a boundary line around Mount Horeb. No one was allowed to cross that boundary except him. On the third day thunder and lightning began; thick clouds enveloped the mountain; trumpets sounded. The entire mountain smoked, gave forth flames, and trembled, and Moses alone climbed up to the summit of the mountain to receive from God the Ten

Commandments, the divine Law. Moses wrote down in the Book of the Covenant every word God spoke.

That is how the myth goes. The Church sees the Ten Commandments as the expression of God's concern for mankind; they are intended to show us the way to a good life. First of all: Were these laws really handed over to Moses by God when he appeared on Mount Sinai? As stone tablets, on which, as it says, "the finger of God had written"?

Perhaps we ought here to explain the word "myth" a little further. What is being said to us here is certainly being expressed in metaphor. This kind of language can express things we find it difficult to describe. The fact that this message is conveyed to us in visionary images does not necessarily mean that this is merely a dream or a legend or a folktale.

We have here an image that refers to a real event, a real entering into history by God, to a real meeting between God and this people—and again, through the medium of this people, a meeting with mankind. This image is mediated through someone who is close to God, to whom it was given actually to hear God speaking and, as the Bible says, to talk with him as with a friend, and who, from the basis of this friendship, was able to become the mediator and to pass on God's message. This is then the essence of the event that is depicted for us in a visionary metaphor.

But to what extent are these Commandments really supposed to come from God?

Today we know that the Ten Commandments, as written in the Books of Moses, are interwoven with the history and culture of the surrounding peoples. The historical struggle is also present in similar advances in the realm of Assyrian culture. Nonetheless, the fact that the Law was given this form and was preserved in this shape in Scripture goes beyond the workings of any mere mutual influence. This is the man who has been touched by God, and on the basis of this friendly contact he is able to formulate the will of God, of which hitherto only fragments had been expressed in other traditions, in such a manner that we truly hear the word of God.

Whether there really were any stone tablets is another question. You know that according to the Sinai narrative Moses first smashed these tablets in anger and then in the end is given some replacements. The essential point is that God, through the agency of his friend, really makes himself known in an authoritative way. In that sense, this mediation is more than a human invention, more even than great human sensitivity to the message of creation.

Are the Ten Commandments still valid today—without qualification?

They are valid. We have already talked about one commandment, which through the encounter with Christ was, so to speak, refurbished and reframed: "You shall not make any graven image." This commandment was given a new meaning the moment God presented himself as his own image. In that way these Commandments are en route; they receive their final form through Christ.

The Sabbath commandment, too, which refers back to the story of creation, retains its fundamental validity but is given a new form when the day of Jesus' Resurrection becomes the actual day of the Covenant. The "route" leads from Sabbath to Sunday—and along the way becomes more profound.

Thus these are not mechanical, already perfectly complete formulae; they belong within the circle of the light of Christ, and there they receive their definitive shape. But the core of them is valid and remains valid.

Have the Ten Commandments never been changed?

No. There are indeed two versions, one in the Book of Exodus and the other in Deuteronomy. They differ from each other in minor externals but are still the same in essence—and of course they cannot be altered by men.

When Moses comes back down from the Holy Mountain, the people are dancing around the famous golden calf. Filled with rage at this idolatry, the champion of God smashes the tablets of the Law. Only the Levites, the descendants of Levi who later constitute the priestly caste, rally around him and thereby take God's side. "Go all around in the camp, from door to door," orders Moses, "and each shall kill his own brother, his friend, or his neighbor."

So, basically, the story of the Ten Commandments began with an enormous violation of commandment no. 5: Thou shalt not kill. Moses really ought to have known better.

It actually begins with a violation of the first, the fundamental commandment: Thou shalt not bow down to any strange gods.

Man is on the right track when he recognizes God as God and lives a life of adoration of God. And he strays into the wrong path, into perversion of his existence, when he worships what is not God. When he makes his divinities for himself and thereby, in the final analysis, worships himself. Starting from this fundamental violation the life of the people is corroded and inwardly distorted. The people have handed themselves over to death. For turning away from

God, who is the source of life, does mean turning away from life.

The story that follows does sound terribly bloodthirsty, and for us it is scarcely comprehensible. There too we have to look forward, toward Christ. He does the opposite. He takes death upon himself and does not kill others. But in this moment of the Sinai story, Moses, as it were, puts into effect what is already present: the other people have perverted their own lives. How far we should take this story literally is another question. The people of Israel stays in existence. What happens expresses the truth that anyone who turns from God not only departs from the Covenant but from the sphere of life; they ruin their own life and, in doing so, enter into the realm of death.

The First Commandment

"I am the LORD, your God. . . .
You shall have no other gods before me."

If you look at it carefully, you see that never in the history of mankind has the dancing around the golden calf been so frantic and so intoxicated as in our own time.

There are no idols that are explicitly presented as such, yet there are indeed powers before whom men worship. Capital, for instance, is one such power and possessions in general. Or let us take the passion for power and status. In many respects, the golden calf has great contemporary relevance in our Western world. The danger is simply there.

But there is more at stake. With increasing frequency, the face of the one God is just obliterated. That happens whenever people say, well, when you come down to it all the gods amount to one and the same God. Each culture has its own particular mode of expression, and it doesn't really matter whether you take God as being a person or as impersonal, whether you call him Jupiter, Shiva, or whatever other name. And it becomes more and more clear that people no longer take God seriously. That they have wandered away from God and now only turn to refracted images in which they see reflected only themselves.

We see that at the moment when man puts God aside, the temptations of idolatry are very great. At present we are in great danger of seeing God as almost superfluous. He is so far away, people say, and worshipping him doesn't seem to bring any results. We pay less attention to the fact that, if we pull away the main supports on which the framework of human life is constructed, then man will gradually disintegrate.

The Second Commandment

"You shall not take the name
of the LORD your God in vain."

We are bound to ask ourselves: If God is so very great, how is it that he is not above my petty blasphemy, the sacrilege of a miniscule earthworm?

It's not a matter of our being able to affect God in some way and his avenging himself. It's a matter of our staying in right order. At the very moment when we dishonor God, disfigure his face, and render him inaccessible to the world, so that he can no longer illuminate it, man loses his own light at the same time.

Martin Buber once said that no word has been so misused as the word GOD. That word is so stained and so disfigured that one can no longer actually use it. I think, he continued, that it is nonetheless not permissible to avoid this word and to omit it from what we say, but we must, with all due respect, attempt to lift it up and set it upright again.

We only have to recall that in the time of the Nazi dictatorship the words "God is with us" were stamped on the uniform belts of German soldiers. While this was ostensibly done to God's honor, he was in fact being misused for other ends.

But each single misuse of God's name, each and every act that obscures his face so that he can no longer be recognized, leaves behind it a monstrous track of filth. The great power of atheism, the rejection of God, and indifference to God are quite inexplicable without this repeated misuse of God's name. His face was disfigured to such an extent that man felt bound to turn away from it. It has in this way long since become clear what terrible effects the breach of this commandment can have in human history.

The Third Commandment

"Remember the sabbath day, to keep it holy."

Many people like Sunday and enjoy the fact that it is different. Others want to go on buying, working, and making noise, without stopping. But perhaps we have simply forgotten what Sunday is supposed to be about.

The Sabbath is introduced in the account of the creation as a time when man is made free for God. Beyond that, and in connection with the Ten Commandments, it is also a sign of God's Covenant with his people. The original idea of the Sabbath is thus an anticipation of the freedom and equality of everyone.

On the Sabbath, even a slave is not a slave; there is rest even for him. In the tradition of the Church this has always been one of its main aspects. As far as free people were concerned, their activity was not work in the strict sense and could thus be carried on. One further important point is that on this day creation should take its rest. It was originally framed in this way so that the commandment held even for cattle.

Today man would like to have total, sole, and absolute dominion over his time. We have in fact forgotten how important it is to allow God into our time and not merely to use time as an element made available for our own private purposes. It is a matter of standing aside from concepts of what is useful or practical—and thereby becoming available for others and for ourselves.

We have already suggested that on the morning of the Resurrection of Christ the Sabbath was renewed in a different form. It is now the morning on which the Risen One enters in among his own, on which we gather together with him, on which he invites us to share with him—to share in the day of worship and in the meeting with God, wherein he comes to us and seeks us out, and where we can seek him, too.

The Fourth Commandment

"Honor your father and your mother, . . .
that your days may be prolonged,
and that it may go well with you."

It is striking that this commandment is the only one that is combined with a promise. Jesus emphasizes again and again how important it is.

I would like to tell a little story at this point. It was when we were on holiday, and I was really happy with my sons. Paul spent hours fishing for little fishes and crayfish; Jakob was digging holes in the sand. We had a little boat, and Paul spent a long time swimming about beside the boat. He had suddenly reached the stage of not being frightened any more, and he was very proud of being able to do this on his own. One time, I sat up above on the cliff and looked at my wife and the children, and they were all so young and beautiful and full of life. And I thought, now the best years of my life are beginning, and I don't want to fritter them away, and how marvelous it is to be, and to be able to be, a parent like that. And suddenly I found myself thinking about my own parents and my grandparents—and in fact about this fourth commandment.

This commandment is in fact the Magna Carta of the family. It lays down a basic framework. The essential life cell of socialization and of society, it says to us, is the family, with parents and children. And only within this basic framework can we learn to practice the fundamental human virtues. Only within the family can the proper relationships between the sexes and between the generations grow and develop.

On one hand, the commandment includes the task of education. This means leading another person into his freedom in the right way, so that he learns the inner structure of rules by which it works and learns properly how to be human. Obedience is instrumental to this process of learning one's own freedom by practicing it. And, naturally, on the part of the children, it is necessary that they accept this education.

There is however a silent admonition, within the fourth commandment, concerning our treatment of the elderly, those who are no longer usefully active, who are now helpless. Great value is placed on honoring elderly parents. Our attitude should not be determined by ideas of usefulness, but in old people we should render honor to those who gave life to us. In his person I can honor the personal value of a human being just at the point where he can no longer fend for himself. This basic and enduring respect for the human being is a most important aspect of this commandment. It implies a determination of our own future, so that later we, too, can go forward with trust into our own old age.

The Fifth Commandment

"You shall not kill."

Hardly anyone would want to quarrel with the meaning of this commandment. Just strange, the way people break it without the least hesitation.

There is no doubt that within ourselves we find it obvious as a basic principle that I should not kill someone else. Even if I have forgotten that it is for God alone to dispose of each and every person, at least I am aware that he has his own right to life, his right as a human being, and that I myself fall short of humanity if I kill him.

In borderline cases, however, we can see that this insight is becoming ever less clear. That is especially true of the beginning of human existence, when life is still defenseless and lies open to manipulation. Here there is a temptation to proceed in accordance with views of practical utility. We want to choose whom we allow to survive and whom not, because they stand in the way of our own freedom and self-realization. At the point where human life is not yet visible in its outer clothing of speech and verbal response, our consciousness of this commandment easily dies out.

The same is true of the end of life. Then we find the sick or suffering persons a burden and persuade ourselves that death would be a benefit for them. That feeling gives us the pretext for helping them on into the next life before it becomes "too difficult", so to speak.

And from that point it all follows step by step. Today ideas about the selective breeding of human beings, ideas with which we became familiar in a most unfortunate time, are making their reappearance. The question is asked whether people who are no longer conscious and can no longer fulfill any social function really should be regarded as people at all.

The further extensions of this notion follow without any real break, especially from the starting point of euthanasia. The question immediately arises: At what point does someone's life become so given over to pain, so burdensome in my eyes, that I may put an end to it? At the two extremes of life, then, this consciousness—a moral consciousness basic to human existence—that no one may simply dispose of another person, is all too easily extinguished. So it is especially important today for us to engage in the struggle for what this commandment represents—for God's rights over all human life, from conception through to death.

The Sixth Commandment

"You shall not commit unchastity"

Our world has made the constant availability of Eros into a virtue. You certainly don't need to be a sex maniac in order to ask yourself: Is unchastity really always a sin?

The original text of this commandment, in the Old Testament, runs: "You shall not commit adultery" (Ex 20:14; Deut 5:18). This commandment has therefore in the first place a quite specific sense. It is concerned with the inviolability of the faithful relationship between man and wife, which not merely protects the future of mankind, but at the same time integrates human sexuality into human existence as a whole and, in that way alone, gives it its true value and stature for humanity.

That is the heart of this commandment. Not in a transitory connection, but within the context of the positive response of two people to each other, who at the same time utter a positive response to children; within the context of marriage, then, is the true place of sexuality, where it gains its true human value and stature. Only there does what is spirit become sensually tangible, and what is sensual become spiritual. Only there occurs that event which we have described as the essence of humanity. It acts as a bridge between the two poles of creation, which mingle together and give to each other their true worth and true stature.

If, then, we say that marriage is the true place for sexuality, that means that a uniting in love and in fidelity, which includes mutual caring and openness to the future and which is thus directed out toward mankind as a whole, is present as a matter of course and that sexuality preserves its real value and is truly humanized only in this context.

There is no doubt that the instinctive drive, above all in a world that is everywhere characterized by eroticism, is very powerful, so that the connection with this original context of fidelity and love is scarcely comprehensible any more. Sexuality has long since become a marketable commodity on a grand scale. But it is also readily perceptible that it thereby becomes dehumanized and that in addition I am abusing other persons when I buy sex from them as I would any other commodity, without showing any respect for them as persons. People who turn themselves into a commodity, who are forced to do it or are traded for this purpose, are virtually ruined. And in the meanwhile, because of the market in sex, a new form of slave trade has even arisen. So the moment I cease to keep sex securely restrained within a context of free and mutually responsible agreement, which creates its own restraints, the moment I no longer maintain its connection with life as a whole, at that very moment there inevitably springs up a whole rationale for considering human beings as a marketable commodity.

To return to the heart of the commandment.

Here the following message of creation is proclaimed: Man and wife are made for each other. We have heard in Genesis that they will leave their father and mother and will become one flesh. Now, we could of course say, from a purely biological point of view, that nature invented sexuality in order to preserve the species. But what we encounter in the first place as a purely natural phenomenon, as a merely biological reality, develops a human dimension within the society of man and wife. It is one way in which a human being can open himself up for another. In which not only can commitment and fidelity grow, but in which, all in all, a sphere can develop where human beings are able grow from conception on into life. Above all, true human companionship develops within this sphere. What was in the first instance a biological law, one of nature's tricks (if you like to put it like that), receives a human dimension, within which the fidelity and the ties of love between man and wife develop, which in their turn make the family possible.

This is the heart of the message that speaks to us from the created order itself. The more we live it out and reflect upon it, the more clearly we can see that other forms of sexuality fail to attain the level upon which man is in fact called to live. They do not correspond to what a fully humanized sexuality can and should become.

We will talk further about sex in a later chapter. But where the Ten Commandments are concerned, one suspects that they may perhaps constitute a law directed against the laws of nature. That would be why we find it so hard to keep them, because they so often run contrary to our human instincts and inclinations.

Of course. To be sure, the sixth commandment in particular carries within it the message of nature itself. Nature has determined the existence of two sexes in order to preserve the species—and that happens in a quite particular fashion in the case of beings who are far from being complete when they emerge from the mother's womb and who need a prolonged period of care and nurture.

Man is the kind of bird that stays in the nest, not the kind that leaves the nest early. From a strictly biological point of view, the human race is so constituted that the enlarged womb of the love between mother and father must continue to be available, so as to facilitate, over and above the first biological stage of development, the growth into full humanity. The maternal womb of the family is practically an existential necessity.

Thus to some extent nature shows man's original face. An enduring relationship with each other is requisite. In this relationship, man and wife give themselves to each other in the first instance—and then give themselves to their children, so that they, too, may find their way into the law of loving and giving and losing oneself. Birds that stay long in the nest need a fidelity that lasts beyond the time of birth. In this sense the message about marriage and family is certainly a law derived from creation itself and is in no way opposed to the nature of man.

But we find it pretty hard to keep.

It remains true that here—just as in all the other areas we have talked about—there is a contrary movement. In this case there is a degree of superfluous power in the biological instinct. In our modern societies—but also in the correspondingly late societies of other eras, as in that of imperial Rome—we can observe a process of public eroticization, which still further reinforces excessive drive and thereby makes the connection with marriage more difficult.

Let's get back to what we said about the four laws. Here we can see two different systems of order in nature. The message of nature refers us to the way man and wife turn toward each other as the inmost natural impulse, which then finally develops into a fully human impulse and creates the sphere within which, as nowhere else, man can truly become himself. The other message is that we tend to a certain extent toward promiscuity, or at any rate toward seeking to make sex available in a way that cannot be brought within the framework of the family.

From the standpoint of our faith it is easy to distinguish these two different levels of natural impulse. One of them truly presents the message of creation—the other, merely man's attempt to control his own existence. Because of this, it will always be a struggle to bring one's behavior within the framework of marriage. Yet we can see that where the struggle is successful, then humanity will fully mature and children can learn about the future. In a society where divorce has become normal, the real damage is always inflicted on the children. On that account, we have yet more evidence, from the children's point of view, that mutual commitment, standing true to each other, is really always the right course of action and the one that best corresponds to man's true nature.

The Seventh Commandment

"You shall not steal"

Respecting other people's property is so banal, so obvious as a moral principle; what's behind this?

The teaching about the universal distribution of goods in creation is not merely a beautiful idea; it needs to work in practice. That is why we find associated with it the truth that each individual needs his own sphere of the basic necessities of life and that there must therefore be some principle governing the disposal of property, which each and every one of us must respect. Corresponding to this, of course, arises a pressing need for social legislation to monitor and restrain the misuse of property.

At present, as hardly ever before, we can see clearly how people ruin their own lives by living only for the sake of what they own, for things, how they are destroyed by this and by making possessions their real god. Anyone, for instance, who lets himself be ruled entirely by the workings of the stock market will basically become incapable of thinking in any other way. We can see how the world of possessions takes powerful hold upon people's lives. The more they have, the more they are dominated and enslaved by what they have, because they have to be giving ever more attention to preserving and increasing those possessions.

The difficulties associated with property can also be clearly seen in the distortion of relationships between the First and

Third World. Here, property is quite clearly no longer subject in an appropriate manner to the principle of the universal distribution of goods. Here again, legal structures have to be found that will help keep this in line, or rather bring it into line in the first place.

You can now see how a vast weight of reality is to be found behind the saying about respect for the possessions of another. It includes both things, not only protecting the principle that everyone should receive what he needs for living (and that his right to this should then be respected). But equally the responsibility to use possessions in a way that does not run counter to the purpose of creation as a whole or to the love of our neighbor.

The Eighth Commandment

"You shall tell no lie", or
"You shall not bear false witness."

Lies make the best stories, they say, but sometimes even little lies grow so big that they can almost topple the president of a superpower or ruling political parties or great media barons. And the strange thing is: nothing stays hidden.

It seems to me that the significance of truth as a fundamental and precious gift for man is rooted here. All the commandments are commandments of love, or are developments of the command to love. In that sense they all have to do quite explicitly with the precious gift of truth. If I creep quietly away from the truth or distort the truth or fall into untruth, I often do harm to someone else—but without fail I also harm myself.

It is well known that telling a little white lie can easily become a habit, a way of cheating one's way through life, helping oneself out with a lie here, there, and everywhere, and then finding oneself caught in a web of lies and living one's life counter to reality. Also implicit in this is not only the fact that every single offense against the dignity of truth is degrading for man, but that each one is a slap in the face of love. For if I withhold the truth from someone, I withhold from him something essential and precious and lead him up a false path. Truth is love, and if love were to turn against truth, it would be mutilating itself.

The Ninth and Tenth Commandments

"You shall not covet your neighbor's wife."
"You shall not covet your neighbor's goods."

These two commandments belong together, and they reach far beyond external and factual matters, touching on our inner thoughts. Here we are told that sin does not begin just at the moment when I commit adultery or unlawfully take away someone else's possessions, but that sins are born of thoughts. It is not enough, then, just to call a halt before the final step, as you might say, because that is not going to be possible unless I have preserved within me an inward respect for the other person, for his marriage, or for his possessions.

Sin, then, does not begin with outwardly perceptible actions, but it begins in that breeding ground of sin, in envious thoughts, in the refusal to seek the good of the other person, in rejecting him. For any human being, a way of life that does not seek to cleanse the inner thoughts is consequently incapable of keeping itself in order on the concrete, factual plane. In consequence this appeals directly to the heart of man. For it is the heart that gives birth to a man's actions.

On this ground alone it must be kept, as it were, clear and pure.

When, in the midst of thunder and lightning, Moses received the tablets of the Law on Mount Sinai, this was the hour of birth of the free individual. That, at any rate, is the theory of the German Jewish popular writer Hannes Stein. From then on, each person was directly answerable to God for himself and for his deeds, whether he be master or slave, man or woman. The Covenant on Sinai is more or less where the autonomous legal person originates. Would it be too bold an assertion to say that the foundation stone of free democratic society was laid, not by ancient Greece, but by the Judaeo-Christian tradition?

I have also read Hannes Stein's book, and I would say that there is certainly some substance in the way he sees things. The original seed of human rights is indeed to be found in the value given to each individual who stands alone for himself before God, who is addressed by God, and who is personally affected by the words of the Covenant—that is to say, the equal value given to each individual—and this has laid the real foundation for modern democracy.

Israel itself was not supposed at first to have any kings, but only judges, who were to apply the law of God and exercise supervision to ensure that it remained in force. What was intended was therefore basically a fully egalitarian society, a kind of anarchy in the positive sense: no one rules except God alone. And he rules through the medium of his law, through his Word and through the Commandments.

This early social order had to give way in the end to pragmatic considerations, in the way we have already discussed. On that account, I would not now wish to minimize the significance of Greek democracy; here too there was significant growth, and a working social model was developed that could later be used as a starting point by others. We should in any case be quite clear that in Greek democracy only the free men had the vote. Women did not take part in politics and thus did not have the vote, any more than slaves did. Because freedom is thus limited, Greece offers the model of a limited democracy. The Word of the Bible, on the other hand, ascribes in fact to everyone who is human, and who as a human being is made in the image of God, the fullness of this individual character. So it does thereby offer a more far-reaching basis for democratic constitutions.

7. Love

The Meaning of Life

The Church says that man is not capable, by and for himself, of giving a meaning to the world or to his own life. Hard to believe, in the face of the vast libraries full of books that have already been written by clever people, and some less clever ones, about life and its meaning.

If there were not already sense and meaning in the world, then we, too, would be unable to make any. We can indeed carry out actions that have meaning and significance within a particular purposive framework, but these cannot of themselves give meaning to life as a whole. Either it has a sense —or it doesn't. Meaning is not something we can simply manufacture. What we manufacture in that way may be able to grant us a momentary satisfaction, but it will not serve to justify the whole of our existence or to give meaning to it.

In all times and all places men have of course asked about meaning and will continue to do so. And in doing so, they will always find fragments of an answer. Of these fragmentary answers, only those elements are valid that men have *discovered*, not those they have *invented*, only what they have found within man as a creature. And what will be of use to them in trying to understand themselves and to live a meaningful life.

What the Church says, that meaning is not created by us but is given by God, should be understood in this fashion: Meaning is something that carries us, that goes ahead of us and beyond all our ideas and discoveries—and only in this way has it the strength to sustain our lives.

If we could express the meaning of life in a single word, then that word would be LOVE. This, so the poets and the scholars of all ages will tell us, is not only the meaning but also the basic principle of living, the one true secret. Someone once said that whoever has felt the infinite power of this love has penetrated to the heart of what faith is about.

Again and again in the course of this conversation we have, I believe, encountered the fact that our life tends in the end toward a discovery of love, toward receiving love and giving love. And the crucified Christ, who presents us with love lived out to the end, as he himself says in the Gospel of John, lifts this principle up into the realm of absolute reality. God himself is love. In this sense, love is indeed both the fundamental rule and the ultimate aim of life.

Here we come again to the mystery of the grain of wheat, to the mystery of losing oneself and finding oneself. And we must link to this the observation that, as we know, no one can make love. It is given to us. It just happens; it comes to me from someone else; it enters into me.

Human love always lays claim to eternity. Love contradicts death, as the French philosopher Gabriel Marcel once said. This human love is turned from a promise into the fulfillment of reality only when it is wrapped in a love that can truly impart eternity. Marcel said that to say to a person "I love you" meant: I refuse to accept your death; I protest against death.

Thus we see that human love, in and for itself, represents an unredeemable promise. It strives for eternity, and yet it can offer only mortality. Yet, on the other hand, it knows that this promise is not meaningless and contradictory, and thereby destructive, since ultimately eternity is alive within it nonetheless. Even from a purely human point of view, then, love is what we are looking for and is the goal toward which our lives are directed. But within its own framework and on its own terms it directs our view toward God and brings us to wait upon God.

Love, it's sometimes so easy to say it. But who really knows what love is? In what sense, for instance, does God love us? We have already talked about the supposedly "angry God". There are people who say that his message is one of threats. What is this love like that God gives us?

The first point is that anger is not necessarily always in contradiction with love. A father, for instance, you know this better than I do, sometimes has to speak crossly to his son so as to prick his conscience, just *because* he loves him. And he would fall short of his loving obligation and his will to love if, in order to make things easier for the other person, and also for himself, he avoided the task of putting him right sometimes by making a critical intervention in his life.

We know that spoiled children, to whom everything has been permitted, are often in the end quite unable to come to terms with life, because later on life treats them quite differently, and because they have never learned to discipline themselves, to get themselves on the right track. Or if, for instance, because I want to be nice to him, I give to an addict the drugs he wants instead of weaning him off them (which would seem to him very hard treatment), then in that case you cannot talk of real love.

To put it another way: love, in the true sense, is not always a matter of giving way, being soft, and just acting nice.

In that sense, a sugar-coated Jesus or a God who agrees to everything and is never anything but nice and friendly is no more than a caricature of real love. Because God loves us, because he wants us to grow into truth, he must necessarily make demands on us and must also correct us. God has to do those things we refer to in the image of "the wrath of God", that is, he has to resist us in our attempts to fall away from our own best selves and when we pose a threat to ourselves.

Sounds very serious.

It is important to recognize that true love carries with it a high seriousness. It desires the true good of the other person, and therefore it has the courage to oppose him whenever he does not see what is good, whenever he is running headlong into misfortune.

In explaining this, we have already said what is positive about love. It likes the other person. It wants things to go well for him, wants him to be happy, to be more truly himself. And for that reason love is good to him. But to be good to that person I must necessarily be guided by what is good, by what is really good for him and make an effort to help him be good. A true act of love is therefore one that springs from goodness and is directed toward what is good. And so, on one hand, self-discipline is always a part of love, giving way oneself for the sake of the other, and, on the other, helping him is always a part. Helping him not to be wrapped up in himself, not just to take for himself, but to learn to come out of himself and to discover the way of the grain of wheat.

The Jewish philosopher of religion Martin Buber once wrote about an important attribute of God's love that he called "bringing out". Buber said: "Bringing out is an essential aspect of God from the beginning. Bringing us out of entanglements, bringing us out of apathy and indifference, bringing us out of our own isolation."

There is a sense in which we could regard the Exodus of the Israelites out of slavery in Egypt as a typical instance. But it is already happening in the call of Abraham. God brings Abraham out from among his family and sets him on a certain path. When it comes down to it, everyone has to undergo his own Exodus. He not only has to leave the place that nurtured him and become independent, but has to come out of his own reserved self. He must leave himself behind, transcend his own limits; only then will he reach the Promised Land, so to speak—the sphere of freedom, in which he plays his part in creation. We have come to recognize this fundamental law of transcendence as being the essence of love. And of course the act of one who loves me is an act of this type. He has to bring me out of the comfortable inclination to stay within myself.

A great authority on the human psyche, Erich Fromm, once posed the question "Why?" about love: Why must we love?

Fromm believed he had found the reason in the appalling experience of isolation, of separation in general, that man has known since being driven out of Paradise. That is the reason for people's need to conform, which goes as far as orgiastic group experiences. Conversely the widespread presence of alcoholism, drug abuse, and suicide in the world today is a symptom of the relative collapse of conformism.

Fromm then takes a further step. He says we cannot solve this problem of separation by means of work, success, conformity, or even orgiastic experiences; all these offer only transient satisfaction. The true answer to this existential question lies solely in union with another person, in love. Fromm says: "The demand for union with another human being is the strongest drive in man. It is the most fundamental demand, the power of which holds together the human race, the clan, the family, and society as a whole. Its denial means madness or destruction—self-destruction or the destruction of others. Humanity cannot exist for a single day without love."

What is interesting is that Fromm talks of isolation as being contrary to man's inmost inclination. If isolation means not being loved, being abandoned, being alone on one's own, this situation is indeed the fear underlying all our fears. Thus we can see again that man is constructed from within, in the image of God, to be loved and to love.

At this point I believe we have to refer to man's being in the image of God. God is love. The essence of love portrays its own nature in the Trinity. Man is in God's image, and thereby he is a being whose innermost dynamic is likewise directed toward the receiving and the giving of love.

The path we follow toward genuine loving leads by way of losing oneself and through all the affliction of an Exodus. Thus along the way lie all those temptations to get there more quickly, to accept substitutes, that you just mentioned.

Only later do we realize that these substitutes bring only enormous disappointment and will plunge us afterward into unbearable loneliness, into the frustration of an absolutely empty existence. They are in fact images of hell. For if we ask ourselves what *being damned* really means, it is this: taking no pleasure in anything any more, liking nothing and no one, and being liked by no one. Being robbed of any capacity for loving and excluded from the sphere in which loving is possible—that is absolute emptiness, in which a person exists in contradiction to his own nature, and his life is totally ruined.

If, then, the essential characteristic of man is his likeness to God, his capacity for love, then humanity as a whole and each of us individually can only survive where there is love and where we are taught the way to this love. We come back to Christ: the saving act of Christ consists of making comprehensible to us the fact that God loves us. He brings this home to each of us, and by his way of the Cross he accompanies each of us along the path of losing ourselves. And by transforming the law of love into the gift of love, he overcomes that greatest loneliness of all, the state of being unredeemed.

How Do We Learn to Love?

But isn't it remarkable, how in spite of our deep-rooted longing for love, we regard everything else as being more important: success, sex, status, money, power. We use almost all of our energy in learning how to reach these goals. And we devote hardly any effort at all to learning the art of loving.

Many of the things you mentioned are short-cuts and substitutes. In these ways we try to save ourselves the trouble and risk of losing ourselves and to reach our goal more quickly and easily. That is one thing. Besides that, it is an essential part of man's calling to develop his capabilities—and only thus can he fulfill his mission of loving.

Man is meant to develop and actualize the potential within him; he is meant to do something in this world. That's because learning work skills and setting about a job in no way conflict with his basic task of loving, but give it concrete shape. I am only fulfilling my mission to love, so to speak, when I become the person I am capable of being. When I am giving what I am able to give. When I open up those possibilities in creation and in the network of human relationships that help us to get through life together and together to shape the fertile capacity of the world and of life into a garden, in which we can find both security and freedom.

This basic impulse goes astray whenever this vocational education aims at no more than the acquisition of skills; whenever mastery over our environment, improving our earning capacity, and the pursuit of power become dissociated from the inner task of loving, from everyone's being there for everyone else. Whenever power gets the better of giving. Whenever self-assertion, turning-in upon oneself, the collecting of things around oneself becomes once more the primary aim and, in this way, man's capacity for loving is choked off. Man is then dominated by things and no longer knows how to value them properly.

It is important that we not see our abilities, our vocational training, as being in themselves merely secondary. Certainly, all our abilities and all the technological capacity of man should be kept in their proper place, in our minds, and ought not to become autonomous. Whenever power becomes autonomous and is the sole category of judgment for man, then it turns into slavery and is the opposite of love.

Let us make the question quite concrete: How is it for a cardinal? Have you been able to learn the art of loving?

You don't have to learn loving in the same way as you learn, for instance, to play the piano or how to use a computer. You have to learn it as you go, so to say, in this sphere or that. And of course you also learn from people who offer you role models. First of all from your parents, who offer you both example and guidance and in whom you see what it is to be human. Later you learn from meeting those people whom life deals out to you. You learn through friendship; you learn through some task that brings you into contact with someone, through some mission. In all this it's not a matter of seeking for oneself but of learning the way of giving and, thereby, the right way to receive.

Now, I don't want to make a judgment about myself, but at any rate I have tried to learn love and, to put it more modestly, kindness, from the picture offered by Christ and the saints, and I have tried to gauge my deeds and actions accordingly. God will judge, other people will judge, how far I have really been able to learn it.

Sometimes one is misunderstood. I cannot forget what I once wrote earlier, in describing you. In doing so, I quoted from the writer Stefan Andres. In a story, Andres gave a sketch of the Spanish Great Inquisitor who had himself portrayed by the great painter El Greco: "He has no share of love."

Yes, that's what the exercise of an office can look like, from outside. At any rate we do try, in those cases where we have, so to speak, to take a critical attitude toward people, to do this in love, which is not just a matter of sweetening the pill but also sets limits beyond which damage may be done and the inner workings of love may be harmed. My fellow workers and I try not to lose sight of the person involved and to do the whole thing in such a way that he can see what we are concerned about. We don't just want to fire off an anathema at him, but to serve and strengthen

Church fellowship as a whole and, ultimately, him. And we feel our duty is above all that of protecting the faith of little ones. Only just lately, an important bishop told me that he saw, in one country in Asia, how a well-known opponent of the Congregation for the Doctrine of the Faith displayed unbelievable arrogance in trampling upon the faith of little people. Then for the first time, said the bishop, he realized that we have an important function in protecting little people from this kind of arrogance.

What I said was aimed not only at the office but also at the office holder personally, upon whom something of the office may rub off.

Yes, of course that is a danger. You can only try to take constant steps to correct this and thus so far as possible escape the danger.

Most people see the problem of love as being in the first instance the problem of needing to be loved *themselves, and not so much their own impulse* to love.

By taking this attitude, of course, you have already distorted the essence of love. If you only want to *have* love, that is just exactly when you never receive it, for it becomes selfish, twisted, and naturally the other person feels this. Learning to overcome oneself and to let go of oneself is an essential part of the process of learning to love, so that one learns to give of oneself, and indeed to do this just when one receives nothing in exchange. That one gives of oneself above all to those people one finds unsympathetic and to the person who simply needs me, someone who is suffering. Think of the good Samaritan. That is when one is truly loving, when one is not thinking of getting anything out of it but just trying to learn to give, to become a person who particularly notices someone being cold-shouldered by everyone, even if—or especially because—he does not seem likeable.

Aspects of Love

Erich Fromm says that the most important sphere of giving is not that of material things. A person is giving most to another when he gives of himself, that is to say, the most precious thing he possesses, his own life. He gives his joy, his interest, his understanding, his knowledge, and of course likewise his humor and his sadness—in short, everything that is in him.

Giving can never mean primarily giving money, that goes without saying. Of course money is also often most necessary. But when money is the only thing that is given, that is often hurtful for the other person. I have seen that again and again in the Third World. If you send us nothing but money, people tell me, then you often do more harm than good. Money is very easily misused in some way and then makes things worse. You must give more than this. You must come yourselves; you must give of yourselves; and you must help, so that the material gifts you bring are used appropriately, so that they are not just something you pull out of a bag in order to buy your way out of the difficulty we represent, the problem we are for you.

As long as we only send money or know-how, we are giving too little. In that sense the missionaries were an example for us, by giving people God, by making love believable for them; their gift to people was a new way of life; they gave themselves wholly and entirely, going out not just for two or three years as an interesting experience, but for their lifetime, so as to belong to those people for always. Unless we can relearn this capacity for self-giving, those other gifts will be too little.

What we have said about things on a world scale is of course equally true concerning individuals. There is a lovely story told by Rilke. The poet tells how, in Paris, he used always to pass a woman into whose hat someone had thrown a coin. The beggar woman was always quite unmoved by this, as if she had no feelings at all. One day, Rilke gives her a rose. And in that moment her face glows. He sees for the first time that she does have feelings. She smiles, and then for a week she is no longer there begging, because someone has given her something that is more than money.

I think that is such a lovely little incident, in which you can see that sometimes a rose, a little act of giving, of affection, of acceptance of the other person, can be more than many coins or other material gifts.

The New Law *that had been promised with the coming of the Messiah was a message of love. Can we say that the Old Covenant was, all in all, pretty well washed-up, more or less at an end; in its worship, in its sacrifice, and equally in its understanding of community life? For obviously the time had come to start something new. Malachi, the last prophet of the Old Covenant, had proclaimed: "Thus says the Lord of Hosts: I take no pleasure in you, and I will accept no more sacrifices from your hands."*

I would not say that the Old Covenant was washed-up. The Jews still live by it and are still able to draw enormous spiritual treasures from the Old Testament. As Christians, though, we would certainly say that it was a path leading to a particular goal, which eventually was bound to be reached, if the path was to have any point to it. What had gone before was not simply broken off or laid aside as worn-out, but it was a path that led to a certain goal and that remains present, so to say, within that goal. Except by that way we cannot reach and enter into the goal.

There is criticism of sacrifices from the beginning of the Old Testament. In the Psalms God says to man: If I were hungry, I would not tell you; I have no pleasure in your bullocks and your burned offerings; that is not what I need; I need your heart.

The offering of sacrifice always included an effort to recognize God's rule and, at least symbolically, to give him what was his own. At the same time, man was somehow aware that God can make nothing of bullocks or of burned calves. Thus it is that the Old Testament rituals transcend themselves, from within, pointing toward him who is the true sacrifice, the Son who gives himself and gives us the Father, who thus begins, so to say, to change the world into a place of love. Love is in this the true sacrifice. It abolishes the despairing gesture represented by the animal sacrifices and renders it meaningless.

It is thus no accident that in fact forty years after the Cross, the Temple disappears for ever from the stage of history, because what it represented is now really present.

Was it for love of mankind that God sent his Son—or was it perhaps only pity for them?

I would not set love and pity in opposition. True pity is much more than mere sentimentality. It is a kind of identification with the suffering of another, and thus it is a true and essential act of love.

In the ancient world Hellenistic thought had expounded the immutability of God and, in doing so, had portrayed him as a pure spirit who could have no feelings, still less suffer. That provoked Christians into asking, what is God really like? And Origen once expressed it beautifully: God cannot suffer (*pathein*), but he can have sympathy. That is to say, he can identify completely with us who do suffer. This is the great act of love by which in Christ he identifies himself with us right to the extent of sharing bodily life—and thereby identifies us with himself and draws us into his love.

So I would say that by setting the power of sympathy, of pity, against the stoic ethic of refusing to recognize suffering, Christianity was proclaiming the power of love. Pity, sympathy, rightly understood, is an act of love.

Part II

JESUS CHRIST

Cardinal, can we picture Jesus Christ for ourselves as being like the image of him on the shroud of Turin?

The Turin shroud is a mystery, an image that has not yet been satisfactorily explained, even if there is much to suggest it may be genuine. In any case, it touches us—by the strange power of this human form with those dreadful wounds.

And with a very impressive face.

In this face we can recognize the Passion in a way that moves us deeply. And we see a great inner dignity as well. In this face there are calm and patience, peace and kindness. In that way it can truly help us to picture Christ.

A man with great self-awareness . . .

If it were merely human self-awareness, it would be present in a surpassing degree. There is something else in this expression, something much greater: Jesus knows that he is at one with someone else, specifically with the Father, with God. This is an intimate unity, surpassing every kind of mystical unity known to us. Jesus has therefore good reason to use the name of God—"I am"—with reference to himself.

But a man who is sometimes brusque and indignant. He says once: "Oh, you faithless and stubborn generation!" And in despair he cries: "How much longer must I be with you? How long must I put up with you!"

I, too, am repeatedly moved by the fact that there is this strictness in the Lord and this impatience with people. We can learn something from this about love, which is not always just being soft-hearted and giving way, but can be demanding.

Jesus looks at people with God's eyes. From this point of view we must recognize how disappointed God must be with people, how anger must build up in him at the sight of what this creature of his is doing with him and with itself. These sayings show how disturbing this attitude of bored indifference toward God, this inability to listen, and man's closed mind must appear from God's point of view.

Jesus' favorite expression is plainly "wailing and gnashing of teeth". Whenever he wants to draw attention to something really bad, he says there will be wailing and gnashing of teeth.

I would not exactly describe it as Jesus' favorite phrase. This is something that appears in Jesus' sayings about limits. "Wailing and gnashing of teeth" portrays the danger, the threat, and finally those who are lost. This depicts well enough the world of those who have fallen victim to drugs or to orgiastic frenzies, for whom, at the moment of awakening out of their ecstatic stupor, the total contradiction of their lives becomes clear.

Hell is usually depicted as fire, as burning. But gnashing of teeth actually happens when you are freezing. This suggests a picture of fallen people, wailing and mourning and crying in protest, shut out in the cold, the cold into which one enters by refusing love. In a world separated from God and thereby from love you begin to freeze—your teeth begin to chatter.

Sometimes Jesus goes in for real wonder-working. When his disciples yet again have no money to pay the Temple tax when it falls due, he says to Peter: "Go to the lake and cast your line; the first fish you pull out, take it and open its mouth, and you will find a four-drachma coin. Give that to the tax collectors to pay the tax for you and for me."

Jesus did not work wonders just because he felt like it, but only in the context of faith. He said explicitly: I did not come to work wonders, but to proclaim the kingdom of God.

The little story you are referring to is in fact something rather different. It is intended to make clear a deeper meaning. We can see here how the Lord, who did not need to pay tax, since the Temple was there for him, does so in deference to the law, but then does it by way of a special gift from God. I can see Jesus quietly laughing about it.

Jesus—An Invention?

Doubts concerning the story of Jesus Christ will never disappear, I'm sure. For some people Jesus is simply invented; for others he is the leader of a kind of religious sect. Others, again, believe Christ to have been yet another of those archetypal figures who succeed in expressing with great clarity something of the drama of human existence: pain, anxiety, love. And many would no doubt say: This teacher is certainly interesting, but what has Jesus to do with me?

It is of course possible to cast doubt on all historical events, as we see again and again. For example, one private scholar denies the existence of Charlemagne; indeed, he alleges that the whole of the history of two centuries is a forgery, and so on. Well, we weren't there at the time. And the historical document may well give us information, but it doesn't bring us into direct contact with the original facts.

So there is room for speculation?

No. Merely by applying the recognized criteria of history, we find the evidence for Jesus to be so early, so extensive and so sound that there is no room for doubt about him as a historical person. And everything that has been transmitted about him is quite different from what anyone might have invented or imagined. It far exceeds any plausible expectations.

And we can perceive here not only the trace of the original event but also the effect it produced. Neither of them can be explained as arising from some synthetic construction, but only by the elemental impetus of something that actually happened. No doubts, then, as to the historical existence of Jesus are in my view at all serious.

But what is really historically reliable in the available sources?

Well, you know that there is more and more digging now into and around the sources. People try to take them to pieces more and more completely and systematically. And in the end we are left with a few miserable fragments, and one suddenly wonders how such events can have grown from such a paltry figure.

There is one thing we should not forget: the First Letter to the Corinthians, which offers a witness to the Resurrection of Jesus and to the institution of the Eucharist, includes texts that Paul found already available to him. The letter was written at the beginning of the fifties, counting from the birth of Christ. The text that it includes goes back to the traditions current in Jerusalem. The basic contents, then, as Paul says, have been handed down directly. Even the linguistic form shows that here we are getting quite close to the events themselves.

I must admit that the more I hear about these efforts of source research, the less confidence I feel in the plethora of hypotheses it has thrown up. And which are then endlessly repeated and refuted. The whole business of constructing a purely historical Jesus, in contrast to the Jesus of faith, which began with the Enlightenment, was already subjected to severe criticism by Albert Schweitzer. He said: We thought we really had him at last, and now he has passed by our age and gone back to being himself.

I think all these attempts are reconstructions in which we can always see the face of the architect. Whether you take Adolf Harnack's Christ—who reflects the typical liberal—or whether you take Bultmann's Christ, who portrays his kind of existential philosophy. All these constructions have been undertaken with one guiding idea: There can be no such thing as God made man. Those events that presuppose his existence cannot therefore have happened. That means that here you are already starting with a presupposition that will, basically, rob the event of its inner force—and, thereby, precisely that which lends it both tension and fullness.

How would you go about it?

I would think it much more appropriate if just for once we asked: Does the portrayal of this person in the New Testament make sense? And my answer would be: only the way he is there makes any sense at all. Only as shown there has he the greatness to be the originator of such events. I am therefore persuaded that—despite all source criticism, from which we still have much to learn—our trust in the Gospels is fully justified. Even if the details of many traditions have been expanded in later periods, we can trust the Gospels for the essentials and can find in them the real figure of Jesus. It is much more real than the apparently reliable historical reconstructions.

And, I would add, the Gospel of John, which for a long time was regarded as a purely theological composition—Bultmann, for example, tried to interpret it in the context of gnostic influences—appears today to have been rehabilitated to an astonishing degree as a historical document. It includes precise geographical details and demonstrates an exact knowledge of Jewish thought and the Jewish way of life at that period. An exegete such as Klaus Berger, in Heidelberg, would therefore regard it as the oldest of the Gospels. Well, I would certainly not go along with him there. Tradition is unanimous in declaring that it was written around the end of the first century. Let's leave it at that. But it is a Gospel that is based on very exact knowledge and does not portray a theological vision that has lost contact with concrete historical reality.

8. Revelation

The French theologian Henri de Lubac once said that the great mysteries were concentrated in the life of Christ. *The actions that took place were indeed genuinely* human *actions, on the one hand, but at the same time they were the actions of a* divine *person. I quote de Lubac: "To grasp the meaning of the life of Christ is to penetrate into the divine reality." Does that mean that, to the extent that we learn to understand the life of Christ, God and, indeed, the whole of our human existence become visible and comprehensible?*

I believe the essential thing is that as we gradually enter our way into and share the life of Christ, we acquire the substance and foundation of life from which we can share in the understanding of God. The words of Jesus have an irreplaceable significance, but we should not reduce Christ to words alone. The flesh, as John says, is part of this; it is the living Word that leads us right to the Cross. Only when we look at the whole figure of Jesus in its living context will the words speak to us with their full power. Thus contemplating the life and the suffering of Jesus is basic to an understanding of his message.

Prophets and Heralds

In that case, let us sketch out the person, the life, and the message of Jesus in somewhat greater detail. Let's start with John. "In the beginning was the Word", his Gospel starts by saying, and then it says, "And the Word became flesh / and dwelt among us, / and we beheld his glory, / the glory of the only Son of the Father, full of grace and truth." This prologue is certainly one of the most sublime things that have ever been written in the world.

The opening words of John's Gospel make a bridge from the creation story, from the foundation of all that is, to what happened in Palestine. They show us that the same Logos, the creative rationality from which the world has sprung, is personally present in this man Jesus. The same power that made the world is itself entering into the world and talking with us. This is the great paradox that meets us here: God is so great that he can become small. And, indeed, so small that he can meet us as a man.

But God doesn't just drop down from heaven and introduce himself; rather, he enters fully into a historical context that offers us a way to approach him, one in which he is expected and in which we are able to receive his message.

John the Baptist is seen as the immediate herald of the coming of Jesus Christ. "He came as a witness", it says in the Gospel, "to bear witness to the light, so that all might believe through him."

In this historical context there is one last prophet, one final witness, who comes before Jesus in history. The Baptist represents a kind of revival movement. At this moment in its history, when Israel is so disturbed, the question about the savior, the Messiah, is now of burning relevance. Israel is occupied by a foreign power, but it still carries the promise within itself and waits for its fulfillment. On the other hand, this is an age with no prophets. It seems as if the light of prophecy has died.

John came out of the wilderness and proclaimed something new. He was, he said, "the voice crying in the wilderness". He baptized people, but he baptized them, so it is written, "on the other side of the Jordan". And when, one day, he saw Jesus coming toward him, John pronounced the mysterious words: "Behold the Lamb of God, who takes away the sin of the world. This is he, concerning whom I said: After me there comes a man who is before me, because he was before me."

John appears in the wilderness as a man dedicated to God. First of all he preaches repentance, purification, and the gathering together of the people for the coming of God. In a sense this proclamation summarizes the whole of prophecy at that very moment when history is reaching its goal. His mission is to open the door for God, so that Israel is ready to welcome him and to prepare for his hour in history.

The important things are first his call to repentance, which continues what all the prophets said, and second his witness to Christ, which again makes prophecy concrete in the image of the lamb, which is the lamb of God. Let us recall the stories of Abraham, the stories of Isaac, the sacrifices that involve a lamb, especially the paschal sacrifice, in which a lamb is sacrificed. These substitutes now find their fulfillment. Basically, the paschal lamb stands in place of us men. Now Christ is sent by God to become the paschal lamb, and he shares our fate and thereby transforms it.

The second sentence is an implicit reference to the divinity of Jesus Christ, even if this has not been fully thought out by the Baptist and is thus not quite explicit. He says that this is not just some historical personage, but is the one who goes before us all, who comes forth from the eternity of God and is an intimate part of that eternity.

The patriarch Jacob had more or less described the time when this Redeemer would come, as in fact it was at the birth of Christ. Many had fallen away from the faith; Pharisees lived a life full of pride and lovelessness, as it says; the rest felt like a flock of sheep without a shepherd. The longing for the Master had grown equally great, both among Jews and among Gentiles. "Drop down the righteous, O heavens, from above!" pleads the prophet Isaiah, "and you, clouds, rain him down!" Yet nonetheless: Might it not be that these prophecies were fabricated in response to Jesus, and in fact only in retrospect?

The first sentence of your question refers to the so-called benediction of Jacob (Gen 49), which consists of a collection of promises, often quite mysterious, for the twelve sons of Jacob. In the blessing of Judah it says: "The rule shall not depart from Judah, nor the scepter from his feet, until the coming of the one to whom it belongs, to whom the obedience of all peoples is due" (49:10). That was then interpreted as a promise concerning the kingdom of David (David belonged to the tribe of Judah), and after this kingdom's disappearance—in the time of Jesus, that is—as the promise of a new son of David, the Messiah, who would also command the obedience of all the peoples of the world, the non-Jews. It is obvious that Christians would see this promise as being fulfilled in Jesus the Son of David. But this text (scholars still disagree about its period of origin) does not go so far as to describe the time of Jesus, and its words point mysteriously to the future, and its meaning only seems clear in the light of Christ.

Now let's take the prophet Isaiah. The original text in fact reads "Drop down righteousness, O heavens." Only after righteousness had come in the guise of a particular person did the Christians read this text with a personalized reference. Thus in this relationship of agreement between Old and New Testaments we can see how the word of Scripture offers a progressive way. The words go to meet him; they seek him out where he is still in obscurity.

It is of course possible to read the Old Testament so that it is not directed toward Christ; it does not point quite unequivocally to Christ. And if Jews cannot see the promises as being fulfilled in him, this is not just ill will on their part, but genuinely because of the obscurity of the texts and the tension in the relationship between these texts and the figure of Jesus. Jesus brings a new meaning to these texts—yet it is he who first gives them their proper coherence and relevance and significance.

There are perfectly good reasons, then, for denying that the Old Testament refers to Christ and for saying, No, that is not what he said. And there are also good reasons for referring it to him—that is what the dispute between Jews and Christians is about. But this is not all. A great part of the purely historical and critical exegesis, likewise, does not read the Old Testament in this sense of pointing the way forward; it regards the Christian interpretation of it as being inconsistent with the original meaning, or at any rate as going far beyond it.

One would have to add this: The Old Testament is not an oracle; it is a path. We still have the freedom to reject it. I would say that the very fact that this freedom is open to us is a guarantee that the texts will stand on their own. It is quite clear that historically the Old Testament precedes Christ; the faith and the Scriptures of the Jews make that as clear as day. The Church Fathers saw it as the historical mission of the Jews that, by saying Yes to the Old Testament and No to Jesus, they give a universal guarantee of the age and authenticity of their sacred books. This, so the Fathers thought, was why they remained Jews and did not become

Christians. The texts stand on their own, but they gain a new significance and a unity of view when we read them with Christ.

Did God Correct Himself?

With the coming of Christ, the Old Testament laws, not only certain laws of ritual sacrifice but also that wretched "an eye for an eye, and a tooth for a tooth", have been superseded. Do we not find ourselves having to say that God corrects himself?

Here again, I would want to talk about traveling a historical path. "An eye for an eye, a tooth for a tooth" sounds frightful, but after all it was at first a principle of justice that contained and directed vengeance. The retaliation must correspond to the offense; it must not run out of control but be limited to what has been done. In that sense, this was a step forward to something that in fact is still recognized in the administration of justice. Besides this progress in legal thinking, we would, of course, have to add that it is only through a love that breaks through the chain of reprisal that anything new can ever really come into being.

In the course of this conversation we have already dealt with the saying: "I have not come to abolish the law, but to fulfill it." Where the question of the Temple sacrifices is concerned, we confront this saying in quite concrete terms. The sacrificial offerings were always only a substitute. And when the one comes who gives the real thing, and who thereby brings man to the point of being able to give himself to God, then the whole meaning of these sacrificial procedures has been fulfilled in him. Now, the whole of what the Temple represented, and was meant to be, is present in him as the living Temple. Thus, something is not simply done away with, but its goal is brought to achievement.

In this way, what the Temple was trying to do is still present in the Eucharist. But now in that meaningful form to which earlier rites were only preliminary approaches. So I would not say that God got it right the second time. We see, rather, how he allows men at first those forms they cannot yet get beyond, as part of a path that carries within it its own inner dynamic and necessarily leads them farther on. What this path truly signified is now fulfilled and receives its rightful place.

The Scriptures speak of the "new Israel, the people of God, whom you have called". Does that mean that with the coming of the Redeemer those people who follow him, the Christians, are the new people of God and are thereby a chosen people?

Yes, you can certainly say so. They are, so to speak, an enlarged Israel. Paul says explicitly that the children of Abraham are not only those who are descended from him by blood, but those who inherit his faith. On this account, the membership of Israel through fellowship with Christ is wider and more inclusive than membership by blood. This fellowship on the basis of a fundamental decision (and above all by way of a gift) has become a people, in that the promise is now given a universal dimension.

The word *chosen* or *elect* has acquired a nasty taste for us, because we interpret it as a form of distinction, as a presumption of superiority. In its original biblical sense it meant that a people was chosen so that something might be required of them, that they might endure something and might accomplish something for others. So that being chosen is always being chosen *for* something. To a certain extent, things are made more difficult for you, because you assume responsibility for others.

It is in this sense that the election and the ideal of Israel have been passed on to those who through Christ belong to Abraham and to the living God. They have not been selected to live a life for others in order to qualify for a special ticket to heaven, but so that they may share in the ministry of Christ, in the service Israel renders to history.

9. The Light

How remarkable: God, the Almighty, chose for himself as the place of his appearance what was very smallest and most insignificant, a wretched stable in Bethlehem. And the Church argues that this is so incredible and paradoxical that it would have to be true on those grounds alone.

This argument, taken alone and unsupported, would not of course suffice to demonstrate that it is true. But it is a fact that the choice of "little things" and "little people" is characteristic of God's dealings with man.

We see this characteristic first of all in the fact that God chooses the earth as his theater of action, this grain of dust in the universe; and in the fact that there Israel, a virtually powerless people, becomes the vehicle for his action; and again in the fact that a completely unknown village, Nazareth, becomes his home; finally, in the fact that the Son of God is born at Bethlehem, outside the village in a stable. All of this is consistent.

God sets against human pride a universal measure, namely, love. Pride is at the heart, and is the content, of every form of sin, in the sense of wanting to be God oneself. Love, on the contrary, does not exalt itself, but stoops down. Love shows that stooping down in that way is the truly exalted thing. That we are sublime when we come down low, when we become simple, when we bend down to the poor and the lowly. God makes himself little in order to bring puffed-up man back into the proper measure. Thus we see that becoming small is the rule, the model of how God acts. It helps us to recognize something of God's nature and of our own nature. In this sense it is quite logical and stands as a rebuke to wisdom.

In this area there is one scene that has become world famous. Musically, it has been immortalized in a triumphant chorus from Friedrich Handel's Messiah. *It's the scene with the shepherds in the field, keeping watch over their flock by night, and an angel appears to them, with the glory of God shining all round: "Fear not!" says the angel, "for I proclaim tidings of great joy." And while he is still speaking, armies of heavenly spirits come to join him, and in a manifestation quite unheard of, they sing the truly sublime words: "Glory to God in the highest, and peace to men on earth who are of goodwill."*

That is certainly one of the most moving scenes in the whole of Scripture. It's not for nothing that Christendom so loves it. From early Christian art onward, we can see that. This scene goes right to your heart, but the message goes far beyond what is merely cheerful and lovely.

Once again, it is the simple people who are called first to the crib. Herod knows nothing of it. Even the wise know nothing about it at first. The news comes to the herdsmen, those who are waiting, those who know they have need of the redeeming presence of God. They are the ones who are open enough and ready to go there. Together with Mary and Joseph, with Simeon and Anna, Elizabeth and Zechariah, they represent the poor ones of Israel—and, thereby, the people of God as a whole. We can see in the Psalms how the expression *the meek* or *the poor* is used as shorthand to refer to the believing core of Israel. And just as Jesus praises the way children are, it is a matter of keeping our simplicity of heart, so that we will be able to see visions and hear the angels.

The second group of people who arrive in Bethlehem, according to the Gospel of Matthew, are the wise men from the East. This is significant. The simple folk come first, but the wise are not excluded. They have a real and genuine wisdom, which makes a person open for Christ. And one more thing is important. The wise men who come to the place where Jesus was born are pagans. To some extent this is the movement of the Church, of the Gentiles, which symbolically takes its beginning here.

The Most Important Moment in History

What took place in this event, in the judgment of the German bishop Rudolf Graber, "is infinitely more important than the creation of the world". Nothing greater than this had ever happened before, and there would never again be anything greater: "For the fact that God's only Son, the second Person of the Godhead, is willing and ready to become man on this tiny little earth simply surpasses all else."

Yes, it really is a valuable lesson, to put our ideas of great and small into proper perspective. By material standards, the creation of the world obviously seems to us immeasurably greater. In comparison with that, this little event in Bethlehem, which was at first entirely overlooked by historians, seems hardly worth mentioning.

Judging by quantitative measurements, then, one is enormous and the other really small. But when we realize that a single human heart stands on a higher scale than the whole extent of the universe, as Pascal expressed it, then we can begin to understand that the act by which God becomes man, that he who is the Creator, the eternal Logos, comes down to enter into human existence and unites himself with it, so that he himself is this man—that this act is an event of a far greater order of significance. God himself comes into the world and becomes a man. This opens up a dimension beside which the apparently immeasurable *material* dimensions represent a significantly lesser order of magnitude.

In the course of two thousand years the birth of Christ has become the greatest myth of all time. This night of all nights has long since become the property of everyone. Nowhere does faith so visibly spill out beyond the threshold of the Church as it does here. Christmas has an incomparable power of symbolism, of values, of morality and melancholy; it is an absolute standard by which humanity is measured. Sometimes I think that although we know Christmas well, Christmas knows us far better.

Perhaps we need to make ourselves clear just once more about the word "myth". Nowadays the word myth is indeed often understood in a positive sense, as a kind of visionary means of expression for realities that go beyond what is visible and tangible; thus, it would embody a higher truth than what is merely factual would. But even in this positive sense, "myth" stands in opposition to history. It refers to a vision, not to facts. The birth of Christ, on the other hand, is a historical event, something that really happened as a concrete event. In the history of religions, this direct connection with real history is among the distinctive features of the Christian faith.

Taking this as understood, it is in fact quite amazing how this night in the stable, in this cave, which was first noticed by the shepherds as a result of the message of the angel, has now become a sign whose significance reaches out beyond the Christian world, a sign hardly anyone passes by without noticing. Although we would have to add that hand-in-hand with this diffusion of Christmas far beyond the range of Christian faith goes a terrible reduction to banality.

It is becoming more and more the trend today to separate this festival from Christianity and to reject its Christian beginnings, like a rocket that thrusts the first stage away from itself when it reaches altitude. In America, in the process of commercialization and the pursuit of sentimentality, the display windows of large shops, which in former years were decorated with crèches at Christmas time, are now equipped with mythological representations, with deer and stags or Santa Clauses, whereby what is truly mythical is set side-by-side with what is Christian. Of course a lingering echo still remains of what touched people when they learned that God became a man. But this is an attempt to keep what is beautiful and touching and to get away from anything in it that makes demands upon us.

Christmas shows us, in the midst of all our great thoughts and great feelings, as well as all the contradictions, the degree of mendacity abroad in the world—and our own doubts and lack of faith, too.

This event touches so many chords of the human heart, speaks to so many great and important human values, that one might almost say at first sight that we could take all these things for their own sake and dispense with the actual event (whereby Christmas, of course, is robbed of what makes it great and falls into a kind of vacuum). But that doesn't change the fact that so much is being said here that is comprehensible and significant far beyond the bounds of Christendom, and what is said will perhaps be able to bring people back to faith again. The mystery of the child, of simplicity, of humility—all of that speaks to us here. And we ought to set these elements that teach about humanity right in the center, so as to show what the human life of God means.

There is a great idea underlying the original custom. This child is God's gift to mankind, and in that sense Christmas is the proper day for giving gifts. But when the giving of presents becomes a matter of obligatory shopping trips, then the idea of presents is completely distorted. Then it is a matter of what Christ said to his disciples: Do not do as the Gentiles do, who invite each other because they in turn receive invitations. As a mere exchange of material goods, Christmas is coming under the power of wanting-for-oneself; it is becoming the instrument of an insatiable egoism and has fallen under the sway of possessions and of power—whereas this event in fact brings us exactly the opposite message. Pruning back Christmas so that it is once again simple would be an enormous achievement.

Light of the World

Christ is not the Enlightened One but is himself the Light. He is not only the Way, but he says he is the End. You once called what happened at Bethlehem the "decisive breakthrough in world history, leading toward the uniting of creatures with God".

It is the tremendous event, God really became man. That he did not just disguise himself as man, did not just play the part for a while in history, but that he truly is man—and that finally, when he stretches out his arms on the Cross, he makes himself into a wide open space into which we can enter.

If, then, this God-Man wants to make us all, as Scripture says, into his Body, to draw us into a living corporate unity, just as, according to the Bible, man and woman become one flesh, then we can see that this is not just a matter of a single event, which happens and then is past. No, it is a breakthrough, a beginning, in which Christ wants to involve us through the Eucharist, through the sacraments, through baptism. In this sense, what happens here is something that surpasses any kind of evolution, the union of God and man, of creature and Creator. Thus it no longer takes place as a step in evolution, brought about by the forces of nature, but as an intervention, a personal act of love, which opens up for man, from this moment on, a new sphere and a new realm of possibility.

You once said that Jesus was "the exemplary man, the man of the future, through whom we are able to see to how great an extent man is a being of the future, a being we are still waiting for". Does that mean that the true potential for development, that being which we are actually called to become, which is truly alive within us, will look just as it was portrayed in Jesus Christ?

It is true that the breakthrough to the new man takes place in Jesus Christ. In him the real future of man, what has yet to be realized, what he can be and should be, has in fact begun.

I would not say that man is capable of being modeled merely in an external sense on the destiny of Jesus. Rather, I would say that the inner self of Jesus, as it is portrayed throughout the whole of his life and finally in his self-sacrifice on the Cross, offers a measure and prototype of future humanity. It's not for nothing that we talk of following Christ, of entering upon his way. It is a matter of inner identification with Christ—just as *he* identified himself with us. I think that is really what man is moving toward.

It is in the great stories of discipleship, which extend across the centuries, that we first see unfolding what is hidden in the figure of Jesus. It is not the case, then, that a schematic pattern is imposed, but that every potential development of true human existence is contained therein. We see how Thérèse of Lisieux or Saint Don Bosco, how Edith Stein, the apostle Paul, or Thomas Aquinas, has learned from Jesus how to go about being human. All these people have become truly like Jesus—and they are nonetheless different and original.

You said once in a sermon that the candles on the Advent wreath should remind children of the thousands of years of human history before *Jesus Christ, remind them of the darkness of history that was unredeemed. Since that time, Christians have given the period since the birth of the Lord a lovely name: "anni salutis reparatae", the years of restored salvation.*

If you picture the time of salvation in a mechanical way, like a rigidly constructed machine in which I only have to follow procedure to get salvation, then we have a false understanding of this idea. We can see how it is constantly contradicted. No century, probably, has fought such terrible and bloody wars as the last one has. Things have happened that are more evil than would have been at all possible in earlier ages, because no one had the capacity to do evil things in such a refined, technologically developed, and rationally systematized fashion.

The salvation that is offered us is no mechanical process or exterior matter. It has been entrusted to our freedom and has thereby also been rendered vulnerable to the fragility of human freedom and of the human character. Salvation begins anew in every man; it is not simply there. You cannot just cement it on externally or control it by the use of power, but always only enter into the freedom that opens up. But above all and in all is the One who comes to meet us and who gives us a hope that is stronger than all the devastation that men can bring to pass.

What Did Christ Bring to Earth?

Jesus is also referred to as the "New Adam". He is said to be the mediator of the whole of revelation and he who fulfills what is revealed. Can we then say, in a few sentences, what was new that came into the world with Christ?

Let's take up the image of the "New Adam". Adam is first of all the symbol for the beginning of human life, for the universal patriarch. When Christ is called the "New Adam", this signifies that the real beginning is here. The first beginning, thus, is a preliminary essay with Christ in view and only becomes comprehensible looking back from him. From that viewpoint we can perfectly well say that the measure and prototype of human existence has been set in Jesus—precisely because he is not just a man, but the God-Man—man is called to share in the union with God.

We ought not to judge the originality of Jesus merely by isolated sayings or deeds. The Cross is something new in the way he accepts it and suffers it. The Resurrection is new. Even the virgin birth is new (although there are indeed myths that point toward it). The message of loving God and loving one's neighbor as fulfilling the whole of the law, or the Eucharist, through which he shares himself in his risen life—these are all enormous innovations that he brings into the world. All of these reflect what is absolutely new: that is to say, that God is no longer just in heaven; God is no longer the Wholly Other, the incomprehensible One, but he is now also the One who is near us, who has become identified with us, who touches us and is touched by us, the one whom we can receive and who will receive us.

In that sense, the entire originality of Jesus lies in himself —as the unity of God and man.

Of course, this God-and-Man also says: "I have come to set fire upon the earth. Would that it were already burning!" And again: "Do you think that I have come to bring peace upon the earth? No, I say to you, not peace, but division."

That is a powerful saying. When he talks about fire, he means in the first place his own Passion, which was a Passion of love and was therefore a fire; the new burning bush, which burns and is not consumed; a fire that is to be handed on.

Jesus does not come to make us comfortable; rather he sets fire to the earth; he brings the great living fire of divine love, which is what the Holy Spirit is, a fire that burns. In an apocryphal saying of Jesus that has been transmitted by Origen, he says: "Whoever comes close to me comes close to the fire." Whoever comes close to him, accordingly, must be prepared to be burned. Especially nowadays, we ought to set these sayings against a vacuous Christianity that renders everything banal, a Christianity that would prefer to be comfortable and undemanding. Christianity is great because love is great. It burns, yet this is not a destructive fire but one that makes things bright and pure and free and grand. Being a Christian, then, is daring to entrust oneself to this burning fire.

We have another saying of Jesus: "Peace is what I give to you, my peace I give to you, not the kind the world gives do I give to you."

We must look at both sayings together in order to let the meaning of what God says shine forth for us. Christ is the one who brings peace. And I would say that this is the saying that is preeminent and determinative. But we only properly comprehend this peace that Christ brings if we do not understand it in banal fashion as a way of cheating one's way out of pain, or out of the truth and the conflicts that truth brings with it.

If a government tried to avoid all conflict and wanted to suit everyone, or even if an individual did the same, then nothing would work any more. And it's the same in the Church. If she simply aims to avoid conflict, merely to ensure that no disturbances arise anywhere, then her real message can no longer make any impact. For this message is in fact there precisely in order to conflict with our behavior, to tear man out of his life of lies and to bring clarity and truth. Truth does not come cheap. It makes demands, and it also burns. The challenge that we find in Jesus' conflict with his contemporaries is an essential part of his message. Here, a rigid and encrusted form of faith, a self-righteous faith, is not conveniently plastered over; rather he takes up the cudgel against it, so that its encrusted shell can be broken and the truth can reach its mark.

Has the peace that Jesus Christ brings the quality of initially arousing conflict?

At any rate it convicts us of our lies. It brings us out of our comfortable indifference into the struggle and the pain of the truth. And it is only thus that true peace can come into being, in place of the apparent peace, beneath which lie hidden hypocrisy and all kinds of conflict.

The saying about fire belongs with the more important

saying about peace, but at the same time it shows that genuine peace does not fear conflict. That truth is worth pain and even conflict. That I may not just accept a lie in order to have quiet. For it is not the first duty of a citizen, or of a Christian, to seek quiet; but rather it is that standing fast by what is noble and great, which is what Christ has given us and which can reach as far as suffering, as far as a struggle that ends in martyrdom—and exactly in that way bring peace.

Good News

Jesus talked about the fire and the sword, but he also says: "Learn from me!" For in this way "You will find rest for your souls." He says he is in truth "kind and lowly in heart". And besides that: "My yoke is easy, and my burden is light." That is the way we picture a message of good news.

Yes, though at the same time we know that these comforting words of Jesus also make a great demand upon us. But in contrast to what we have just been saying about the pain of the truth, about the fire of Christ, they show what it all comes down to *in the end.*

Christ embodies the great and undiluted loving-kindness of God. He doesn't want to make things difficult for us; on the contrary, he comes to help us bear the load. He does not do this by simply taking away from us the burden of being human; that remains heavy enough. But we are no longer carrying it on our own; he is carrying it with us. Christ has nothing to do with comfort, with banality, yet we find in him that inner calm which comes from knowing that we are being supported by an ultimate kindness and an ultimate security.

We see that the entire structure of the message of Jesus is full of tension; it is an enormous challenge. Its nature is such that it always has to do with the Cross. Anyone who is not ready to get burned, who is not at least willing for it to happen, will not come near. But we can always be sure that it is there that we will meet true loving-kindness, which helps us, which accepts us—and which does not merely mean well toward us but will in fact ensure that things go well for us.

10. The Way

Gospels and Gospel Writers

There is little in the life of Christ that would have been likely to leave any concrete traces on this earth. Jesus did not build any temple; he conquered no cities and struck no coins. To be sure, no manuscript of any classical author has been transmitted in anything remotely approaching the number and variety of documents as have the writings of the New Testament. Their numbers run into thousands, and the oldest among them are separated from the time of Jesus by only a few decades.

We have already talked about historical and critical research, which feeds people's doubts as to the truth concerning the person and the message of Jesus. It is not certain, scholars say, where or when Jesus was born or whether he did in fact preach the Sermon on the Mount in exactly that form. It is even improbable, so the more recent researchers say, that he understood himself to be the Messiah. Much can only be understood, we are told, in terms of a period in which apocalyptic expectations had risen to a peak. This is the point I should like to develop a little: Does modern scholarship betray history, and in particular does it betray faith?

Historical and critical scholarship has undoubtedly rendered great service. It has taught us to understand many things much more accurately. But it also has its limits, especially with respect to a text of this kind. The scholarly method refers to researching the past by the study of texts in general, and in doing this it assumes that certain rules about history hold good. The events recounted in the Gospels break right out of these general rules in any case and thus run counter to the generalized application of this method, which admits no exceptions.

In the course of time people have sought to discover and to distinguish within the texts various sources; and much of this work is important. But these remain, on the whole, mere attempts at analysis that are quickly replaced by others, and one should not overestimate the probability of their being correct. It is particularly the case that the question of who actually created the Gospels leaves us with more questions and uncertainties than if one simply accepted the texts as a whole as being credible and historical. For if this were not so, then there must have been at that period, within a very short time, an enormous plethora of brilliant literary creations. How could the text of the Gospel become established so quickly? Who were the writers capable of producing such a thing? How does it come about that a uniform structure, the Church, arose from this foundation—there are no answers to any of this here.

Where, then?

The text has its own specific character, and this demands to be respected. The texts as a whole communicate a reality that breaks right out of the ordinary course of history. This reality is internally consistent, and on this account we are as much justified as we ever were in trusting them as a whole.

We must add that there is no such thing as *the* historical-critical method, no such thing as *the* results. There are scholarly writers who, just as in the past, regard the text as very trustworthy and who are able to advance objective methodical arguments for doing so. And there are others who leave hardly anything remaining—and who are then obliged to resort to complete reconstructions in order to explain how everything came about. Thus they are drawing their bow at a venture, because there are no sources for this, so that these attempts basically become sheer fantasy.

Let us look a little more closely at the evangelists. There is Matthew. He has a double name, which was unusual at that period, that of Matthew-Levi. A customs official who pockets some of the money he handles, someone who works for the enemy, the Roman authority. He is the one of whom the Gospel says: "And when Jesus was sitting at table for a meal in his house, many tax collectors and sinners came and sat down to eat with him and his disciples." Not exactly the upright citizen or trustworthiness personified.

I'm afraid we will have to go into the question of sources a little further. Earlier, the Gospel of Matthew was held to be the oldest of the Gospels. A note by a second-century writer, Papias, says that Matthew first of all wrote this Gospel in Hebrew, and then it was translated into Greek. On account of its detailed information, its structure, and the way it was so readable, it was seen as *the* Gospel of the Church, and its text was the one generally used in quotations. Luke and Mark were also acceptable, but Matthew was held to be the oldest and the one that offered most, the one most immediately directed to the Church as far as her liturgy and her faith were concerned.

According to the results of research, the texts of the three synoptic Gospels—Matthew, Mark, Luke—are intertwined with one another in some kind of close relationship and are interdependent. The question of how Matthew came to be written has been completely reopened. Nowadays the greater number of scholars are of the opinion that one cannot ascribe this Gospel to the apostle Matthew, that, on the contrary, it originated rather later and was written down toward the end of the first century in a Syrian Jewish Christian congregation.

The origin and growth of the Gospels as a group now appears to us to be a very complex process. At the beginning there were probably collections of the sayings of Jesus, which were at first memorized and handed on orally but quite soon were also written down in a set form. The Erfurt exegete Heinz Schürmann, who died just recently, showed how it is probable that the disciples deliberately memorized sayings of Jesus as far back as during the lifetime of Jesus himself. In the beginning, then, there was oral tradition. Besides the transmission of sayings, there were stories about events, stories with a local connection, and so on. It was not the individual who undertook the handing on of sayings and stories, but the congregations of believers and, embodied in them, the common Church. Then came the process of setting things down in writing, when people were already able to build upon a wealth of traditional material. This was far from being the private activity of a few authors, even though the process of editing undertaken by the evangelists was most important. Their activity was in each case the vehicle of expression for a particular theological vision. With respect to the individual Gospels, today we assume that not Matthew but Mark is the oldest of the Gospels. Matthew and Luke have, so to speak, taken Mark as their basic framework and have enriched it with other traditional materials that were available to them. The Gospel of John, now, had a separate origin and development and is homogeneous. It is important that the first three Gospels were not just written by *one* writer in each case but were based on the transmission of material by the whole believing Church—a process, that is to say, in which material slowly crystallized in particular traditions that were finally brought together to form the text of the Gospels.

In a certain sense, then, the question about particular people is secondary. Certainly, we can clearly recognize the individual character of Luke. He is the undisputed author of the third Gospel and the Acts of the Apostles. Mark, too, as a pupil of Peter, clearly has his own profile as an evangelist. It is no longer clear, today, who was responsible for the final editing of the Gospel of Matthew. What is fundamental is that oral transmission came at the beginning, as is so characteristic in the Orient. That guarantees the close connection with the historical origin. The texts that grew out of this oral tradition were subject to community control (a process that led, in the particular communities that picked up these traditions, to a specific coloring, but without affecting their fidelity).

And concerning the personality of this Matthew-Levi, you have only portrayed his past. Through his meeting with Jesus, Matthew became a quite different person. He accepted Jesus as his way of life and renounced what he had previously been doing. Within the fellowship of the Twelve, in fellowship with the risen Lord, and finally in his missionary work, he showed that he was truly "made new" and that we can believe this new man.

Luke the Evangelist was a doctor; he wanted to show his readers above all how Jesus came into the world as Savior, to redeem both body and soul. For him, Jesus was full of sympathy and love for people on the margins of society.

But let's turn to the Gospel of John. You have just said it is homogeneous. At any rate it is quite different, with a deeply reflective tone. In the synoptic Gospels we meet the Son of Man; in John the disputes with the scribes shine forth—and above all the entire glory *of the Son of God. I can imagine that this is your favorite Gospel.*

I am very fond of it, but I must say that I am also very fond of Luke. There we have these marvelous parables of Lazarus the beggar, of the Good Samaritan, of the Prodigal Son. He is such a great story teller that there are real "pearls" in it. The childhood stories, too. Each evangelist shows his own face. I must say that I love Luke especially on account of the deeply penetrating humanity there is in it, a humanity that at the same time illuminates horizons in eternity. I regard the Synoptics, taken as a whole, as showing an irreplaceable beauty, precisely because they are not individual compositions, but because we can sense here the handing on of traditions within the living Church, in a way that leads eventually to their coalescing into a coherent text. But without doubt John is still a book with unfathomable depths that continues to fascinate me.

There are times when the story of Jesus strikes one as somewhat artificial. For instance, Jesus keeps strictly to the Old Testament's use of significant numbers. He was forty days in the wilderness; he did exactly seven miracles; he told twelve parables; he appointed twelve apostles . . .

What all the evangelists know and recount is the appointment of twelve apostles. And that is not surprising. If Jesus really wants to constitute a new Israel, if he is aware that God has sent him to have Israel renewed and then to have the light carried to the nations, then he will quite obviously base his actions on the old symbolism of the twelve tribes of Israel and will, so to say, call twelve new patriarchs and thus represent the foundation of the new Israel in a symbolic action.

The forty days in the wilderness take up Israel's forty years in the wilderness. The number of miracles and parables we are told about varies from one evangelist to another.

Even so, the Gospels always read like teaching material. Partly, even, like a stage production, a piece designed to agitate, for propaganda purposes.

Yes, they are teaching material but are also simply a witness. John himself says that he wants to bear witness. That is the basic category within which we should read them. They want to show us Jesus himself, with his word, his work, his suffering. They intend to do far more than teach. They intend to make it possible for us to encounter an event, an event that does of course have a spiritual content and does transmit a theory of knowledge. They speak both to our heart and to our understanding.

The Way, the Truth, and the Life

There are marvelous synonyms for Jesus: he is the Bread of life, *the* Salt of the earth, *and the* Light of the world. *Jesus says of himself:* "I am the Way, the Truth, and the Life. *Whoever believes in me, will have eternal life.*"

Two thousand years after his birth, is it at all still possible to give an authentic answer to the question of who Jesus really was?

If we had to dig back now through two thousand years, purely by means of history, then, as we have just mentioned, the historical method runs up against its limitations. But it's not like that.

We can see how the living agent that arose as a result of the preaching, the Church, has preserved her identity, and how she is present in this identity from the beginning. By the same token, the Church is contemporary with Jesus, and this is a relationship of contemporaneity that persists through time.

Accordingly, we are not separated from him by the great yawning gap of two thousand years. The agent that gives living witness to him, and which, as it were, speaks with the same voice as she spoke in the very beginning, has never ceased doing this. The knowledge of his presence has remained alive in her. In her we can look at the fount from which this knowledge comes. Naturally, faith is involved in this, but without some kind of sympathy, of faith, I cannot know or recognize any other person at all.

I once saw a picture in the church at Nazareth, it showed the little boy Jesus, hovering awkwardly around by the workbench. Mary sits there anxiously, even suffering, while Joseph the carpenter already has quite clearly the attitude of a man who has realized early on that this offspring of his will never make an artisan. Even at twelve years old, Jesus wanted to run off ("I must be in my Father's house"), and when he was thirty the people of Nazareth wanted to throw him off a cliff.

At first, within the Christian tradition, stories about Jesus' childhood were not handed down for public hearing. Not until Matthew and Luke do they appear in two variant modifications of the tradition. The Gospels were not intent on giving some kind of biography of Jesus, as a historian might write it, but on giving witness to those things that are essential for us. And so they had no interest in recounting the story of what happened during this period of silence; rather, they wanted, on one hand, to show his divine origin in the childhood stories, the star, which stands as a sign over his life from the beginning, and then also to show him with his message.

What we see in such "Holy Family" pictures is the pious fantasy that has, especially since the nineteenth century, taken up the theme of Nazareth and has pictured it in terms of people's own life stories. As against this, we must remember that in Palestine at that time there was no such thing as the nuclear family as it is here portrayed. Instead, the more extended family lived together as a sort of clan. And that's where the reference to Jesus' brothers comes from.

The nineteenth century saw everything in a different light. We see the climax of this interpretation with Charles de Foucauld, who extrapolated from Nazareth a message of tranquility, of recollection, and of humility. He certainly discovered some precious things, but ones that do not constitute the center of the message set before us in what the Gospels say.

Why did Jesus not begin his public ministry until he was thirty? Did he have just three years to proclaim his message up to the time of his death?

It was quite clear that in the world of the time, in the complex relationships of Israel, it was not possible for just any young man to appear. Someone who wished to act as rabbi, even if Jesus was not a rabbi in the strict sense, had to be at least thirty years old. That's why he made his appearance then and not before. The message of Jesus had its own inner dimensions, and this amount of time was ultimately enough for these.

Once, when Jesus was visiting his hometown, people went into a huddle, just as we know inquisitive neighbors do: "Is that not the son of the carpenter? Where has he suddenly got so much wisdom and power?" And the Bible quotes them further: "Is his mother not called Mary, and aren't James, Joseph, Simon and Judas his brothers? Don't his sisters all live among us?"

In this place alone, four brothers are named, and an unspecified number of sisters. If I recall correctly: Has the Church not always spoken of an only son of the Virgin Mary?

In a little village like Nazareth everyone naturally knows everyone else. Obviously, someone who has hitherto lived in tranquility like all the others is looked upon with amazement if he suddenly appears making such demands. And when you know someone so well, then you don't believe any of it. It seems to be in contradiction with how he was before, and people try to drag him back down to what is ordinary, so to say. On this account, Jesus answers with the saying: "Nowhere is a prophet less welcome than he is in his own country." As concerns the brothers and sisters of Jesus: the Church still believes that Mary gave birth *to him* as a virgin, to him and no other. On his account she belonged to God and could not then, as it were, go back into an ordinary family life.

The phrase "the brothers and sisters of Jesus" is accounted for without difficulty in terms of the family structures of the time. And there are enough indications that these children were not seen as belonging to Mary. There is a reference, for example, to another Mary and other things. We have only oblique references to specific family relationships. But they do show us that several families belong together here. When Jesus, hanging on the Cross, gives his Mother John as a son, we can see that she is standing there as a figure apart and belongs to him in a quite particular way.

From a purely historical point of view we certainly cannot arrive at a definite answer. You cannot demonstrate the uniqueness of the motherhood of Mary. But, on the other hand, you cannot prove that the people referred to are full brothers and sisters of Jesus. There are enough indications, however—Josef Blinzler wrote a good monograph on this—to suggest that these brothers and sisters belong to other families and are referred to as brother and sisters within the clan, as it were. And besides that, this notion of *brothers and sisters of Jesus* is also an idea that was important in the early Church, when there were tensions between these relatives of Jesus, who took a strict view of what Jewish Christianity should be, and other tendencies within the growing Church.

Who Was Jesus Really?

Sometimes Jesus behaved like a raging half-wit. When he was coming back into town one morning, hungry, and found no fruit on a fig tree, but only leaves, he began to curse: "No more fruit shall you bear, to eternity." The fig tree withered on the spot.

The business with the fig tree is "typological", that is to say, it's a matter of a symbolic act, of a kind that was typical for prophets in Israel. In this case, the fig tree represents Israel, and the story is linked to the Passion, in which the struggle for the Yes or the No of Israel reaches its dramatic climax. But the significance of the barren fig tree as a symbol reaches far beyond this situation and exemplifies the question of fruitfulness in general.

There is no question at all of a sudden fit of anger; rather, it's a symbolic gesture by which Jesus shows that peoples, communities, groups, who can bring forth nothing but leaves, who only display themselves, and from whom nothing else comes forth of any use to others dry up and wither. There is also a kind of Christianity that brings forth only leaves—of paper—and then withers. In this sense we must see this action from the perspective of the Son of God, who in this way sets up a symbol we can see right across the centuries.

Once, he reproaches entire towns for not having repented: "And you, Capernaum, do you suppose that you will be lifted up to heaven? No, you will be cast down into hell."

Here, Jesus is speaking to towns that are closely connected with his life and from whom he might particularly expect faith. But he can see that this syndrome of "knowing the prophet" is at work here, too. They don't really take him seriously; their faith cannot grow. So these places are lined up with cities that have become a byword for acts of judgment, for failure, for being lost.

And again we can see the same thing: wherever a person or a society refuses to take God's business seriously, in some way or other the fate of Gomorrah overtakes them again. When any society turns away from fellowship with the living God, it cuts the inner roots of its social organism.

We can see such retribution at work even today. Think of atheist societies and of the problems in the states that succeeded the Soviet Union, which show this process of collapse after fifty years of Marxist rule. In this case societies that turned away from God truly pulled the ground of life from beneath their own feet.

But even toward Peter, on one occasion Jesus is extremely angry, even wounding. "Away with you, Satan", he hisses. "Get out of my sight! You are tempting me."

Jesus has an especially close relationship of trust with Peter; that's how such language is justified. We can see how Peter takes it. He understands that he was quite in the wrong. What is at issue here is that he would like to prevent Jesus from taking the way of the Cross. He says, that's not consistent with your mission; you must be successful; you cannot go to the Cross. Thereby Peter repeats the temptation from the days in the wilderness, which is presented to us as Jesus' one temptation, to be a Messiah of success, to climb on the political bandwagon.

This is a temptation that crops up again and again. For instance, too, if someone were to conceive a Marxist version of Christianity, which would finally create the ideal society. The same idea of salvation is at work here: Mankind would be saved if everyone had enough money and possessions. It is this idea that Jesus opposes. In that way, at the moment when he suggests this model, Peter so to speak takes the role of Satan in the wilderness. Peter understands this; even if, to the last, he has again and again to grapple with the scandal of the Cross and has to learn what is different about Jesus, as against that other conception, which is so very human.

Jesus has a genuine aversion to many people. He calls them "a brood of vipers and serpents" and "blind leaders". "You strain gnats out and swallow camels", he rages. "Woe to you, scribes and Pharisees, you hypocrites. You lock people out of heaven." Jesus is obviously an advocate of frankness and veracity, of the unity between talk and action, between what we preach and what we practice. He detests the scribes: "You bind heavy burdens together and lay them on people's shoulders, but you yourselves do not lift a finger to help them carry them."

I think that in these sentences we can hear the anger of God over counterfeit piety. From the perspective of God, such people are repugnant to Jesus. He shows them in dramatic fashion how this apparent piety, or even learning, completely misses its task. And there, too, he speaks down all the generations. We know that Luther referred these things directly to the Catholic hierarchy and said it was all equally applicable to them.

We ought not to be so simplistic. But all those who serve the Word of God ought in fact to feel themselves shaken by such words and should always be ready to ask whether this does not also apply to them. There is a little book by the Church Father, and Father of monasticism, Maximus the Confessor. In this work he addresses an uncomfortable speech to his monks. He says this saying is far more true of us now than it was for the Pharisees then. We are worse than they were if we live out all this distortion, narrowness, and pretense of piety, because we have been given a greater light.

And for the scribes, they know every single letter of Scripture, so to speak; they are exegetes, Bible specialists, who can tell you right off which prophet said what and where. But it is all dead knowledge. They only dissect and analyze the Scriptures and no longer find life in them. Thus, the danger of any and every specialized exegesis is made visible in this figure of speech. People know everything, but Scripture is treated like a laboratory specimen, like a skeleton, that can be used for developing all kinds of things. However much people may know in detail, in this way they have strayed a long way from the message of Scripture. When simple people listen, on the other hand, they often understand the real message better than those whose extensive learning has become blind and deaf to the heart of the matter.

Jesus is, obviously, also an impatient man. On one occasion he commands his chief apostle, Peter, to walk across the sea. Come!

he calls to him. And Peter comes. He climbs out of the boat and finds he can in fact do the impossible; he walks across the water. He does so, at any rate, up to the moment when he gets anxious about the wind, which is getting stronger. He starts to sink in the midst of the waves. Jesus shakes his head: "Man of little faith, why did you doubt?"

He is just showing what had been going on in Peter's soul. There's a similar incident another time in the storm on the lake, when the disciples are in despair because Jesus does not stir, not even when the boat is filling with water. And after he has stood up and he saves them, he says: "How could you doubt?"

Jesus assumes that his disciples really ought to know him. That they ought to know he will not let them drown. He shows them in this way that their faith in what he is, and in what they have actually recognized and accepted, is still so minimal that a puff of wind can, as it were, blow this faith away.

The scene described here is concerned with the way Peter no longer looks at Jesus but has earthly elements in view. Naturally, then, by any reckoning of probability, he is bound to sink as soon as he gets out onto the water. But he has left out of this the essential point, that he has been called by Jesus, who is the Lord. Together with him, and by his power, in relation to him, he will so to speak be able to walk right over even what is deadly in this world.

This story offers another profound parable. If we look at the element of probability in natural phenomena, and at everything we can know about it, then Christianity appears as extremely improbable. And if we let our gaze be captivated by the tendency of the moment, by the wind that is blowing around our ears, then really our faith can only sink out of sight. We would necessarily find ourselves saying, with Peter: It doesn't work any more! If we do that, then we have already lost our true anchor, which consists in depending on our relationship to the One who can overcome brute force, the brute force of death, the brute force of history and its impossibilities. Faith means resisting the brute force that would otherwise pull us under. Faith means fellowship with him who has the other kind of power, one that draws us up, that holds us fast, that carries us safely over the elements of death.

One time, when Jesus was among the Gentiles in the neighborhood of the cities of Tyre and Sidon, he was unwilling either to teach or to work miracles. Even when a mother absolutely implored him to heal her daughter, who was being horribly tortured by an evil spirit, Jesus brusquely rejected her: "I have been sent only to the lost sheep of the house of Israel."

One of the characteristic features of the life of Jesus is that he himself does not embark on the mission to the Gentiles. Not until after his Resurrection does he entrust his disciples with this mission. First of all Israel, we might say, takes priority. This is the people chosen by God, the point at which God decides to start work. And so Jesus keeps to this prerogative that Israel holds in the history of salvation. In his earthly life, Jesus engages in a struggle for the heart of Israel; he struggles to get Israel as such to recognize him as the Promised One and to unite with him so that, beginning from there, history can be transformed.

Paul, too, keeps to this scheme at first. Wherever he goes, he always starts his mission in the synagogue. Even when he comes to Rome, he first of all calls his Jewish compatriots together. And only when he fails to unite the fellowship of faith in Jesus with the history of faith in Israel does he then turn to the Gentiles. Paul himself, the one responsible for overcoming the hesitation in taking the great step, says that the message is first meant for Israel and then for the Gentiles.

Thus one of the rules of salvation history is being adhered to. God remains faithful to himself, and Jesus is faithful. Even if he does renew and transform the Jewish Law from within, he is not simply a rebel who wants to do everything differently, but acts on the basis of this inner faithfulness. Thus, the confirmation of God's faithfulness removes any appearance of betrayal from the imperative transition to the Gentiles—and lets it appear, on the contrary, as part of the logic of his Resurrection, whereby in the final analysis the death of the grain of wheat becomes the transition into greatness and universality.

Jesus travels through the countryside. He urges people to humble themselves and repent; he teaches them to pray; he warns them against pleasure-seeking and hard-heartedness. He tells the story of Lazarus the beggar, who goes to heaven, while the wealthy reveler has to go to hell—in fact, a real traveling preacher.

He is a wandering preacher, that's true. He preaches first of all in Galilee and tries to gather people together with his Word. Then he extends his preaching activity to Jerusalem as well. He knows that he has been sent to Israel, and he wants to bring to everyone the new message he has to deliver. At its heart is the kingdom of God, the renewal of the world through the merciful acts of God.

The individual elements you referred to all fit into this wider view. Jesus lives and works in faithfulness to the history of God's salvation, on one hand; he also keeps the pattern of Israel's feasts; he makes pilgrimages, keeps the Passover. He lives absolutely as a pious and faithful Jew. And at the same time, as the Son, who is the new Moses. Who ranks *above* Moses. Who does not merely interpret the law as the scribes do; but as the Son who is himself the lawgiver, he lifts it onto a new plane.

A rebel?

It's not simply a liberal or rebellious attitude, attacking this and that, barging around and not wanting to accept things; rather, this is the perspective of the lawgiver, of the Creator himself, who tears up what is temporary and introduces us to what is permanent and, in doing so, sets an example of a deeper faithfulness. I believe we must be able to see the way apparent rebellion and real faithfulness go hand-in-hand if we really want to understand the person of Jesus. What has gone before is not abolished—"Not a jot, not a tittle shall be removed", he says—but for the first time its full depth is revealed.

It's obvious that Jesus takes particular delight in children and in people with a simple faith. He is—something we rarely see with him—downright enthusiastic: "I praise you, Father, Lord of heaven and earth, because you have hidden all this from the wise and the learned and have revealed it to the little ones."

Yes, here again is the mysterious pattern of the way God acts: the whole magnitude of it is more easily grasped by simple people than by those who, with a thousand distinctions and diverse intellectual baggage, ferret out each little bit on its own and are no longer capable of being overwhelmed by the magnitude of the whole.

No rejection of intellectuals, or of detailed knowledge of Scripture, is intended here, but a warning not to lose our inward simplicity, to keep the meaning of the whole in view, and to allow oneself to be impressed, to be ready to accept the unexpected.

It's no secret that for intellectuals this is a great temptation. When we look back on the history of the ideologies of the past century, we can see that simple people have often judged more soundly than intellectuals. The latter always want to make more distinctions, to find out more about this and that—and thereby they lose their overall view.

"To you it is given", says Jesus to the disciples, "to learn the secrets of the kingdom of heaven. To other people, however, these can only be told in parables; for they will look and not see, they will hear and will not understand. This is the meaning of the parable: the seed is the Word of God." Even so, there must be something peculiar about the language of the Gospel. All the people of the world, of no matter what culture and no matter in what century they have lived, can understand it.

The saying you have quoted comes originally from the prophet Isaiah. He pronounces this threat of judgment at a moment when Israel has failed. What he means is, You all hear the truth, but in the end, obviously, it has only been told to you so that you fail to understand.

A mysterious saying.

Jesus says, In the end, what has been given for understanding develops in your case into a hardened determination not to understand. You are welcome to hide behind the words in the foreground; just stay there, and shut yourselves off from understanding. Thus the Word that is given becomes a Word of judgment, because people want only to look at its outer shell and not to hear the heart of it.

In themselves, the parables are there to bring what is intangible closer to people. Just from an educational point of view, they are marvelous. The great and eternal mysteries are told us in everyday stories, which suddenly become transparent vehicles for God's mystery. And the very greatest things can be seen in the simplest, in sowing and reaping, in stories like that of Lazarus or that of the Good Samaritan.

God comes to meet man in Christ; he makes the Word palatable for him; he translates it into terms that everyone has experienced and known, everyday matters, so that through the familiar everyday terms people can make their way toward the essential matters and see them. In this manner we have indeed sayings that transcend their own time and speak to every culture, because they start from the basics of human life.

There is obviously another level to the parables, another code built into them. You once said that fully understanding them was "bound up with life in Christ": "They will not open themselves to someone who tries to comprehend them from a purely intellectual, historical, or speculative point of view."

If I read Scripture in terms of the concrete pictures it offers and lose my sense for any deeper meaning within these simple stories, then I refuse to take the path the parable opens up for me.

A parable takes me along a certain path. At first I see what everyone sees, what I already knew. Now I realize that there is more to this. I have to learn to go beyond what I see daily. If, on the contrary, I hold fast to the superficial level and refuse this path, then I cannot see the deeper meaning in these stories, especially since the parables always relate to particular circumstances in the life of Jesus himself. Some of them constitute something like Jesus' secret autobiography, whose meaning is only unfolded in his own life and suffering.

The Multiplication of Loaves

There is one story in the Gospel that is told quite straightforwardly, without any frills or profundities: the Feeding of the Five Thousand.

It happens at an out-of-the-way spot somewhere in Galilee, and many people have gathered around Jesus. They have probably been listening to him, fascinated. Suddenly it is evening, and somehow no one has realized what time it is. The disciples urge Jesus to send the people back to their villages immediately; there is nothing to eat out here and no way of buying anything. Jesus stays calm. He just says: "Give them something to eat."

They have just five loaves of bread and two fishes, that is, seven items. "And he took the five loaves and the two fishes," it says in Holy Scripture, "he looked up to heaven and gave thanks, broke the bread, and gave it to his disciples. In this way they could all eat their fill, five thousand men and a large number of women and children. When they collected up the remains, there were even twelve basketfuls left over."

One on hand, we have the facts; on the other, a deeper dimension of symbolism in this story. People expected that in the messianic age the miracle of the manna would be repeated. The Messiah, so they believed, would prove his identity in that everyone would have enough to eat and bread would once more come down from heaven.

Jesus' intention is to transfer this manna miracle onto a different plane. And to do it with the Eucharist. With the bread in which he gives himself, and in which accordingly the multiplication of loaves takes place henceforth throughout history, down to our own day. He can, in a certain sense, be shared with others to an infinite extent.

In this sharing of bread, Jesus is making an advance with this renewed manna miracle, in that he repeats the old manna but also leads to a quite different, shall we say more humble, and at the same time more demanding, form. In its profundity this is a far greater miracle. And also in that bread does not just fall down from heaven; but sharing human togetherness, mutual giving—things that do not just fall down from heaven—are also made part of it.

In this miracle we are offered a many-faceted view of human life and of the Church that was to come. And this story is preliminary to a separation of spirits. There are some who say, Yes, he is the Messiah, and who then want to make him king and force him to seek political power. And after he will not accept this, then a dissatisfaction with the miracle arises, and the opinion surfaces that, in that case, he is not the Redeemer. And from this moment dates the separation of the ways: one leads to rejection, the other to the Passion.

Is this just symbolic, or did it really happen?

Many exegetes today, who believe in the laws of nature and think something like that is impossible, are tempted to take this feeding miracle as merely a kind of pictorial representation, and indeed there is a great deal of symbolic content in it. But we ought not to be in too much of a hurry to deny possibilities to God. Similar things have happened in the story of the Church.

I was recently in Turin, and there one of the old priests told us how twice in the life of Don Bosco quite similar events occurred. On one occasion, by an oversight, not enough hosts had been consecrated. Although an enormous number of people had come to take Communion, young people, there were in fact only ten or twenty hosts. Don Bosco in any case made no stir or fuss. He said: "Don't worry, just share them out, and there'll be plenty for everyone." And there was.

The other time, he promised a lad, after a hard day's work, that they'd all have dried chestnuts. He therefore said to his mother to get the chestnuts ready. But she misunderstood him and dried only just enough for ten boys. When she realized her mistake, the mother was furious. But he only said, "No bother, just share them out, there will be enough, even some for seconds." And in fact that's what happened again this time. There are a whole lot of witnesses to this, who were there at the time.

So we should never start out by denying that God may be able to do something that normally doesn't happen.

Jesus and Women

Jesus frequently transgressed conventional boundaries. He made a point of associating with sinners and poor people. And he obviously had a quite special relationship with women. Jesus "was no ascetic, but was quite attached to all the joys of life", so the Jewish biblical scholar Shalom Ben-Chorin believed. However this may be, women for their part found the Son of Man quite fascinating. Can we not suppose that Jesus had a sexual or erotic relationship?

The sexual or erotic dimension plays no part in his kind of friendship. On this point Jesus simply belongs to another order of being. But we can see, in his relationships as portrayed by the Gospels, that he was capable of deep personal friendships and of real love. And it is also true that women in particular were sensitive to the new, different, noble, and mysterious something that made its appearance in him, and in special ways he drew them into his company.

In contrast to the contemporary Jewish custom, by which women were viewed as being of secondary status, Jesus achieved something like an emancipation of women. Because of this social status, women belonged somehow in this category of little ones, who were assured of God's special love and his special attention. And by doing so he called forth the charism of the women. In their meeting with him, the two women from Bethany come especially into our field of vision. They show us how, from then on, women play an essential part, as living and active members, in the building up of the Church.

It was the women who stayed by Jesus faithfully, to the foot of the Cross. In contrast to them, the disciples had all long since made themselves scarce. From Mary Magdalen, Jesus had driven seven evil spirits that had spiritually devastated her. And she in particular, not Peter or John, was now the first person permitted to report his Resurrection. A remarkable fact, when we consider that in the Orient women were simply not considered capable of bearing witness in court. On that account Saint Augustine called Mary Magdalen the Apostle of the apostles.

And that title has remained. Right up to 1962 the Preface of Apostles was read in the liturgy on her day, because she was reckoned as being "the woman apostle". The fact that Mary Magdalen was the first to bring the message of the Resurrection to the apostles shows once more the especially close and warm relationship Jesus had with this woman. We can also detect that in the dialogue, when he simply says, when she does not recognize him, the name "Mary". And then she recognizes him and falls at his feet: "Rabboni, my master." That expresses reverence, distancing herself from his greatness, yet at the same time her deep love for him who as God is Man, and yet as Man, God.

I would like to go into the position of women in the Church later. Here, just briefly: Are there any stories by Jesus or about Jesus in the Gospels that we are likely to have to give up in the future because they are contradicted by new historical knowledge or by newly discovered evidence, for example at Qumran?

I know of none. Perhaps there are certain shades of meaning that these texts allow us to understand differently. But what the Gospels say was formulated directly in the period itself and thus cannot be contradicted by new contemporary evidence. The witness of the Gospels to Jesus Christ remains and is still valid.

The Meeting

Your Eminence, you once said that faith in Jesus Christ unlocks the world to man. It shows us how everything is built up, how things relate to each other. Can we also learn from it how to live our lives better?

The decisive moments of our lives are beyond our control. We can determine neither our birth nor our death. But part of the task of a biography is to find out who we are and what our calling is; what path we should take. Can the Christian faith really help an individual a little?

Faith is not, of course, a substitute for our own reflection. Or for learning with and through other people in history as a whole. God doesn't take our labors away from us. Faith is not a magic formula. But it does give us the key to learning for ourselves. So that we can get answers and find out for ourselves who we are.

It is always the case that a person first recognizes himself in others and through others. No one can arrive at knowledge of himself just by looking within himself and trying to build up his personality from what he finds there. Man as a being is so constructed for relationships that he grows in relation to others. So that his own meaning, his task in life, his advancement in life, and his potential are unlocked in his meetings with others.

From the starting point of this basic structure of human existence we can understand faith and our meeting with Jesus. Faith is not just a system of knowledge, things we are told; at the heart of it is a meeting with Jesus. And what I was trying to express then was that this meeting with Jesus, among all those other meetings we have need of, is the truly decisive one. All our other meetings leave the ultimate goal unclear, where we are coming from, where we are going. At our meeting with him the fundamental light dawns, by which I can understand God, man, the world, mission, and meaning—and by which all the other meetings fall into place.

The Wilderness

The teaching of Jesus Christ is called by the apostles, literally, the "New Way". This New Way begins, after Jesus has been baptized, in the wilderness itself. It is, we might say in boxing parlance, the interval before the final round, before Jesus gets up to suffer his Passion. Forty days in the wilderness—once more a mighty symbol.

The number forty has indeed great symbolic significance. Elijah likewise, to take just one example, was on the way to the holy mountain for forty days. Again and again, this period is the time required for learning, preparation, growth. The original image is that of Israel's time in the wilderness, during which the people learned to know God's order and his will and were thus prepared for life as a people and for being entrusted with God's promises.

In his forty days in the wilderness, Jesus resumes the forty years in the wilderness of Israel. He retraces, so to speak, the whole of this historical path and thereby shows us, too, that without a period of renunciation, of tranquility, of going forth, and of recollection, no great mission can fully ripen. Fasting and praying, Jesus faces up to the whole abysmal emptiness of the wilderness. It symbolizes, on one hand, a special meeting with God, but at the same time the dangers of the world. It is the place where there is no life, no nourishment, the place of solitudes. Thus he walks through the whole world of perils, of human failure, of abandonment, the wilderness of hunger and of thirst. At the same time Jesus takes upon himself human temptations; he suffers them himself, so as to start from there in bringing his great Word and the sublime message.

After forty days and forty nights of fasting, Jesus is led into temptation by the devil. At first, Satan wants Jesus to make bread out of stones. A pretty stupid devil, obviously.

This account shows the alternative programs, the temptations, to which Jesus, as the Redeemer, was exposed during the whole of his three-year journey, which are also the permanent temptations in the history of the Church. Accordingly, Jesus says at another time: "You have endured my temptations with me." And he says to Peter: "You are now Satan; you bring these temptations to me." Even the five thousand who have just been fed, who want to make him king and thereby a provider of bread, bring temptation to him. We can see here preliminary sketches of what has to be resisted again and again on the path of Jesus and also in the Church.

What do you mean?

I mean for instance making oneself useful by reforming the social order of the world and creating the ideal state. It is important for the Church to work alongside others to improve society, but the real healing of mankind cannot begin from external social structures, but only from within. Even though the hunger of men must touch the heart of the Church, in all ages, even if she has to struggle to find hands to multiply the loaves—nonetheless she must not be diverted in that direction, to be merely a social organization, to concentrate only on material things as if this were the real matter of redemption, and to forget, in doing so, that man does not live by bread alone, but by every Word that comes from the mouth of God.

The same is true of the other two temptations, being encouraged to jump from the pinnacle of the Temple in order to test God, so that he is forced to show his hand, and finally the dreadful temptation to seize power over all the world: "Worship me, and I will make you lord over all the earth", the devil promises him. That means worldwide rule based on power, and even if it is for the sake of whatever ideal end, but sought apart from God, then it corrupts any man.

In the course of history we have had more than enough of these experiments in doing without God, and giving man what he wants by sheer effort, through the structures of power. All these experiments have shown, in a negative sense, what it's really about. They hold up a mirror to the Church and to each individual: whenever we try to do without God, try to bypass him and to put the world right by our own systems, whenever we think that the satisfaction of material needs is the real key to the problem, then we solve nothing; we destroy things; we do the work of Satan.

After his experiences in the wilderness, the first disciples begin to come to Jesus. They ask him: "Master, where do you live?" And Jesus gives a very brief answer: "Come and see."

Yes, the experience of being with him is necessary there. Jesus cannot be located at a fixed point. He lives on the way, going on before. Only in following him, by accompanying him on the way, do we learn where he lives. And then we will see him. If we want to understand him and his teaching purely on the basis of theory and reflection, we don't get to know him.

The first disciples whom Jesus intends to make "fishers of men" are Andrew and John; later Peter is added, Andrew's brother. It is striking that the Master did not surround himself with learned men, but with upright, simple folk. They were not especially clever, not even particularly bold or alert, and they obviously could not preach without the help of the Holy Spirit. Again and again they were tormented by doubts and lack of faith. Was Jesus not very deft at choosing his people?

By all means, they were not persons of consequence, able to undertake a worldwide mission on the basis of their own knowledge and ability. Even if, as Saint John Chrysostom says, they did "make the great cast of the dice", it was by another power. Thus the choice of these simple folk, who were not politicians and were not learned, seems to me to say a great deal. It becomes clear: They could not have done this on their own. They were touched by someone greater than themselves and were led and supported by him.

Nonetheless, we can see in this society, in which diverse elements are brought together, a certain argument in favor of the disciples. On one hand are anti-Roman fanatics, ready to use force. Simon the Zealot, perhaps. The zealots are the party of those who want to bring in the messianic age by force. In the case of Judas Iscariot, too, the name suggests membership in a similar party. These are men of the extreme left, then, as we would say nowadays. They are ready to take part in a resistance movement and probably expect something like that from Jesus. On the other side, we have Levi, the customs official, who is one of the collaborators, one of that class of wealthy people who are always hand-in-hand with power.

A sort of proportional choice.

Right away, in constituting this circle of followers, Jesus achieved a reconciliation. People can come from every side, and there is a path to or from him from every starting point. Thus we can imagine the inner tensions within this group of disciples.

Besides that, all these disciples, as you said, are grown men with their own lives. Peter, for instance, has a fishing cooperative, and in that sense he has a small business. These are people who are part of practical life, with a sense of concrete realities, without being smothered in the narrow-mindedness of purely pragmatic realism. They have kept alive their hope of something better. They have not fallen victim to some kind of magic, but have put all their powers at the service of their calling. They give us an example of how God can do what only he himself is able to do by working through quite ordinary people, but also of how greatness is hidden in ordinary people.

People nowadays, in contrast to these disciples following Christ, have the idea that they can work out their path, put their lives together, by their own unaided efforts. They think that in any case no one has any clear identity any longer. Life is a flowing stream of illusions, according to what task or what scenario confronts us—or what desire. An either-or decision is in any case passé in the modern world; instead of that there is the new possibility of neither-nor.

Flexibility has become the all-sufficient watchword. We want to be able to react to new demands, and we hope, by changing jobs fast, to be able to climb the ladder as quickly and as high as possible. But I think there are still callings that demand the whole of a person. Being a doctor, for instance, or a teacher, is not something I can do just for two or three years, but is a calling that requires my whole lifetime. That is to say, even today there are tasks that are not a job that runs *alongside* my life, so to speak, in order to ensure I have money to live on. For a true calling, income is not the criterion, but the practicing of some skill in the service of mankind.

What would Jesus say about it?

Jesus would not want to stop anyone reacting to flexible challenges. His own disciples had to be flexible enough to turn from their everyday lives as fishermen to accompany him on a way that was mysterious, toward a goal they could not yet see—and then in the end to make the great leap out of the heart of Judaism, where they all had deep roots, into the mission to the Gentiles.

At the same time, they had to be steady and faithful as far as their basic decision was concerned. To that extent, we should not set faithfulness in opposition to flexibility. It is faithfulness in particular that has to show its worth in changing situations. Anyone who lives fifty years today as a priest, or as a faithful marriage partner, has to live through many changes in that time. He has to mature as he passes through each alteration and to develop his complete identity.

It is unfortunately often the way in the modern situation that only change, only flexibility for its own sake, counts for anything. I would like to disagree with this. Today, if ever, we need people to stand by their mission, their calling; today above all we need people who give themselves entirely. Let's think back again to development aid. It is useful if people go and do something for two or three years, but we also need very many who give themselves entirely. There are callings that demand the whole of a person.

Lives that follow such a course are not a sign of a lack of imagination or of rigidity. In this very faithfulness people can become inwardly so broad and mature and noble that change and continuity become interwoven. The two together build true greatness.

To stay with paths in life: many people have the notion that their life is a kind of film. And in this biographical filmstrip they suppose they should be able to make all the cuts and supervise the production of each scene themselves. One cannot avoid the thought: Why should I go out of my way in life, make special efforts, seek anything out, show self-control or faithfulness? That is, set out on this difficult path that the disciples follow with Jesus. Why should my life not just be simple and easy?

That is something only those people can afford who are born to luxury. That is a fantasy of people with property, which takes no account of the fact that, for the great majority of mankind, life is a struggle. On those grounds I would see this idea of choosing one's own path in life as a selfish attitude and as a waste of one's vocation.

Anyone who thinks he already has it all, so that he can take what he wants and center everything on himself, is depriving himself of giving what he otherwise could. Man is not there to make himself, but to respond to demands made upon him. We all stand in a great arena of history and are dependent on each other. A man ought not, therefore, just to figure out what he would like, but to ask what he can do and how he can help. Then he will see that fulfillment does not lie in comfort, ease, and following one's inclinations, but precisely in allowing demands to be made upon you, in taking the harder path. Everything else turns out somehow boring, anyway. Only the man who "risks the fire", who recognizes a calling within himself, a vocation, an ideal he must satisfy, who takes on real responsibility, will find fulfillment. As we have said, it is not in taking, not on the path of comfort, that we become rich, but only in giving.

Power and Possessions

There is one saying of Jesus about "lords and servants". Christ says: "You know that the rulers of the world oppress their people, and those who have power over others misuse it. It must not be so with you, but whoever among you wishes to be great must be your servant, and whoever wishes to be first among you must be your slave. For even the Son of Man did not come to be served, but to serve and to give his life as a ransom for many." Serving and obedience are important characteristics in the teaching of Christ and in the life of the Church. These ideas are not especially popular nowadays. What underlies this?

From the point of view of the Gospel there is indeed a scheme of life that runs counter to the prevailing trend among modern people, a sort of healthy unmodernity that pulls us out of the trend toward domination and manipulation. And anyone who is not numbered among the powerful will be thankful whenever he sees someone powerful not helping himself at life's table. When the powerful person sees the power or possessions that have been given him as a mandate to be of service to others.

I believe that in this saying about the lord who should serve others, and also in Jesus' own actions in doing so himself, we see the true revolution that can and should change the world. As long as power and wealth are seen as ends in themselves, then power is always a power to be used against others and possessions will always exclude others.

At that moment when the Lord of the world comes and undertakes the slave's task of foot-washing—which is, in turn, only an illustration of the way he washes our feet all through our lives—we have a totally different picture. God, who is absolute power itself, doesn't want to trample on us, but kneels down before us so as to exalt us. The mystery of the greatness of God is seen precisely in the fact that he can be small. He doesn't always have to take the highest place or the box seats. God is trying in this way to wean us away from our ideas of power and domination. He shows us that it is in fact a trifling matter if I can give orders to a great crowd of people and have everything I could want—and that it is truly great if I undertake the service of others.

A tremendous provocation.

Accepting this is, and will certainly remain, revolutionary. You can never simply do it like that, because it always requires an inner conversion—but it is the healthiest and most essential conversion there is. Only when power is changed from the inside, when our relationship to possessions is changed from within and we accept Jesus and his way of life, whose whole self is there in the action of foot-washing, only then can the world be healed and people be able to live at peace with one another.

A manifesto.

Jesus shows us what man ought to be, how he ought to live, and what we ought to work toward.

11. The Truth

In your office as Prefect of the Congregation for the Doctrine of the Faith, you are for the Church the chief guardian of truth. It is your task to defend the truth of the faith. Do we really always know exactly what is true and what is not?

Each individual must always keep in mind his own fallibility. On the other hand, it is not the case that as believing Christians we are just fumbling around in the dark for what we actually believe. The impression has gradually arisen that no one actually knows exactly what it is we believe and that consequently everyone should be able to choose for himself. If it really were true that we no longer had any common, recognizable identity, if the faith had lost any kind of shape, then Christianity would have lost any justification for its existence. It would have to admit its bankruptcy, that it no longer knows itself what it wants.

As Catholics we can say—others will be able to say something comparable in their own way—that an identical faith has been expressed since apostolic times in terms of content, and this was also formulated in words. As early as the sixth chapter of his Letter to the Romans, Saint Paul says that in baptism, we "have become obedient . . . to the standard of teaching" (v. 17). In other words, Paul can already see a distinct identity of content in Christianity, which comprises everything handed down to us from Christ (including the Old Testament). These *formulas* of faith, which according to Paul offer a basis for the action of baptism and define its meaning, developed at an early stage from the words of

Scripture into a *profession* of faith and then, somewhat more broadly expressed, into a *rule* of faith, which has a genuinely apostolic origin.

Can we see here the identity of the faith?

Yes. Certainly, the faith has been further developed and defined in the course of centuries, but it has not thereby evaporated into uncertainty. In that sense we have to oppose these ideas of leveling-down, these notions that faith is incomprehensible. Faith has something to say. And since the faith can be described, we can also assign limits to it. We can say from what point onward someone quite clearly does not share this faith. And when someone does not believe this, can no longer believe this, then he should have the courage to say, I can no longer live within this identity; I no longer accept it as being true, and should separate himself from it. But a kind of fog, in which the whole thing degenerates into an indefinable network of customs, is no use to anyone.

Your motto as a bishop runs "co-worker of the truth". How did you come by this expression?

I am of course, as is only right, a keen reader of Holy Scripture, and I came upon this phrase, which somehow fascinated me right from the beginning, in the Third Letter of John. Its meaning is in the first instance rather limited. Whoever receives the messengers of the good news becomes thereafter a fellow worker for the truth. And by accepting the messengers he himself is already sharing in this work, in this world.

I must say that I felt very strongly within myself the crisis of the claim of truth during the decades of my teaching work as a professor. What I feared was that the way we use the idea of the truth of Christianity was sheer arrogance, yes, and even a lack of respect for others. The question was, how far may we still use it?

I have really thoroughly explored this question. In the end I could see that if we abandon the concept of truth, then we abandon our foundations. For it is characteristic of Christianity, from the beginning, that the Christian faith does not primarily transmit practices or observances, as is the case with many other religions, which consist above all in the observance of certain ritual rules.

Christianity makes its appearance with the claim to tell us something about God and the world and ourselves—something that is true and that enlightens us. On this basis I came to recognize that, in the crisis of an age in which we have a great mass of communications about truth in natural science, but with respect to the questions essential for man we are sidelined into subjectivism, what we need above all is to seek anew for truth, with a new courage to recognize truth. In that way, this saying handed down from our origins, which I have chosen as my motto, defines something of the function of a priest and a theologian, to wit, that he should, in all humility, and knowing his own fallibility, seek to be a co-worker of the truth.

Son of God

At some point in his travels through villages and countryside, Jesus suddenly pauses. "Who do people think the Son of Man is?" he asks his disciples. Well now, they reply, "some say he is John the Baptist, some say Elijah, or Jeremiah, or one of the other prophets." "And who do you say I am?" is what he next wants to know. Peter says: "You are the Messiah, the Son of the living God." Jesus is pleased: "Happy are you, Simon Bar-Jona; for flesh and blood have not revealed this to you, but my Father who is in heaven."

A clear and important distinction is made in this story about Peter: What do people say—and what do you say? Jesus is referring to the fact that there are two ways of knowing him. Those people who have perhaps been present at a miracle, at one sermon, those who have heard about him, have a certain knowledge of him; they put him among the great figures in the history of religion.

It's still the same today. People want to put him in one of the recognized categories. He is one of the models of what it is to be human, the philosopher Karl Jaspers says, for instance; he is one of the prophets, or the founder of a great religion, is what others think. Jesus says that this is the perception of those people who know me at secondhand. But what do you say about me? That is, what do those who know me inwardly say?

According to Luke, this scene belongs together with Jesus at prayer. He makes it clear in this way: those who also know the communication he has with his Father, who come to know the real Jesus, know this most intimate relationship, they will also be truly able to recognize who he is. Thereby they go beyond any general categories and discover the unique and particular character of this figure—he who is the Anointed of God, the Son of the living God. This passage, which is transmitted by the three evangelists in a different form in each case, was the starting point from which the Christian profession of faith developed. Peter is seen as taking the lead in making this profession and, thus, also as the one who has been given particular responsibility for this.

The Doctors of the Church say about Jesus: "God from God, Light from Light, true God from true God, of one substance with the Father."

If we compare the three Gospels, then we can see how this profession of faith gradually grows and gains depth through the further experiences of the disciples and of faith. At first, in Mark, it says: "You are the Messiah"; in Luke, "the Messiah of God"; in Matthew, "the Messiah, the Son of the living God".

What does this mean? Here it gradually becomes clear that Jesus is not merely the Messiah, as Jewish expectation sees him, but that two kinds of expectation come together in him. On one hand, there is the expectation of a new David or a new Moses, of a new king or a new lawgiver, someone who is the friend and mediator of God, just as David and Moses were. The other expectation is that God himself would take direct action and would take the business of the world in hand. These two expectations flow together into the figure of Christ. There is a man, but in this man God himself is directly involved.

The sum total of our meeting with him, starting from the Galilean preaching, by way of his message, and then his trial before the Jewish court, in the course of which he is confronted with the question of whether he is truly God, right up to the Cross and in the meeting with the Risen One, implies that Jesus is rightly described in the words "Son of God, Light from Light, true God from true God, begotten, not created". Even the Jewish authorities can sense that a claim is being made here that goes beyond anything human, and which they therefore understand as blasphemy; perhaps they could only understand it as blasphemy. And in that sense they have rightly understood him. Jesus agrees with them. He says, Yes, I am!

The Trinity

In Ireland the shamrock, because Saint Patrick used it as a picture for the Holy Trinity, is the national emblem. For ordinary mortals, or at least for those who are not Irish, it is hard to understand: Father, Son, and then the Holy Spirit as well—three beings, and yet again just one. And it gets complicated, even for saints. There is a picture by the artist Pinturicchio in which a bishop is standing on the edge of a bay, with his hands lifted in puzzlement, more or less staring into space. The picture has the title: "Saint Augustine on the Seashore, Reflecting on the Mystery of the Holy Trinity". Does the teaching on the Trinity arise simply from speculation about God?

I would like to stay with Augustine just for a moment. This picture is represented in my coat-of-arms by a seashell, and in this way I wanted to express my sympathy with Augustine.

Augustine wrote his great work on the Trinity; he struggled with it and, then, had to recognize that it was beyond him. A legend developed, from this struggle of his, that he found beside the sea a boy who was digging a hole and who then tried to scoop the ocean into the hole with the seashell. When he saw that, the saint realized within himself that, just as the ocean cannot be put into this hole, no more can the mystery of God be put into your brain; it's too small for that.

I believe this legend hits the nail on the head about our limitations. The ocean just cannot go into the little seashell of our thought, even if we make it as big as possible. God, as the Wholly Other, remains beyond our comprehension.

You see, it's not just for ordinary people but even for the very cleverest that this mystery, that God is truly only one but that he nonetheless exists in three Persons, in this threefold relationship of love, is in the end insoluble. What is important is that the Christian faith holds fast to both things: there is one God, and he is the ultimate unity. But this very highest unity is no longer an indivisible unity, but a unity that takes its being from the dialogue of love. God, the One, is at the same time in himself relation, and on this account he can make relationships. We can in some way dimly grasp that this makes sense, even if it remains for us an insoluble puzzle.

Well then, how did the teaching on the Trinity come into existence at all?

From familiarity with Christ. From the fact that he, who says *Father* to God and who refers to himself as *the Son*—and Christ definitely does not refer to himself as "a son of God"—shows himself to be identical with God.

Many questions arose in consequence: What is the real truth about this? Is Christ *a* God, then? Are there two Gods? Is he something quite different? Was he being presumptuous? Is what he says true at all? Well now, there is one item of empirical evidence, that is, Jesus' dialogue with the Father, and besides this there is the claim that he makes, which comes from within this dialogue of Father and Son, in his words to those who are listening to him, so that here we meet on one hand similarity, unity, and divinity within the uniqueness of God, but on the other hand also distinction and diversity.

In addition there is the fact that Christ himself talks about the Spirit of the Father, which is at the same time his Spirit. The fact that this duality of Father and Son also included someone else, the Holy Spirit, was of course much more difficult to understand. One could have experience of Christ as a person; the Spirit is present in his effects, so to speak, but is for us less easily comprehended as a person. For this reason there were disputes for a long time about the Spirit's quality as a person. But when Jesus talks about the Spirit as the "Paraclete", as the advocate he is giving us, as the Comforter, then it becomes clear that he belongs with him in the same rank of being, and that this being-in-relationship within God is expressed in the threefold structure of Father-Son-Spirit.

The repeated attempts made in theology to depict the inner harmony upon which the relationship of the Trinity rests are both moving and impressive. These offer us substantial help in thinking about this and make it possible to see something of the ocean, however far distant it may be from the little hole we have dug. The essential point is that the teaching about the Trinity was not invented but results from experience. It arose from the encounter with what Christ says and does and what, then, through a growing familiarity with these words and deeds in faith and prayer, was gradually able to be formulated. We must not overlook the fact that the formula of baptism stands right at the beginning: "I baptize you in the name of the Father, and of the Son, and of the Holy Spirit." This form of words comes straight from the commission given by the Risen One. Even if their implication is not yet made clear, nevertheless these words, from the very beginning, help shape the structure of Christian prayer and Christian faith.

Our Father

The Our Father is the only prayer that Jesus taught his disciples, and for two thousand years it has been an essential part of every worship service. This prayer—just like the Creed, like the tribes of Israel, like the apostles and the Zodiac—comprises twelve clauses in all. And these twelve clauses, in turn, contain seven requests. There must be a great secret here.

I didn't know there were twelve clauses. To what extent that is true of the Greek text is another question. If it is true, that is in any case an interesting structure. In fact we have the Our Father in two versions, those of Luke and of Matthew. I find it lovely, the way that the whole range of human requests is covered in seven petitions, and also the inner ranking of those petitions, and how each word has its own inner depths.

Just the word *Father*, through which we put ourselves in the relationship of children to God, is inexhaustible. But the word *our* is no less a part of it. Not in saying "I", but in saying "we" am I included in this filial relationship. And thus the structure of this prayer holds riches that the explanations and interpretations of all the centuries have only gradually revealed.

The Our Father obviously never gets old . . .

There is no end to the books written about it, because each of us finds himself in it in a quite personal way. That is why what is true of the Word of God, of the Christian Creed itself, is also true of the Our Father: on one hand, it has a fixed shape—it is always the same—and yet it is inexhaustible and is ever new. It always leads us farther on. We are not just chained to a past in which there is nothing more to be discovered; it is rather a whole country of discoveries, in which each of us can also find himself anew.

And why does the Church pray this prayer day after day in the Mass? Just because Jesus gave it to us?

I would say that is quite reason enough. It is the original prayer, within which we know ourselves to be most completely praying together with him and praying along the right lines. Gregory the Great once expressed the opinion, in a letter, that the Our Father is so essential in the Mass because in the end it is the prayer Christ made himself. It is exalted above every prayer that men have composed, he said, even above the liturgical prayers.

It says at one place in the Our Father: "and lead us not into temptation." Why should a loving God want to lead us into temptation? Is that a mistake in translation? Frère Roger, the founder of the Taizé movement, an ecumenical religious community in France, suggested that we might pray: "And do not leave us in temptation."

That's been worked over a great deal. I know that Adenauer pressed Cardinal Frings hard on that point, that it couldn't be right the way it is. And we're forever getting letters to the same effect. "Lead us not into temptation" is in fact the literal translation of the text. And then of course we ask what it actually means.

The person praying knows that God does not want to force him into what is wrong. He asks God here for his guidance in temptation, so to speak. The Letter of James says explicitly that God, in whom there is no shadow of darkness, does not tempt anyone. But God can put us to the test—think of Abraham—in order to make us more mature, in order to bring us face-to-face with our own depths so as then to be able to bring us back to himself more completely. In that sense, the word "temptation" has various shades of meaning. God never wants to lead us onward to what is evil; that's quite clear. But it could well be that he does not simply keep temptation away from us, that, as we said, he helps us in temptation and leads us through it.

In any case, we ask him not to allow us to get into temptations that might make us slide into evil ways; that he not subject us to tests that strain us beyond our powers; that he not set aside his power and leave us on our own, that he knows our weakness and therefore will protect us so that we are not lost.

In short: the prayer stays the way it is?

I would say yes. It would not be entirely wrong to make translations consistent with the meaning, like that of Roger Schütz and other suggestions. But it seems to me better to have the humility to leave the original words and to pray oneself into its depths.

The Father-Son Principle

"No one knows the Son except the Father, and no one knows the Father except the Son", it says in the Gospel according to Matthew. Obviously, the analogy of the fatherhood of God is more or less the key to understanding the generations, or to understanding the processes of coming to be and passing away. The apostles call the Father "the origin and the goal of all things" and say that only in him can man see and recognize himself. Is this a relationship that is, somehow, engraved deep in the substance of life?

First of all it seems important to me to highlight the unique nature of this quite special Father-Son relationship. There is first of all a quite universal rule of knowledge expressed in this sentence about "no one knows the Father except the Son; no one knows the Son but the Father". It signifies that like can only be recognized by like. Where there is no inner correspondence to God, there is no possibility of knowing God. God can be known, in a strict sense, only by himself. Consequently, knowledge of God is bestowed on man, then that assumes that God draws man into a relationship of kinship and that there is then so much alive in man that resembles God that cognition and knowledge become possible. And then Jesus continues: "No one can know this except those to whom you choose to reveal it." In other words: Recognition and knowledge can only dawn within a community of will.

But isn't this Father-Son relationship also exemplary for human life?

It can be regarded as that. It is used, first of all, as a model for talking and thinking, so that we are enabled to see a little bit into God, as if through a distant window—always being aware, of course, that the *dis*similarity of God with anything in our lives is, as the Fourth Lateran Council says, much greater than all the similarities. But, on the other hand, the pattern of relationships between father and son could not serve as an analogy, to pass on to us even a distant glimpse of the inner mystery of God, were there not a trace of God himself to be found in it.

This specific relationship of father to son—which is a relationship of giving, of receiving, and of giving in return—is basic to human life. If one continues to philosophize on this basis, then one must of course pose the whole question of the human family, and then one also inevitably runs into certain limitations. It is in any case right that this particular type of relationship is of such great extent that it can reach right up above, like an outstretched index finger.

With the crisis in fatherhood in modern civilization, and the loss of the traditional role of father, the concept of authority has also got out of kilter. It seems as though, because of this, we have forgotten an enormous amount of traditional wisdom, or just casually pushed it aside. We had somehow come to feel uncomfortable about trusting anything traditional. And so, to stay with this image, we have more or less thrown out the baby with the bath water.

God gave fathers their mission, it used to be said. And indeed, down the line from father to son, the transmission of the inheritance has been carried on since time immemorial, a handing down that is almost always a dramatic process, a struggle, a matter of restraining and of guiding, a process in which you have to resist in order to grow.

Erich Fromm once sketched out the difference between the love of a father and that of a mother in this way: a mother, he says, loves on principle. Her love is a free gift. It is almost a kind of blind love. And there is no moral obligation bound up with it. A father's love, on the other hand, is conditional love. It is a love one can earn by trying to live according to the rules.

These are very profound anthropological questions. How is the process of handing on the way to live, handing on human wisdom and experience, actually carried on? How are the basic relationships of father, mother, and child, of father and son, of mother and daughter, established for us? What can they tell us about the mystery of God, and what can they not tell us? In the first place, I would like to emphasize yet again the infinite dissimilarity that is part of our relation to God. That it is still the Wholly Other who appears in the guise of what is similar and that we must therefore be extremely cautious in making analogies and comparisons. The more we understand about human beings, about the father-child relationship and the mother-child relationship, the more we feel we can see something of God in them. Perhaps that God has a mother-love for us, although—as we said earlier—the word "mother" is not used to refer to him in prayer.

What you have just quoted from Erich Fromm, something I wasn't familiar with, I find most interesting and worthy of reflection. At first glance I wouldn't entirely agree with it. I do think that in a mother's love, which is in the first instance simply a natural feeling—she has after all carried this child within her, it is her flesh and blood—we find not merely the biological given of sympathy and love. She is also responsible for this child, for his being given not only biological life but also an appropriate love and thereby a way to grow to human maturity.

I believe there is a moral demand deeply embedded in this from the start. Human motherhood is never a purely biological phenomenon, but is at the same time a spiritual undertaking. The mother carries the child within her; she gives birth to him; and in doing so she has to come to terms with the child on a spiritual level. This is an undertaking that involves the whole of her as a person.

There is no doubt that the father-son relationship is different and more complicated. A theologian has said that today we ought to supplement the story of the Prodigal Son with that of the prodigal father. Fathers are often entirely occupied by their work and give more wholehearted attention to their work than to their child, more to achievement than to gifts, and to the tasks implied by those gifts. But the loss of involvement of the father also causes grave inner damage to the sons. If we look for a moment at pagan mythologies, then the father-god Zeus, for instance, is portrayed as moody, unpredictable, and willful: the father does incorporate power and authority, but without the corresponding degree of responsibility, the limitation of power through justice and kindness. The Father as he appears in the Old Testament is quite different, and still more in what Jesus says about the Father: here, power corresponds to responsibility; here we meet a picture of power that is properly directed, that is at one with love, that does not dominate through fear but creates trust. The fatherhood of God means a devotion toward us, an acceptance of us by God at the deepest level, so that we can belong to him and turn to him in childlike love. Certainly, his fatherhood does mean that he sets the standards and corrects us with a strictness that manifests his love and that is always ready to forgive. The story of the Prodigal Son is probably the most impressive presentation of the portrait of God the Father that we have from the mouth of Jesus in the entire New Testament.

In that sense our human experiences of fathers and fatherhood are corrected; a standard is set up by which they may be measured. The picture of God the Father that we find in the Bible is not a projection upward of our own experiences; rather, the contrary: we are told from on high, in quite a new way, what a father really is and what he could be and should be among us human beings.

12. Life

I believe everybody would love to know how life really works, its inner workings, how it can go well, how we can come to terms with it and really feel good about it. The great actor Cary Grant wrote a very moving farewell letter to his daughter, Jennifer, before his death. He wanted to give her just a few bits of advice to help her along the way. "Dearest Jennifer," he wrote, "live your life to the full, but without being selfish. Be temperate in your attitudes; respect the trouble taken by others. Strive after the best and what is in good taste. Keep your understanding clear and your conduct sober." And farther on: "Be thankful for the faces of good people and for the sweet love behind their eyes. . . . For flowers that dance in the wind. . . . Yet a little sleep, and then I awake for all eternity. If I do not awake, as we understand it, then I still live on in you, my dearest daughter." That sounds more or less Catholic.

It is in any case a beautiful letter. How Catholic he may have been or not, I don't know. This is certainly written by a man who had grown wise and who had been granted a sense for what is good and had tried to hand it on, and to hand it on in marvelously loving fashion.

The Life of Man

If we look at the life of man from a wider perspective—what is it? Is life basically more a sort of game we have to play? Is it just a feather in the wind? At the mercy of instincts, of various forces, of a man's origins, of the bite of a malarial mosquito, which can throw it off-track? Or, is the course of all our lives maybe long since fixed?

Like a railway schedule, I might say, which God in his unfathomable counsel has long ago written into his secret Book of Life? *Michelangelo used to say, "The figure is already there, within the stone. I only have to chip away the rest of the block."*

You have packed a very complicated program into a single question, there. I think if we're going to ask "What is life?" then we ought first of all to note how many different levels of meaning there are in this concept.

In the first place life is biological. It ultimately comes from inorganic matter and establishes a new level of being. The capacity for reproducing itself and that of self-contained functioning are among the principal indications of the presence of life, so that what we have is no longer a machine, but an organism. So first of all we have the biological level, which begins with the simplest kind of single-cell creatures and then develops ever higher and more complicated life forms, becoming ever more wonderful, richer, and more mysterious.

Man introduces a new level of being. This is spirit, which lives and is itself life. Spirit is fused with biological existence and thus gives life another dimension.

Besides this, Christian faith is persuaded that we meet with yet another level of being, and that is in our encounter with Christ. We can already get some idea of this in the phenomenon of human love: here, whenever I am loved by another, the Thou of the other person adds a further dimension to the activity of the spirit. Something similar happens when God himself turns to me, in Christ; my life thus becomes a life lived in community with the creative life that is the origin of all.

That means that life has many levels.

And it reaches its highest level when it becomes life with God. It is in this that the whole thrill of the human adventure resides. Man can be and should be a synthesis, comprising every floor in the whole building of creation. He can, and he should, enter into the living God and pass back to him whatever has come from him. We have already said that the element of freedom plays a part in the dynamic of every life, and this element is opposed to any absolute predetermination.

On the basis of the Christian idea of God, there can be no immutably fixed plan for life. For this God is so great and is so much the Lord of all, on account of his very essence he is, to such a degree, love turned toward freedom, that he is able to grant man the power to dispose of his own life. Even if he still holds this life in his hands and surrounds and supports it, nonetheless freedom is more than just a fiction. It even stretches to the point of allowing man to wreck God's whole project.

What is important is that life takes place on these various levels. By way of the higher levels, it finally reaches out beyond death into eternity. In any case, death is the necessary fate of all merely biological life.

If freedom is more than just a word, then how can I get my life really straightened out? How can I take control of my life, manage all those stations, passageways, and crossroads that are so important in life? When is any life a success? Can we tell that, on the basis of the teachings of Christ? Would it have to be something like Mother Teresa's life?

That is one possibility. But if we look at the great gallery of saints, shall we say, or at the gallery of those great people who have, in whatever way, succeeded in life, then we can see that there are many kinds of calling. Not everyone has to be a Mother Teresa. A great scientist, a great scholar, a musician, or a simple artisan, a laborer, all can represent a successful life, people who live their lives honorably and faithfully and humbly . . .

Once again, that sounds a bit old-fashioned.

It may sound like that, but that is how you find a way to live a successful life, whether yesterday, today, or tomorrow. Each life has its own calling. It has its own code and its own path. None is just an imitation, stamped-out along with a mass of other identical ones. And each one requires the creative courage to live one's own life, and not just to turn oneself into a copy of someone else.

If you look at the parable of the lazy servant, who buried his talent so that nothing could happen to it, that expresses what I am trying to say. Here is someone who will not take the risk of living his life in its proper originality and letting it develop; or of exposing it to the dangers that necessarily arise with that.

In this sense there are a multitude of callings. I said in our book *The Salt of the Earth* that there are just as many ways to God as there are people. In this case we would have to add: There are just as many ways of living a successful life as there are people.

Is man, then, what we might call a creative blank?

No, all this does not mean that we are thrown, clueless, into an ocean of indeterminacy, as Sartre says, for example. Sartre thinks freedom is damnation. A cow does not need to think how to go about being a cow, but man has to invent himself. It really isn't like that, with man having to come from nowhere into life, with no plan or guide.

There is a basic pattern. Each individual person tries to find someone who can explain things to him, whom he can ask, How did *you* do it; how did *he* do it; how can *I* do it? How can I get to know myself and learn my own capabilities? We are convinced that the fundamental, authoritative source of information is Christ. On one hand, he gives us the broad common outlines, and, on the other, he comes into such a close relationship with us that with him and in the community of the believers we can come to know our own originality—and can then reconcile community and originality.

In earlier times, people just wanted to be upright, honest folk and to make their lives fairly secure. That was enough. There was a time to plow, a time for sowing, and a time for reaping. And it said in the Bible how life should be. Today, everything seems to have become much more complicated. At any rate, the red thread of life, the main plan and direction of one's life, which hitherto gave one something like an identity, seems harder and harder to spin.

It seems to me indisputable that life, in our complicated society, has itself become more complicated. In spite of this, we ought not to throw out the baby with the bath water and regard the constant elements as being nonexistent. We have already meditated on the Ten Commandments, which reveal their meaning anew to every generation and in each individual life, but which still hold a clear and unchanging message.

We would have to reiterate that Christianity is not evaporating into formlessness and no longer able to make any pronouncement. Christianity in particular has a definite shape, which, on one hand, is broad enough to leave room for originality but, on the other, can set the standards required for its development. Especially in a confused and complicated world, we are able to, and ought to, rely that much more on the great unchanging elements in the Word of God, so as to find the red thread once more. For if we don't do that, then the nihilistic creativity of the individual quickly turns into a mere imitation that becomes subject to generally applied criteria and only undertakes whatever the age and its possibilities have to offer.

If we leave aside the specific message of faith, then we do not become more original, but rather, according to the fashion of the times, we are leveled-down into uniformity. We experience this reduction to uniformity quite clearly in the uniformity of modern existence. I therefore believe it to be more important than ever to see how the constant elements of revelation and of faith point us in the right direction and offer us handholds by which we can haul ourselves up and at the same time give us enough light to see how we can develop our own wholly personal calling.

The Jesus Principle

Jesus always wanted to show men the way; show them the handholds for a successful life, as you just said. Once, he climbed up a mountain, and his Sermon on the Mount may be said to have opened a new chapter. Its effect, in any case, must have been revolutionary even then. It says: "When Jesus had finished saying all this, the crowd was very much struck by his teaching; for he taught like someone who has authority from God, and not like their scribes."

The Sermon on the Mount certainly has an especially symbolic place. Jesus presents himself as the New Moses. And in place of Mount Sinai we now have the Mount of the Beatitudes as the height from which he gives guidance to men. In doing this, he makes use of the structure of the Ten Commandments, but he also deepens and renews it; in the Sermon on the Mount he gives it a new breadth, so that it makes a new claim on us. More than that, he makes the breakthrough to a new level of humanity, which is made possible by God's uniting himself with man.

Jesus declared publicly: "It is not from myself that I have my teaching, but from the One who sent me. Anyone who does the will of God will know for himself whether this teaching comes from God or whether the teaching I give is my own."

He doesn't merely place himself on a level with Moses, which already would have been less than easy for his audience to cope with, but on a level with the real lawgiver, God himself. Jesus interprets the law with divine authority. "You have been told", that is to say, "God has told you", he says, and continues: "But I say to you". In that sense, the Sermon on the Mount is in many respects the clearest expression of his claim to divinity; his claim that the Old Testament Law is now being given its most profound interpretation and most universal application, no longer by way of human mediation, but by God himself.

People can sense that. And they also sense very strongly, shall we say, the double implication of the Sermon on the Mount, that this is, on the one hand, the message of a new inwardness, a maturity, and kindness, bringing freedom from superficiality and external things, yet at the same time making a more serious claim on us. And this claim is so great that man, were he left on his own, would be crushed by it.

When it is said: I no longer merely say to you, you may not commit adultery, but that you may not look on a woman with lust; when it is said: not only may you not kill, but you may not even be angry at the other person; and when it is said: an eye for an eye, a tooth for a tooth is no longer enough; on the contrary, if anyone strikes you on the cheek, you must offer him the other cheek—then we are confronted by a demand so great that it amazes us but that also seems to ask too much of men. Which would at least be asking too much of them if it were not in the first place lived out in Jesus Christ and if the whole thing were not the result of a personal encounter with God. We see here in fact the divine authority. That he is not one of the messengers but the One in whom God is expressing himself.

The place in John that you quoted gathers this all together in a formula. You must try to live it, it means, and if you live out my Word, then you will see you have taken the right path.

The Sermon on the Mount does not necessarily correspond to traditional suppositions. Indeed, it contradicts our definition of happiness, of greatness, of power, of success, and of righteousness. Jesus is obviously concerned with different categories. And at the end of his speech he offers his public yet another summary of what is important, a law of all laws so to speak, the golden rule of life. It runs thus: "Everything you would expect from other people, do that to them! The whole Law and the prophets are comprised in this."

The golden rule existed before the time of Christ, at any rate in its negative form: "Whatever you would not want someone to do to you, do not do to others." Jesus transcends this with the positive formulation, which of course makes a far greater claim on us. Everything you would like people to do to you, he now says, do that to others. That calls forth, so to speak, the creative imagination of love. In that way this rule becomes the *law of freedom*, as the Letter of James summarizes the Sermon on the Mount and the message of Jesus as a whole. Because in the end this opens up an infinitely broad field within which the creative potential of goodness can be developed.

The marvelous thing about it, I think, is that no one reckons up any longer who has done what to whom; that we no longer hamper ourselves with distinctions but are able to see our essential task: that is, to open our eyes, to open our hearts, and to discover the creative potential of goodness. It's no longer a matter of asking myself what I would like, but of making what I would like available to others. And this real self-giving, with all its creative imagination, with all the possibilities that open up to us, is expressed in a quite practical rule, so that it doesn't remain just an idealistic dream.

The great Sermon on the Mount begins with the Beatitudes. It is interesting that there are just nine of them. Nine, again, is reckoned to be the number of the angels, because their world of being is divided into nine orders. And it is also the number of perfection.

The Beatitudes are a remarkable passage because they diverge so widely from our ordinary standards. The rich are not mentioned as being blessed—there is a distinction between blessed and happy—but the poor; and not those who are free from suffering, but those who suffer. Hunger for righteousness is included, a pure heart, and much more.

The Pope has said in one of his encyclicals that the Beatitudes are actually a silent autobiography of Jesus. We do indeed find the individual sections of the Beatitudes realized in him. It is he who is poor in the Holy Spirit. It is he who comes from among the poor. It is he who is concerned for the righteousness of others. It is he who makes peace. It is he who suffers for the sake of truth. I believe we only understand the Beatitudes rightly if we understand them from the viewpoint of the Person of Christ. It is in him they are lived out, and it is through him that they are able to show us the way. In all this, individual callings are of course various. For one person one of them will stand out, and for someone else, another one. It is important to understand them as being embodied in the figure of Christ and thus to find they can be lived out in following him.

Can we assume that each of the clauses in these Beatitudes is the key to a corresponding special mystery?

Yes, only we ought not to understand this in any esoteric sense. It is, rather, a key to unlock life for us, and then mysteries are opened up that hitherto were not revealed. It is less a matter of an occult form of enlightenment or cryptic teachings. It is an insight into life, and each of these several steps offers us, as we take it, understanding and knowledge.

True and False Cares

Let's come to some of the "practical instructions" in the Sermon on the Mount. At one point there is mention, literally, of true and false cares. *Jesus says, we should take no care about what to eat or what to wear, since life is more important than food or clothing. Only pagans are concerned about all these things. Our heavenly Father already knows, he says, all the things that his children need: "Look at the birds of the air", he advises us; "they do not sow, they do not reap, and they do not gather supplies in barns; your heavenly Father gives them food. Are you not worth far more than they are?"*

That sounds good, but anyone following that advice would presumably soon bite the dust.

In a world built on planning for the future and hoping to make the world a better place by precaution, thus, by care, that has of course become totally incomprehensible. We have, I think, to read the text most attentively. And then there is indeed a key to be found in it. Jesus also says: Seek first of all the kingdom of God, then the rest will also be given you. That is to say, there is an ordering of priorities. If we exclude the first priority, namely, the presence of God in the world, then we can be as active as anything, even do many useful things, yet somehow it disintegrates in our hands. And we can see that there's something lacking. Even if the efforts at technical improvement make many things much easier in the world, nonetheless they make life darker and more difficult in many respects.

I believe it all comes down to this priority: the kingdom of God first. This has to be our basic concern, which then shapes all other concerns from within, from the viewpoint of the kingdom of God. Of course we don't just grow wings. We are concerned about tomorrow; we have to take care that the world proceeds in the right direction. But these cares become freer and are less oppressive if they are combined with the first priority. And conversely, they wear a man out and consume him if he loses sight of this priority.

Judging

At one point, high up on the mountain, Jesus says: "Do not judge, so that you will not be judged! For in the same way that you judge, you will be judged, and with the same measure that you measure and give, it will be given to you." That's easy to say. But do we not have to judge?

That is not disputed. Jesus himself, in Matthew 18, gave the basic points for keeping order in the community, when he says, for instance, that you should first admonish someone before two witnesses, and then before the community, and so on. Man needs order and, therefore, needs a system of justice. This concerns another level, namely, that we should not constitute ourselves as a court for final judgment of the world, but that in judging others we should respect the fact that we do not know everything about them. Even if a system of justice has to do it, for the sake of keeping order—it never judges persons, but only certain acts, and tries to find an appropriate response—we ought always to respect what is secret, the fact that there are things hidden from us, which only God can judge.

The second clause of this instruction then further asserts that we should always recall that we are going to be judged and that we will be judged according to the standard that we ourselves have applied. In this way it exhorts us to use a true standard, to keep a limit, to have a proper respect for others. Thus Jesus gives us an inner standard for making those judgments that are indispensable. It consists of always recognizing these final limits of what God reserves to himself.

The Two Ways

Jesus once says: "Go in through the narrow gate! For the gate is wide that leads to destruction, and the road to it is broad, and many go that way. But the gate that leads to life is narrow, and the road to it is narrow, and only a few people find it."

We might conclude from this that hell is completely full, and heaven half-empty. But that's certainly not what is meant here. The Lord says to us elsewhere—we always have to read all of his words together, this basic rule crops up again here, clearly—that many will come from east and west and will sit at table with Abraham, Isaac, and Jacob. The Apocalypse, in its vision of the future, tells of an innumerable throng assembled around the throne of the Lamb. What we have here is a quite practical warning: If we just do what *everyone* does, if we take the comfortable way, the broad road, that's more pleasant for the moment, but we are turning off the right road. It means, the difficult narrow road, the narrow gate I find it hard to get through, that's the right thing to choose.

We have here an image, graphically vivid as oriental picture-language normally is, which makes clear a basic rule for everyday living. Letting oneself be pushed, going with the tide, letting oneself be submerged in the crowd leads only again to the crowd and then into nothing. The courage to climb higher, to face up to difficulty, that is what brings me onto the right road.

The False Prophets

Christ says: "Beware of false prophets; they come to you like (harmless) sheep, but in reality they are ravening wolves. By their fruits you will know them. Do you pick grapes from thorn trees, or figs from thistles? Every good tree brings forth good fruit, but a bad tree bad fruit." That sounds like a reference to sects and heresies.

You can hear it like that. But it's also first of all a simple rule. This was an age of many wandering philosophers, quack healers, alleged saviors. They all promised salvation and the true path, wanted to make a good impression on men and, apparently, to bring goodness and righteousness, yet often they were really concerned for their own advantage. They were ravening wolves, destructive.

Jesus warns against these "charlatan saviors". He says that the criterion is: How does he live himself? What kind of person is he really? What fruit does he bring, and what kind of fruit do you see in his own circle? Check on all that, and you will see where it is all leading. This practical criterion, suggested in the context of the moment, yet again reaches out into the perspective of history as a whole. Think of all the people who proclaimed salvation in the course of the past century, whether Hitler or the various Marxist prophets, who all come saying, now we're bringing you the real thing. In a certain sense, they make their appearance like pious sheep, but in the end they're great destroyers.

But it has an even wider application to the many little preachers, false prophets, each of whom says, I have the key, you should do it like this, then you will very quickly be happy, rich, and successful. In contrast to them, Jesus urges us to approach such promises of salvation in a spirit of discrimination and with caution. Not just to fall in with them, but to preserve the vigilance of our reason and our common sense, and not to let ourselves be taken in by some movement or other that looks good but leads in the end to nothing or finishes in destruction. He wants us above all to ask about the constant elements of God's Word, about the fruits they produce.

Is that equally true of movements within the Church?

It is always true that the fruits are one criterion. Within the Church, one will above all have to look at whether someone is only proclaiming himself, trying to force his own personal views upon me. Or whether he has the humility to put himself at the service of the faith of the Church and become a servant of the common Word, the only Word.

There are many similar aids to practical life in the Sermon on the Mount. I would like to add just one more sentence from it here. Jesus says something that is hard to understand and harder still to follow: "Love your enemies, and pray for those who persecute you." And then it adds that God makes "his sun rise upon the wicked and the good, and he sends rain upon the righteous and the unrighteous."

Loving one's enemies is truly a great and a new step forward. The spirit of vengeance is taken away from us. We must recognize in our enemy the man who is God's creature. That does not mean that we should allow evil to befall us without attempting to oppose it. But it does mean that in dealing with him, we should preserve at a deeper level this respect for him. That we should aim at what is good even for our enemy, aim to bring him to what is good, finally to turn toward Christ. In that sense, praying for him is one of the basic factors in our attempt to do him good. In making a positive intervention on his behalf before God, and in trying to ensure that he does not remain our enemy but should abandon his enmity, we have already changed our attitude toward him.

The reference to a God who generously shares the gifts of creation even with the wicked is found elsewhere in the ancient world. Here it is sometimes used as an example of the indifference of God toward good and evil. Jesus lifts it up onto a different level by showing the enormous goodness of God, who wishes to include everyone in goodness, gives everyone a chance, provides good things for everyone. And even when he, so to say, punishes us, he does it so that we may listen better. As Creator, he can do no other than to love his own and to wish them to find the way. Any kind of vengeance is completely unthinkable for him.

When we have sat on this mountain and listened to Jesus and have thought about it all, and if we are now somewhat exhausted but also happy; when we know that we do not come from this world and do not remain here, not a single one of us, the Master gives his listeners what is practically a sure pledge for what he has said. These are not the usual bits of advice and counsel that one is not obliged to follow; he says he can guarantee that: "Whoever hears my words and acts upon them is like a wise man who builds his house upon a rock."

And the other man builds upon sand, and then when the great storm comes it is swept away. The solid house with good foundations stands upon the rock. That corresponds to what we heard just now in the passage from John: Whoever lives with the gospel, whoever dares to give it a try, whoever truly builds on this word, knows that he has chosen firm ground to build on.

There is another connection being made here. The saying about the house built on rock makes another appearance in the conversation with Peter, when Christ says that he is building the house—his Church—on solid rock. In that way this saying can remind us that we do not have to build alone. Anyone who wants to build his life as a private dwelling has already moved away from the rock. Building our life always really means building together. Working together to build up the one house of God, which stands upon his Word and thence provides us with a secure dwelling place.

We could go on endlessly talking about life, how you go about it and make it good and free and also exciting and fun. William Shakespeare, who was obviously a Catholic, experienced the twists and turns of life to the full. The titles of his plays read almost like a symbolic biography, from Much Ado about Nothing, *through* Measure for Measure, *right up to* All's Well that Ends Well. *As a good educator he delivered a recommendation at the end, something like the distilled essence of his earthly wisdom: "Buy terms divine in selling hours of dross."*

This is a wise saying, as one would expect from a great man. The time we make best use of is the time transformed into what endures; the time we receive from God and give back to God. Any time that passes him by just expires and becomes mere past.

13. The Mother of God

Basically, the story of our way of reckoning time began with a woman. "And the angel of the Lord brought the message to Mary", the Gospel tells us. She was a girl from the unknown little town of Nazareth, and she obviously had no idea what was happening to her.

The true stature of this event has only gradually been recognized in the course of history. First there is the meeting with the angel, when Mary is, as it were, suddenly overcome by this unusual message: She has found favor with God; she has been specially selected to be the Mother of his Son. That must have been a terrifying moment for Mary.

A human being as the Mother of God!

This is in fact the great paradox. God becomes small. He becomes man; he accepts thereby the limitations of human conception and childbirth. He has a mother and is thus truly woven into the tapestry of our human history, so that in fact a woman is able to say to him who is her child, a human child: The Lord of the world is within you.

For a long time, there was a great deal of controversy about the expression *Mother of God*. There were the Nestorians, who said she did not of course give birth to God; she gave birth to the man Jesus. Accordingly, she can be called Mother of Christ, but not Mother of God. It was basically a matter of the question of how profound a unity there is between God and man in this person Jesus Christ, whether it is so great that we can say, Yes, the one who is born is

God, and so she is God's mother. Obviously she is not God's mother in the sense of his having come from her. But she was in the sense of having been the mother of that man who was entirely at one with God. In this way she entered into a quite unique union with God.

Mary is honored as Queen of heaven, *as the* prototype of the Church, *and likewise as* Mother of mercy. *The power and outreach of this Madonna, who again and again provides the motivation for millions of people, cannot be measured by conventional standards.*

What happened has been understood in history, to an increasing extent, as at the same time honoring woman. The original image of woman is expressed in Mary, the pure figure of humanity and of the Church. And while Eve, the original first woman, the "mother of all", as they call her nowadays, the mother of all the living, gives birth in the end only for death, now Mary, in giving birth to the Savior, who rises from death and who brings life, becomes truly the pure fulfillment of what was meant with Eve, with the promise of woman and of her fruitfulness. She becomes the Mother of the One who is life and who gives life, Mother of life and of the living.

Ave Maria

The angel's greeting to Mary has become a fundamental prayer of the Catholic Church. Some of the greatest geniuses of mankind, Mozart, Rossini, and others, have set the Ave Maria *to music: "Hail Mary, full of grace! The Lord is with you. Blessed are you among women, and blessed is the fruit of your womb, Jesus." And the angel then says: "Do not be afraid." And what does Mary say then?*

"Behold, I am a maidservant of the Lord." Yes, she does learn this fearlessness. For we see that throughout Holy Scripture, whether in the case of the shepherds or that of the disciples: when man becomes aware of the closeness of God, he is afraid. He realizes how small he is, and he is terrified by the overwhelming glory and holiness of God, since he plainly recognizes his incommensurability. This appears as one of the first messages of the gospel: "Do not be afraid." This God has not come to frighten us; rather in his greatness he makes himself small, puts aside what makes us afraid, because he comes to save us.

John Paul II took up the saying "Do not be afraid, have no fear of Christ" in one of his first addresses as Pope. I would say that this is a thread that ought to run throughout Christianity. We do not need to be afraid of this God, as if he were going to take something away from us or to threaten us, for it is from him that we have the security that overcomes even death.

As concerns the *Ave Maria*, the Church's prayer, it is composed of two pieces. One part is the angel's greeting; the other is what Elizabeth says when Mary comes to visit her: "Blessed is the fruit of your womb", and Elizabeth then adds: "All generations will call you blessed", thus also predicting the devotion offered to Mary. That is spoken prophetically, in the Holy Spirit. In other words: Christians will also give praise to God by rejoicing over people in whom he has shown how great and how good he is.

What does Mary mean to you, personally?

An expression of the closeness of God. It is with her involvement that the Incarnation becomes really concrete and comprehensible. It is very moving that the Son of God has a human mother and that we are all entrusted to her care. The saying of Jesus on the Cross, when he gives Mary to John as his mother, far transcends that moment and reaches right down through history. With this handing over of Mary, the prayer to Mary opens up for everyone a particular aspect of trust and intimacy and our relation to God as such. Personally, my attitude was shaped from the beginning by the strongly christocentric aspect of the liturgical movement, and this has been further strengthened in dialogue with our Protestant friends. But over and above the liturgical feasts of Mary, the May devotions, the October Rosary, the places of pilgrimage—the popular devotion to Mary, that is—have always meant a lot to me. And the older I am, the more the Mother of God is important to me and close to me.

There are really not many places in the Gospels where we are told about Mary. There are important parts of Jesus' life during which she doesn't appear at all, and if she does, then it's not always a positive appearance as the loving mother.

That's correct, in the Gospel tradition Mary is quite marginal. In Matthew the Mother plays almost no part; the story of Jesus' childhood is written more from the point of view of Joseph. Obviously, I would say here, people were discreet so long as she was alive. And obviously she herself was always discreet.

Jesus is building a new family, and whenever the woman who gave him birth and who suckled him is praised, he corrects the traditional view of family and upbringing. He says what is important to him: "Blessed are those who hear the Word of God and follow it." That is the new family membership, the new motherhood. He describes it in this way: Whoever does my will shall be brother, mother, sister to me. Understood thus, the departure from the normal human familial relationship, moving toward the great family of community with the will of God, which is now to be built up, is essential. Luke, who tells us about this reprimand, has in any case linked this saying on a literary level with the childhood story, with the meeting with Elizabeth. There, Mary appears as the Mother who embodies not only physical motherhood but also quite fully the hearing and believing, as the one who stands within the divine community. She is portrayed by the Gospel of Luke as the one who hears and keeps the Word in exemplary fashion.

With other women, Jesus shows himself to be sensitive and close to them. His mother, on the other hand, he often brusquely corrects. At the wedding in Cana, for instance, when she asks him to do something to prevent the wine from running out for the guests, he addresses her imperiously: "Woman, why do you turn to me?" Did he really treat his mother so harshly? Did he, from time to time, perhaps even refuse to have anything to do with her?

You are referring to a passage in the Gospel of John. Saint John has a quite particular mariological understanding. In his relatively late Gospel, the role of the Mother has been more clearly worked out than in Matthew, for instance. John, for instance, wherever Jesus speaks to Mary, uses the word *gynē* [Greek] for "woman" (*Frau*; at an earlier period, translated as *Weib* in German). We can perceive a theological image in this. For if Mary is addressed simply as *gynē*, "the woman", if she plays a role beyond that of an individual, from Cana to the Cross, then the image of the New Eve is already making an appearance. We have to reread all the various scenes in relation to each other, in this case the scene at the Cross together with the scene at Cana, in order to see that Jesus first of all comes forth from his family, until at the proper hour—at the Cross—the new family begins, in which Mary holds a new and essential place.

But even at Cana this apparently harsh saying, which seems at first almost a repudiation, has hidden layers of meaning. Jesus says here that he is simply bound to time. He cannot, so to speak, look to family necessities first. In the second place, however, at her request he nonetheless performs the miracle and, so to speak, anticipates his proper hour. When Mary's request is at first refused, she is merely being brought into her proper place—and immediately appears as the Woman, as prototype of the interceding Church, which can then, like Mary herself, plead for an anticipation of her appointed time. This is, then, a most profound passage, which offers yet more opportunities for reflection and comment.

To descend for a moment from these theological heights, I should just like to mention here a little meeting I had that gave me some idea of this picture of Mary. I well remember a visit I made to the pilgrimage shrine of Altötting in Bavaria. It was cold, and I was walking across the main square to the famous Chapel of Grace. The little building was full to overflowing. Inside it was dim, and candles were burning everywhere. There were almost all women in the chapel. They were praying together, and of course they also sang their lovely hymns to Mary, Salve Regina, mater misericordiae, *Hail Holy Queen, Mother of mercy.*

At first you feel a little strange and put off, but these were really lovely songs: "To thee do we cry, mourning and weeping, in this valley of tears." And, remarkably, I suddenly found I could understand these women quite well. In its own way, this sounded very true, very beautiful, and it had the key to touching your heart and releasing feelings of happiness. You could feel a kind of healing power, springing from ancient forms of prayer and blessing. You are not alone, these beautiful feelings said. Someone is with you who knows you well. He likes you. He understands you. And if it comes to the worst, he is always on your side.

Well now, I had the feeling that this was a form of speech that not only hits man directly on his weak spot, but at the same time, as we say, applies an ointment. And perhaps in the devotion to Mary we can see a remedy for this development in the Church that wants to strip the faith of much of its holiness and mysticism, and which has perhaps already done so. Is this in a way a kind of pious protest on the part of simple folk against the religion of the professors?

I certainly think you can say that. The figure of Mary has touched the hearts of men in a special way. On one hand, the hearts of women, who see themselves in this and feel very close to Mary, but also the hearts of those men who have not lost their appreciation for mother and maiden. Mariology has expressed the inmost feelings of Christianity. Here people can have direct experience of Christianity as the religion of trust, of certainty. And these really ancient and simple prayers, which developed within popular piety and have never lost their freshness and immediacy, keep them steady in their faith, because through the Mother they find God so close that religion is no longer a burden, but a matter of trust and a help in coping with life. And think of all the other prayers—"Mother most kind, stand by me"—where we can hear this trust expressed.

There is, on the other side, a kind of purist Christianity, a rationalizing, that can seem a bit cold. Of course the feelings

—and we must allow this to be the task of the professors —have to be scrutinized and purified, again and again. This must not deteriorate into mere sentimentality, which no longer keeps in touch with reality, which can no longer acknowledge the greatness of God. But since the time of the Enlightenment—and we are now involved in another enlightenment—we have experienced such an enormous trend toward rationalizing and puritanism, if I may so express it, that the heart of man sets itself against this development and holds tight to Mariology.

"Non-Catholics are accustomed to regard devotion to Mary as encroaching upon the position of Jesus", wrote the great English cardinal John Henry Newman. And even today, sceptical persons believe that an overflowing Marian devotion will supplant the true essence of Christianity, the gospel of Christ himself.

There is one thing we must not forget: it has always been the Mother who reached people in a missionary situation and made Christ accessible to them. That is especially true of Latin America. Here, to some extent, Christianity arrived by way of Spanish swords, with deadly heralds. In Mexico, at first, absolutely nothing could be done about missionary work—until the occurrence of that phenomenon at Guadalupe, and then the Son was suddenly near by way of his Mother.

This was the remarkable discovery of an image of the Madonna. You can say that it turned things around completely, and without it the christianizing of the continent would have been unthinkable.

Yes, and suddenly the Christian religion no longer wears the terrible face of the conqueror but the kindly face of the Mother.

In Latin America, even today, these two foci of popular piety are influential: first, a love for the Mother of God; second, identifying oneself with the suffering Christ. In these two figures, in which faith is able to express itself, people have been able to grasp that this is not a God of conquerors, but the true God, who is also their Redeemer. That is why Mary is so dear to Catholics in Latin America especially. And we ought not to accuse them, from our rational perspective, of having thereby distorted Christianity. On *that* point in particular they have understood it aright. They have, that is, recognized the true countenance of God, who wants to save us, who is not on the side of the destroyers. Thus they were able to become Christians on the basis of their own seeing and understanding, without having to suffer the gospel, so to speak, as a religion of colonialism.

Protestants seem to have long ago suppressed any part Mary might play in their faith. She no longer has any place there, even though Luther himself never abandoned his devotion to Mary. For the Catholic Church, the myth of Mary is neither hocus-pocus nor an incidental matter. It is one of the essential elements of faith. Its mysteries are even guaranteed as dogma with the seal of infallibility.

Once again, concerning the word myth: if myth means that this is a story that transcends the factual element, then we can use the word here. It is in any case important that we are not concerned, here, with an invention, but with real history.

A remark concerning Protestants: it is true that a puritan tendency took the upper hand. People were afraid in the first place that Mary would to some extent take Christ's place. In due course, such a radical sense of *solus Christus* (only Christ) developed that people thought the two were in competition, instead of being able to recognize—as we have just seen in the example offered by Latin America—that the face of Christ himself appears in the face of his Mother, and its true message becomes clear in this way.

Nowadays Protestants are making some timid efforts to recapture the figure of Mary. People have realized that the complete removal of the feminine element from the Christian message is a shortcoming from an anthropological viewpoint. It is theologically and anthropologically important for woman to be at the center of Christianity. Through Mary, and the other holy women, the feminine element stands at the heart of the Christian religion. And this is not in competition with Christ. To think of Christ and Mary as being in competition means ignoring the essential distinction between these two figures. Christ gives John, and through John all of us, the Mother. That is not competition, but a most profound kind of intimacy. The Mother and Virgin forms an essential part of the Christian picture of man.

The Dogmas

Where Mary is concerned, many people have a mental block, a phobia, which is often clothed in sarcasm. Let's look quickly at a few dogmas, so that we can better understand the image of Mary. Let's start with the most controversial, the most challenging dogma of all, the dogma of perpetual virginity *from the year 553. Is that a matter of biology? Or is it about something else?*

When we were talking about the brothers and sisters of Jesus, we mentioned that the Gospels do not provide any evidence that Jesus had real brothers and sisters or that Mary bore any children after him. On the contrary, the special and unique nature of his relationship as her son is so clear that we can only properly understand the notion of siblings within the framework of clan thinking. Mary was *his* mother and could not afterward belong to anyone else.

Why not?

For one thing, because this birth came about, not through any relationship with a man, but by the intervention of God. If today some say this could not have to do with biology and were to thus push biological factors aside as unworthy of God, then they are taking a Manichaean attitude.

Man is a biological creature. And if he is not physically, biologically involved, then the material world is being somehow despised and ignored, then the Incarnation is just a matter of appearance. So I oppose this line of argument. The whole man is involved—that is the answer. God took life, including physical, biological, material life, in his hand and set a sign in it.

The Church Fathers found a lovely image, I think. In Ezekiel chapter 40 there is a vision of the new Temple, where the "east gate" is mentioned, through which gate only the king may enter. The Fathers saw an image here. They started with the assumption that the new Temple is a living Temple: the living Church. The gate through which he entered, and through which no one else may come—who or what can that be if not the Mother, Mary? She, who has borne God, cannot return to ordinary status. She remains in the same reserved position as the gate, which belongs to the king alone. And who thus became the actual door into history, through which the One came for whom all was waiting.

It stays like that: virgin birth is virgin birth?

Yes.

What was the dogma of the Immaculate Conception *of 1854 trying to say?*

The background of this is the teaching on original sin. This says that every man comes forth from a background of sin —a "damaged relationship", we called it—and in this way is burdened with a disorder in his relation to God. In the course of time the idea developed within Christendom that the one who, from the beginning, is there to serve as a gate for God, who was specially intended for *him*, could not be affected in this way.

There was a great dispute about this in the Middle Ages. On one side were the Dominicans. They said, No, Mary is a human being just like any other, so she also suffers from original sin. On the other side were the Franciscans, who upheld the other view. To cut a long story short, in the course of this dispute people came to see that Mary belongs to Christ more than to Adam. And further: that her being set apart for Christ was already there in advance—for God is always already ahead of us, and his thoughts shape our lives from the beginning—was the characteristic trait of her life. Since a new beginning takes shape in her, Mary cannot possibly belong to this sinful state of things: her relation to God is not disordered; she stands from the outset, in a special way, in the sight of God, who had "looked upon her" (*Magnificat*) and allowed her to look upon him.

More than this, her belonging in a special way to Christ brings with it a complete state of grace. Those words of the angel, at first sight so simple, "You are full of grace", can then be interpreted so as fully to comprehend her entire life.

In that sense it expresses, in the end, not merely a privilege for Mary, but a hope for us all.

To make it still more challenging: What does the dogma of the bodily Assumption of Mary into heaven *mean? It was set forth very late, in the year 1950. It is a strange fact that from the beginning there was neither a grave nor any relic of Mary.*

This dogma is obviously especially difficult, for all of us, because we cannot imagine heaven. And still less can we imagine some kind of body being located there. Seen in this way, the dogma poses a challenge to our understanding of what is meant by heaven, by body. To our understanding of man and of his future . . .

And how do you personally respond to the challenge?

Saint Paul's theology of baptism helps me here, where he says "God has raised us up with Jesus, and in Christ Jesus he has enthroned us with him in the heavenly realm" (Eph 2:6). That is to say, as baptized believers our future is already arranged.

The dogma says, then, that in Mary's case what baptism ensures for us all, that is, dwelling "enthroned" with God "in heaven" (God is heaven!), has already been put into effect for Mary. Baptism (being united with Christ) has achieved its full effect. With us this being united with Christ, being raised up, is still shaky, very inadequate. Not in her case. Nothing more is lacking. She has entered into full community with Christ. And part of this community is another corporal identity, which we cannot imagine.

In brief: the essential point of this dogma is that Mary is wholly with God, entirely with Christ, completely a "Christian".

Meanwhile, more than a million people are urging that the Catholic Church should raise Mary to the status of "Co-redemptrix". Will the Church go along with this desire—or is this an error?

I do not think there will be any compliance with this demand, which in the meantime is being supported by several million people, within the foreseeable future. The response of the Congregation for the Doctrine of the Faith is, broadly, that what is signified by this is already better expressed in other titles of Mary, while the formula "Co-redemptrix" departs to too great an extent from the language of Scripture and of the Fathers and therefore gives rise to misunderstandings.

What is true here? Well, it is true that Christ does not remain outside us or to one side of us, but builds a profound and new community with us. Everything that is his becomes ours, and everything that is ours he has taken upon himself, so that it became his: this great exchange is the actual content of redemption, the removal of limitations from our self and its extension into community with God. Because Mary is the prototype of the Church as such and is, so to say, the Church in person, this being "with" is realized in her in exemplary fashion. But this "with" must not lead us to forget the "first" of Christ: Everything comes from him, as the Letter to the Ephesians and the Letter to the Colossians, in particular, tell us; Mary, too, is everything that she is through him.

The word "Co-redemptrix" would obscure this origin. A correct intention is being expressed in the wrong way. For matters of faith, continuity of terminology with the language of Scripture and that of the Fathers is itself an essential element; it is improper simply to manipulate language.

The Miracles

No one is held in such honor in the Church as the Mother of God; with innumerable churches and altars, hymns and litanies, Marian feasts and pilgrimage festivals. The thousands of shrines of Mary to which people make pilgrimages are spread like a network of nerve cells over the whole face of the globe.

And no one supposedly works so many miracles as Mary. The places where she has appeared are filled with the documentation and testimony to inexplicable events. Bernard of Clairvaux, for instance, attributes incredible powers to Mary: "Ask of her, and you are never without hope", he says. Cardinal, are all the miracles real?

Well, we can't check everything in detail. It will often be a matter of marvelous coincidences, which we perhaps ought not to describe as miracles in the strict sense. All of these things are in any case the expression of the special trust that people have placed in Mary. Through Mary they are able to look upon the face of Christ and of God, so that they are able to understand God.

In the realm of those facts you have just listed for us, we confront the point that the mystery of the Son and the mystery of God are made accessible to men in a special way through the Mother. That is the basis for this quite special trust people have in her.

Mary is the open door to God. In talking to her we can be completely unselfconscious, we can come begging to her like little children, trustingly, in a way people often would not dare to do with Christ. This is the language of the heart. The way this language has expressed itself in a network of pilgrimage shrines shows again and again how the heart of man has been touched by this. This is the faith that Christ tells us can move mountains.

To what extent, then, miracles in the strict technical sense occur is another question. It is important that there is great trust here, and that this trust is answered. Faith becomes such a living thing in this trust that it spills out into the physical, everyday realm and thereby permits the kind hand of God to become actually effective, through the power of the kindness of this Mother.

Let us take Fatima: on the thirteenth of May 2000, Pope John Paul II pronounced the children of Fatima to be "Blessed". He himself ascribes his survival, after his attempted murder in Saint Peter's Square on the thirteenth of May 1981, to a miracle worked by the Mother of God of Fatima. And he even says that this encounter had a determinative effect on his entire pontificate.

What happened? Around noon on the thirteenth of May 1917 three children who were herding goats in the hitherto completely unknown Portuguese village—Lucia (10) and the sister and brother Jacinta (7) and Francisco (9) had a remarkable experience. They told how there was a bright light over an oak tree, surrounding a "marvelously beautiful woman". "Do not be afraid", they say she said; she had come with a message that would bring peace to mankind. At first the children were scoffed at and made fun of on account of their story. But at any rate, on October thirteenth of the same year around seventy thousand people came to test the truth of their story as eyewitnesses.

According to the reports the spectacle began at about midday. It had suddenly stopped raining. The clouds parted, and all at once the sun began to spin around at a terrific speed, like a wheel of fire. Trees and people were suddenly bathed in a fantastic, unreal light. The crowd broke out in a cry of fear. Because for just a moment, it seemed as though the sun would fall on them.

Whatever happened or did not happen on that October thirteenth, from a purely scientific point of view, we have no way of knowing for certain. What matters is that people were visibly moved by the unique experience of that moment. They were able to realize, something is happening. And in some way or other the sun became for them a sign of the mystery that lies beyond it.

The Apocalypse talks of a woman who is clothed with the sun and who stands on the moon. This stands, in the first place, for the people of God in the whole of the Old and the New Covenant, but also in a special way for Mary. The sun in which she is arrayed refers to Christ as the true Light of the world. This therefore expresses her radical connection with Christ. The moon—image of the past, of transience—is beneath her feet. In this image we see such magnitude that it is at first frightening, but it then becomes for us a power enthroned. And those people who make pilgrimages to Fatima or to Lourdes or to Guadalupe experience the greatness of this figure, as well as the consolation and healing it brings.

I believe we cannot talk about Fatima without touching on the famous "Secret of Fatima". We are talking about the messages the children who saw the vision received in 1917. The first "secret" is a glimpse into hell ("You have looked into hell, where many poor sinners are going"). The second is a prediction of the end of the First World War, which was in any case to be followed ("unless people stop causing pain to God") by another "still worse" war. Included in this is a prediction of the conversion of Russia. But John Paul II was the first to mention this conversion in an act of dedication to Mary; a year later, Gorbachev introduced his Perestroika, and ten years later the iron curtain fell.

For decades there was only speculation about the third secret, for instance about whether it predicted the catastrophes of the Apocalypse, or at least the end of the Church. This message, it was said, was meant only for whoever was pope at the time, and therefore it was not published. On his third visit to Fatima, the Pope himself disclosed this secret. On behalf of the Pope, Cardinal Sodano outlined the contents of this secret and declared that the vision the children had of "a bishop clothed in white who was hit by shots and fell to the ground, obviously dead" was a prediction of the attempted murder of Pope John Paul II.

Basically, the message of Fatima is not very complicated at all. It was expressed in this way by the three children who saw the visions: "I am the beloved Lady of the Rosary! . . . I have come so that men may become better. They must stop giving such pain to God."

Indeed, the message itself is quite simple. And Lucia, the only surviving one of the children, has placed more and more emphasis on this simplicity and has said, Don't take any notice of all the other things you are told about; it's all just a matter of faith, hope, and love. I too have been able to have a brief conversation with her. She said it then with great emphasis: Tell people that!

What she meant was: the angels we saw at first helped us to learn to practice faith, hope, and love, and the content of the whole message is that we should learn this. That is what the Mother of God wants to make us aware of and, by doing this, to purify us and convert us. Penitence is in fact this inward conversion of our existential attitude, stepping outside of the current trend, which leads away from God and leads us only to ourselves. Penitence is conversion, coming out of oneself, self-giving, which becomes love and which in turn presupposes faith and creates hope.

I believe that all these appearances of Mary, so far as they are authentic, do not bring us something to set *beside* the gospel. They offer no satisfaction to people's curiosity, no sensations or anything like that, but bring us back to the simple and essential things, which we are so easily inclined to overlook. Nowadays especially, with the complexity of all our problems, Christianity often becomes so complicated for us that we can no longer see the forest for the trees. It is a matter of being led back to the simple heart of it, not to anything else, but to the essentials, to conversion, to faith, hope, and love.

Meanwhile, the Congregation for the Doctrine of the Faith made available to the press the full text of the so-called third secret of Fatima, at a press conference on June 26, 2000. At the same time the Congregation was responsible for a booklet being published in the major languages of the world, in which the text in Sister Lucia's handwriting is reproduced in facsimile, so that there can be no further reasonable discussion as to the authenticity and the completeness of this text. In this booklet not only the sequence of visions but also the series of pieces written about them by Sister Lucia, and what happened to the account of the third secret, are carefully recounted. Furthermore, the address you referred to by Cardinal Sodano is reproduced; and I personally have provided an attempt at interpretation of the text. Since this booklet is available to anyone, I can be brief here.

The vision shows a bishop clothed in white (whom the children themselves identified as being a pope), making his way with difficulty up to a mountaintop crowned with a cross; the path leads through a town that is half-destroyed. Bishops, priests, lay people, and finally even the pope are killed. But the blood of those who are executed is collected by angels, and it becomes fruitful for the world. We can see in this text a brief snatch of a vision, in symbolic images, of the Church of the martyrs of the twentieth century; Professor Riccardi (the chairman of the Community of Saint Egidius) has meanwhile brought out a book about the martyrs of our century who died under the various dictatorial regimes, which demonstrates in a most impressive manner the reality of what is seen here in imagery. But it becomes clear, from the whole drift of the three parts of the secret, that the call to repentance is central, and this makes clear at the same time that the story does not unfold with an inescapable determinism, as if everything were in any case already unalterably written, but remains a story of freedom: repentance can change the vision.

The whole secret is a dramatic call to the freedom of men, a call to change themselves, and thus to change the course of history; and that is something this text has in common with the Apocalypse. If the Pope finally escaped death, then we may see this as a sign of how history can be changed by prayer.

Let's pay just one last little visit to Lourdes. The greatest center of pilgrimage in the world, greater even than Mecca, lies dreaming off the beaten track in the French Pyrenees. Eighteen times, so people say, Mary appeared between February and July of the year 1858 to the young girl Bernadette, and ever-increasing crowds of people were able to share in the ecstasy of the simple miller's daughter. "The Lady wore a white dress, a white veil, a blue girdle, and a yellow rose on her foot", Bernadette recounted. And on the very spot where, at the command of the Madonna, she then uncovered with her hands a little spring of water, ever since, 30,000 gallons of wonder-working water have gushed forth daily from the ground.

The Jewish writer Franz Werfel made a solemn vow that if he were rescued from the Nazis, then he would commemorate the life of Bernadette in a novel, and he kept his vow. Things very quickly calmed down again around Bernadette herself. "You see," she said, before her death, "my story is quite simple. The Virgin made use of me. Then I was put in the corner. That's my proper place; I'm happy there; that's where I'll stay."

The story of Lourdes is for me personally a particularly moving story. And by the agency of Werfel, as probably for many other people, it has come really very close to me, for he tells it from the standpoint of sharing it at a profound inner level. Even if, to demonstrate his solidarity with the Jewish people, he did not want to become a Catholic, yet nonetheless he has obviously shared Bernadette's vision of Mary within himself and has believed and trusted in her.

I should say that we ought not to get lost in mere quibbling, explaining things away here. This simple girl, who brought nothing for her part but a great inward purity, surrounded in the century of rationalism by a very crude and anticlerical rationalism, but also confronted by sceptical Church authorities who at first, quite rightly, acted only with great caution, in this somewhat cold spiritual climate, in fact almost freezing, she was able to introduce the face of the Mother of God. And in the sign of the living, healing water she also shows us a sign of Mary for the saving power of creation, which is reawakened by Mary herself.

That Christianity is made comprehensible as a religion of the heart, and as a healing reality, deliberately or precisely in this rationalistic context, in which the simple soul becomes the seeing soul, remains for us a great sign. And on that account it is perfectly normal, and something quite positive, that people still come into contact there, again and again, with the mystery of Christ. In this healing water they are referred back anew to the great and healing waters of baptism, which is the real new wellspring, a gift to us from Christ.

Mercy

In the Gospel it says: "Brothers and sisters, what use is it if someone says he believes, but does nothing. Can faith save him?" In Matthew it is written that the Son of Man, as heavenly judge, will keep account of everything and one day will draw up a reckoning. For: "What you have done for one of the least of my brothers, you have done for me." Since, according to this, faith on its own is dead, the Church has extrapolated from the Gospel the seven corporal works of mercy. *These are, in detail:*

To feed the hungry
To give drink to the thirsty
To clothe the naked
To give shelter to the stranger
To set free the prisoners
To visit the sick
To bury the dead

The first saying comes from the Letter of James, which has a strong Jewish-Christian flavor. James was the Bishop of Jerusalem. In the history of the Church, he represented that kind of Christianity for which it is of great importance that faith take concrete shape in one's life, that faith bear fruit, that it demonstrate itself in action.

The second saying is from the Gospel itself. It tells the parable of the final judgment, where the Lord identifies himself with the needy and says: In the needy, you are encountering me. And this became a saying that in the course of

Church history has taken fire anew, again and again. People have recognized that, whenever we meet someone despised, someone suffering or poor, then Christ is waiting to meet us in them. In the parable the Lord himself talks of various forms of mercy: "I was naked, and he clothed me; I was sick, and he helped me; I was in prison, and he visited me. . . ." He offers us there a little classification of the needy people through whom Christ is represented in the world.

Let's pick out one of these works: "Clothing the naked". That surely doesn't mean giving away old clothes.

Of course this saying is meant in a more inclusive sense. Certainly the gift of old clothes can be a good thing, if it is done from the heart; we ought not to undervalue little things. But here it's a matter of more than that. On one hand, it has always to do with real practical help. What matters is that we shouldn't just hold fine principles and, from time to time, make a donation, but we should be on the lookout to see where people need me in my own life. That is usually uncomfortable and inconvenient. Think about the priest and the Levite who pass by the man who has been attacked and robbed. Each of them probably has an important appointment, or maybe they're afraid something could happen to them if they stop for too long in this frightening place. There's always a reason.

Jesus' parable of the last judgment, like the list of the works of corporal mercy, says to us, on the contrary, in a practical way: This doesn't just include mankind as a whole, but right there where I meet someone in need is where I must help, even if it doesn't suit, even if I have no time right then, or I think I can't afford it. I have to think about particular cases, not just about general measures.

That is what distinguishes the Christian exhortation to love from the Marxist one, which refers precisely to general plans and structural modifications and overlooks individual cases. But, on the other hand, it does of course mean that we must also take an interest in systems and structures on the wider scale, must try to undertake not just individual help, however important that may be, but also help to ensure that people in need are offered fundamentally improved opportunities. In the Church this has produced hospitals for the sick, schools for the poor, and much more. In that sense the two things go hand-in-hand: both an eye open for my immediate neighbor, whom I must not overlook on account of my plans for social and structural improvement, and also the overcoming of inequitable structures and systems and structural help for those who need, so to speak, to be clothed.

Besides the corporal works, there are also the seven works of spiritual mercy. *These are:*

Giving advice to those in despair
Teaching the ignorant
Rebuking sinners
Consoling those in mourning
Forgiving injustices we suffer
Being patient with those who are troublesome
Praying for the living and the dead

What matters is that mercy cannot be concerned only with material things. If we provide only what is materially necessary, we have done too little. In development aid it has therefore always been clear to the far-sighted how important it is to give people training, so that they will be able to see to things for themselves. Only if we help people's spirit, if

we help the whole person, are we really helping. F
reason it is all the more important to bring God to p
Setting moral standards is in fact the most prominent work of mercy.

Let's pick out one of them again: "Teaching the ignorant". I think the recipients would, as a rule, hardly experience such teaching as a work of mercy.

Let's stay with development aid, in Latin America. Here, both the Church and also left-wing groups have made literacy campaigns a major element of their activities. And why? As long as people are ignorant, they remain dependent. They cannot get out of this situation, which is a sort of slavery, by their own efforts. Not until they have access to education are they really being helped, because they are then in a position to get on equal terms with others and properly develop their country and their society. And there, people really have experienced what it means to teach the ignorant, that through this they find access to the world of the spirit, the key to what moves the world today.

Even if we think about earlier, corresponding movements in Europe, Jean-Baptiste de la Salle, for instance, who started the charity schools in France, for the poor, who had lived in a dependent condition for generations, being able to learn was an enormous opportunity. The basic capacity to offer the chance of learning, opening the door to the world of the spirit, that is the basic work of spiritual mercy—always supposing, of course, that you not only teach people to read, but introduce them to a meaningful spiritual context, that is to say, not just pass on an ideology to them, but open up for them the way to faith.

The Rosary

A quite special prayer of the Catholic Church, the Rosary, is directly connected with the mystery of Mary. It's a kind of litany, which is prayed with the help of a string of prayer beads, "phrase" by phrase, starting with the cross (standing for the Creed); and continuing with the Ave Marias *of the three divine virtues, hope, faith, and love (for Christian life); all the way through three sets of five "mysteries" connecting Mary with Jesus, which recount the whole New Testament story in a few concentrated sentences.*

In all periods, great thinkers and mystics have appreciated its multifaceted potential and its spiritual power. Nowadays, the Rosary strikes some people as being irritatingly old-fashioned, but others as being a supernatural promise, to which they ascribe help in their everyday lives and a development in their awareness. I don't know, perhaps you have to spend a certain length of time with it, just as Tibetan Buddhists do, to discover a meditation in it. Perhaps you have to pray the Rosary a hundred times, or a hundred times a hundred, before you begin to share in this prayer; and, conversely, you will also begin to know yourself a little better and to find the heart of your own self. What do you think is the secret of the Rosary?

The historical origin of the Rosary lies in the Middle Ages. This was a time when the Psalms were the normal form of prayer. But the great number of unlettered persons of that period could not take part in the biblical Psalms. Therefore people looked for some kind of Psalter for them and found the prayers to Mary with the mysteries of the life of Jesus Christ, strung out like beads on a necklace. They touch you in a meditative way, so that the repetition allows the soul to settle into tranquility and, holding fast to the Word, above all to the figure of Mary and to the images of Christ that pass you by, make your soul calm and free and grant it a vision of God.

The Rosary does in fact provide a link for us with this primitive knowledge that repetition is a part of prayer, of meditation, that repetition is a way of settling oneself into the rhythm of tranquility. It's not so much a matter of consciously concentrating on the meaning of each single word, but allowing myself on the contrary to be carried away by the calm of repetition and of steady rhythm. So much the more so, since this text does not lack content. It brings great images and visions and above all the figure of Mary—and then, through her, the figure of Jesus—before my eyes and in my soul.

These people had to work hard. They could not expect to accomplish great intellectual tasks in prayer as well. On the contrary, they needed a prayer to bring them calm, to take them out of themselves, away from their troubles, and set before them consolation and healing. I think this basic experience in the history of religion, of repetition, of rhythm, of words in unison, of singing together, which carries me and soothes me and fills my space, which does not torment me, but lets me be still and comforts me and sets me free, this basic experience has here become fully Christian, in that people pray quite simply in the Marian context and in that of the appearance of Christ to men, and yet at the same time let this prayer be internalized in them—going beyond the intellectual level to where the soul becomes one with the words.

Do you have a particular way of praying the Rosary?

I do it quite simply, just as my parents used to pray. Both of them loved the Rosary. And the older they got, the more they loved it. The older you get, the less you are able to make great spiritual efforts, the more you need, rather, an inner refuge, to be enfolded in the rhythm of the prayer of the whole Church. And so I pray in the way I always have.

But how? Do you pray one Rosary, one set of mysteries, or all three?

No, three are too much for me; I am too much of a restless spirit; I would wander too much. I take just one, and then often only two or three mysteries out of the five, because I can then fit in a certain interval when I want to get away from work and free myself a bit, when I want to be quiet and to clear my head. A whole one would actually be too much for me then.

To close this part: How long does someone actually need in order to comprehend a little of the mysteries of faith and also of the art of believing? Two years, five years, longer?

That can vary. There are people with religious gifts who respond with an inner immediacy. There are others for whom it is harder. It is important not to let oneself be put off, to stick with it. And then you can see how you gradually grow into it.

Naturally, there are favored periods, and there are dry periods. There is a time when you are truly, inwardly moved, and you begin to see something—and then other times may come when it is very difficult.

It is important for the process of spiritual growth that you don't just pray and study your faith at times when it happens to cross your mind, when it suits you, but that you observe some discipline. Guardini always laid great emphasis on that. Faith can lose its way if I only pray according to mood and whim. Faith also needs the discipline of the dry periods; then something grows in the silence. Just as in the winter fields, despite appearances, the growth lies hidden. "Bread grows in winter", is what Ida Frederike Görres said.

And how should we begin? With questions?

I should say, never begin with thinking alone. For if you try to pull God toward you in the laboratory of rational thought, and to attach him to you in what is to some extent a purely theoretical fashion, you find you can't do it. You always have to combine the questions with action. Pascal once said to an unbelieving friend: Start by doing what believers do, even if it still makes no sense to you.

But everyone has his own starting point, I think. For many people—history shows this—looking at Mary is first of all a door by which to enter. For others, Christ is the proper beginning, meditating on the Gospels. I should say that reading the Gospels is always a way in for people. It cannot, of course, be a purely theoretical reading, the way historians do it, wanting to take the text apart and to show what sources can be found in it, but must be a reading with Christ in view, in the course of which one is always moving over into prayer.

I should say it's a kind of to-and-fro between steps—even if, sometimes, these are stumbling steps—the steps of religious practice, and those of searching through reading and reflection. You can never look for faith in isolation; it is only found in an encounter with people who believe, who can understand you, who have perhaps come by way of a similar situation themselves, who can in some way lead you and help you. It is always among us that faith grows. Anyone who wants to go it alone has thus got it wrong from the very start.

14. The Cross

We are used to thinking of suffering as something we try to avoid at all costs. And there is nothing that many societies get more angry about than the Christian idea that one should bear with pain, should endure suffering, should even sometimes give oneself up to it, in order thereby to overcome it. "Suffering", John Paul II believes, "is a part of the mystery of being human." Why is this?

Today what people have in view is eliminating suffering from the world. For the individual, that means avoiding pain and suffering in whatever way. Yet we must also see that it is in this very way that the world becomes very hard and very cold. Pain is part of being human. Anyone who really wanted to get rid of suffering would have to get rid of love before anything else, because there can be no love without suffering, because it always demands an element of self-sacrifice, because, given temperamental differences and the drama of situations, it will always bring with it renunciation and pain.

When we know that the way of love—this exodus, this going out of oneself—is the true way by which man becomes human, then we also understand that suffering is the process through which we mature. Anyone who has inwardly accepted suffering becomes more mature and more understanding of others, becomes more human. Anyone who has consistently avoided suffering does not understand other people; he becomes hard and selfish.

Love itself is a passion, something we endure. In love I experience first a happiness, a general feeling of happiness.

Yet, on the other hand, I am taken out of my comfortable tranquility and have to let myself be reshaped. If we say that suffering is the inner side of love, we then also understand why it is so important to *learn how to suffer*—and why, conversely, the avoidance of suffering renders someone unfit to cope with life. He would be left with an existential emptiness, which could then only be combined with bitterness, with rejection, and no longer with any inner acceptance or progress toward maturity.

What would actually have happened if Christ had not appeared and if he had not died on the tree of the Cross? Would the world long since have come to ruin without him?

That we cannot say. Yet we can say that man would have no access to God. He would then only be able to relate to God in occasional fragmentary attempts. And, in the end, he would not know who or what God actually is.

Something of the light of God shines through in the great religions of the world, of course, and yet they remain a matter of fragments and questions. But if the question about God finds no answer, if the road to him is blocked, if there is no forgiveness, which can only come with the authority of God himself, then human life is nothing but a meaningless experiment. Thus, God himself has parted the clouds at a certain point. He has turned on the light and has shown us the way that is the truth, that makes it possible for us to live, and that is life itself.

INRI—The Passion of the Lord

Someone like Jesus inevitably attracts an enormous amount of attention and would be bound to offend any society. At the time of his appearance, the prophet from Nazareth was not only cheered, but also mocked and persecuted. The representatives of the established order saw in Jesus' teaching and his person a serious threat to their power, and Pharisees and high priests began to seek to take his life. At the same time, the Passion was obviously part and parcel of his message, since Christ himself began to prepare his disciples for his suffering and death. In two days, he declared at the beginning of the feast of Passover, "the Son of Man will be betrayed and crucified."

Jesus is adjusting the ideas of the disciples to the fact that the Messiah is not appearing as the Savior or the glorious powerful hero to restore the renown of Israel as a powerful state, as of old. He doesn't even call himself Messiah, but *Son of Man*. His way, quite to the contrary, lies in powerlessness and in suffering death, betrayed to the heathen, as he says, and brought by the heathen to the Cross. The disciples would have to learn that the kingdom of God comes into the world in that way, and in no other.

A world-famous picture by Leonardo da Vinci, the Last Supper, *shows Jesus' farewell meal in the circle of his twelve apostles. On that evening, Jesus first of all throws them all into terror and confusion by indicating that he will be the victim of betrayal. After that he founds the holy Eucharist, which from that point onward has been performed by Christians day after day for two thousand years.*

"During the meal," we read in the Gospel, "Jesus took the bread and spoke the blessing; then he broke the bread, shared it with the

disciples, and said: Take and eat; this is my body. Then he took the cup, spoke the thanksgiving, and passed it to the disciples with the words: Drink of this, all of you; this is my blood, the blood of the New Covenant, which is shed for you and for many for the forgiveness of sins. Do this in remembrance of me." These are presumably the sentences that have been most often pronounced in the entire history of the world up till now. They give the impression of a sacred formula.

They *are* a sacred formula. In any case, these are words that entirely fail to fit into any category of what would be usual, what could be expected or premeditated. They are enormously rich in meaning and enormously profound. If you want to get to know Christ, you can get to know him best by meditating on these words, and by getting to know the context of these words, which have become a sacrament, by joining in the celebration. The institution of the Eucharist represents the sum total of what Christ is.

Here Jesus takes up the essential threads of the Old Testament. Thereby he relies on the institution of the Old Covenant, on Sinai, on one hand, thus making clear that what was begun on Sinai is now enacted anew: The Covenant that God made with men is now truly perfected. The Last Supper is the rite of institution of the New Covenant. In giving himself over to men, he creates a community of blood between God and man.

On the other hand, some words of the prophet Jeremiah are taken up here, proclaiming the New Covenant. Both strands of the Old Testament (Law and prophets) are amalgamated to create this unity and, at the same time, shaped into a sacramental action. The Cross is already anticipated in this. For when Christ gives his Body and his Blood, gives himself, then this assumes that he is really giving up his life.

In that sense, these words are the inner act of the Cross, which occurs when God transforms this external violence against him into an act of self-donation to mankind.

And something else is anticipated here, the Resurrection. You cannot give anyone dead flesh, dead body to eat. Only because he is going to rise again are his Body and his Blood new. It is no longer cannibalism but union with the living, risen Christ that is happening here.

In these few words, as we see, lies a synthesis of the history of religion—of the history of Israel's faith, as well as of Jesus' own being and work, which finally becomes a sacrament and an abiding presence.

The disciples go with Jesus to the Mount of Olives. There Peter asserts passionately that he will never betray the Master. Jesus wants to pray in the Garden of Gethsemane. He is deeply moved and at the same time under great strain. Sorrow and anguish come upon him. "My soul is afflicted unto death", he says to two disciples; "stay here and watch with me." They go off a couple of yards, and he throws himself to the ground. He prays, and perhaps he also weeps. "Father", the two hear him say, "if it is possible, let this cup pass me by. But let not what I want, but what you want, be done."

That is one of the most moving, and the most disturbing, passages in the New Testament. We can only try to meditate ever anew on this mystery of the anguish of Christ, as the great believers have done.

To a certain extent I see here the struggle between the human and the divine soul of Jesus Christ. Jesus can see the whole abyss of human filth and human awfulness, which he has to carry and through which he must make his way. In what he sees, which goes far beyond anything of which we can be aware—and even we can feel horribly sick if we take a look at the awfulness of human history, into the abyss of denial of God, which can destroy people—in this he sees how dreadful is the burden that is being laid upon him. This is not just anguish in the face of his execution; it is being confronted with the entire, fearful, abyss of human destiny, which he has to take upon himself.

The Greek theologian Maximus the Confessor depicts this process in a particularly impressive way. He shows us how the "alchemy of being" is accomplished in the prayer on the Mount of Olives. Here, Jesus' will becomes one with the will of the Son and, thereby, with the will of the Father. All the rebelliousness of human nature, which shuts itself against death and against the horrors he can see, comes to the surface in this prayer. Jesus has to overcome man's inward resistance against God. He must overcome the inner temptation to do it some other way. And now this temptation reaches its zenith. Only the breakdown of this resistance makes a Yes possible. It ends with the fusion of his own individual, human will into the will of God and, thus, with the single petition: "But let not my will, but your will, be done."

Jesus' disciples are a pretty tired bunch. When the Master comes back again, he finds them sleeping. Jesus is disappointed. "Could you not even keep watch with me for one hour?" he says.

Yes, he is disappointed. And believers in all ages have seen how this saying of Jesus reaches beyond the context of the moment into the entire history of the Church. Again and again, the disciples are sleeping. Again and again, there is a grave threat to God's work, and his people are sleeping. He has brought them quite close to himself; they are supposed to lessen the burden of being alone; but they are obviously not affected by the awfulness of the moment.

And Christ says further: "Watch and pray, that you may not fall into temptation. The spirit is willing, but the flesh is weak."

This saying harks back to what God says after the flood: "I can see that they are but flesh; they are weak; they need forbearance and pity." In the end, his disappointment is swallowed up in pity.

Judas makes his appearance with a great troop of armed men. He goes up to Jesus and kisses him. That is the sign. When the soldiers seize Jesus, Peter intervenes, grasps his sword, and strikes off the ear of one of the slaves of the high priest. Jesus just says: "Put your sword in its sheath, for all who take the sword will die by the sword."

Peter wants to demonstrate that his courageous words about never betraying the Master are true. That he is ready to risk death at this very moment. Certainly, he will soon have to learn that striking out boldly very quickly becomes a very small thing if striking out boldly doesn't work.

Above all, Jesus is once again speaking out to the whole of history here: God's work, he warns us, cannot be defended with the sword, as has unfortunately been attempted again and again. Anyone who wants to defend God by force is already by that very fact opposing him.

After the arrest of their Master, the disciples take flight. All of them, without exception. Jesus is taken before Caiaphas, the high priest, and formally examined. But the case against him is shaky; the witnesses' statements are fabricated. At last they find an offense to charge him with: blasphemy. The high priest presses him: "I adjure you, by the living God, to tell us, are you the Messiah, the Son of God?" And Jesus responds coolly: "You have said it."

As high priest, Caiaphas is responsible for the faith of Israel. Naturally it doesn't occur to him that he might really be condemning the living Son of God to death. He sees in Jesus someone who has done injury to the very heart of the Jewish creed, the belief in one God, by the presumptuous claim to be himself God's Son. And, certainly, he does this in a state of blindness, unable to perceive the mystery; his faith is encapsulated in a formula. We ought not to be too ready to condemn him, since in some way he believes, of course, that he is acting responsibly on behalf of religion.

The martyrdom begins. The scribes and the elders are the first to spit in Jesus' face. They cover his head and give him a slap: "You, Messiah, you're a prophet, aren't you; who hit you?" Peter, who is hanging around in the courtyard, is recognized and denies knowing his Master. When he realizes what he has done, he goes out and weeps bitterly. Even Judas is not happy about his treachery; he is terribly sorry for what he has done. He throws his silver pieces into the Temple and goes and hangs himself.

Here we see all the drama of human weakness: Peter runs away at first, but comes back to see what is happening. In his eyes, his denial of Jesus is only a little lie he tells so as not to be discovered and thus to ensure he is able to stay near him. Yet under the gaze of Jesus he realizes how cowardly he has been and how he has now deserted him.

What I find fascinating is the difference between the two people who have fallen into sin. One finds his way to repentance, and in this way he is once more accepted. He is ready to receive forgiveness. He does not despair. He suffers and thus becomes a penitent who reforms. The other is so horrified by his betrayal that he no longer believes in forgiveness.

That, I would say, is the real difference. Two kinds of regret, of self-accusation. One does not become nihilistic but allows itself to be picked up again. And one in which the belief in forgiveness has been extinguished, which destroys itself and thereby fails to take the path of renewal, which would have been open.

I believe that is an important lesson for all men who have fallen, for everyone who feels guilt in any way or who is overcome by guilt. It shows us that a mistakenly exaggerated self-condemnation, which grows in the end to a total denial of oneself, is not the appropriate way to deal with guilt.

Jesus is dragged before the Roman governor, Pontius Pilate. "Are you the king of the Jews?" he mocks. "Yes, I am a king," Jesus replies, "but my kingdom is not of this world. For this I was born, and for this I came into the world, to bear witness to the truth. Anyone who belongs to the truth hears my voice." Pilate obviously cannot understand the answer and asks sceptically: "What is truth?"

Jesus has first of all been through a Jewish trial, which ends with a verdict of guilty. Remarkably, the Jewish authorities do not carry out the sentence; instead of that, they transfer the matter to the secular Roman court. At this second trial there is a different charge. Here Jesus is no longer accused of offending against the Jewish creed, which would have been a matter of indifference to Pilate, but is accused of being a political usurper who is undermining Roman rule. The religious trial is turned into a political one.

The indictment is certainly thin, and the Roman judge, who is in fact himself a cynic, has at first not the slightest desire to act as a lackey for the Jewish authorities. In this, the figure of Pilate seems very modern. When Jesus talks about the truth, he answers like a typical sceptic: Well, what is that in fact, truth? Only a deluded madman would assert that he is acting as witness to the truth and would go to his death for it.

The Roman declares to the crowds that he can find no fault in the man, but he is offering, in view of the religious festival that is coming up, to release a prisoner, and they can choose now between this Jesus and the violent criminal Barabbas. The crowd howls: "Barabbas! Barabbas!" "And what shall I do with Jesus, then?" asks Pilate. And again the response is unmistakable: "Crucify him! Crucify him!" Pontius Pilate pays tribute to the mob, but he washes his hands publicly and symbolically, as a sign of his own innocence.

This passage is a real object lesson about crowds. There are, probably, people in the crowd who were quite harmless before, people like those who liked Jesus and cheered him. We can see how a crowd destroys the conscience. How it alienates people from themselves and can turn them into instruments of evil.

Just as the priests did earlier, the soldiers now make fun of the prisoner. They take his clothes off, dress him in a purple cloak, and weave a crown of thorns for him. A stick in his hand serves as a scepter, and the grinning hirelings go down on one knee before him. "Hail, king of the Jews." Then they spit on him; they take the stick and beat him about the head with it. Again it is Pilate who asks for pity in the face of this picture of misery: "Ecce homo—look at the man."

All these passages open up unfathomable depths. With their many levels, they lead us through the whole scale of behavior, from the banality of evil to the humility of divine power and love. We see first of all the inhuman attitude of such a death squad, for whom cruelty has become their daily bread. But there is probably more than that, so that, through the mockery, we glimpse something more profound. For the very person they have crowned so as to mock him is the true king of the world. That man, who wears the crown of thorns and, with it, takes upon himself the crown of the suffering of mankind, is the truly crowned head of all. And what Pilate says, again, has a very complex meaning over and beyond what he intends to say. Somehow, it is saying: "Yes, *that* is man", a pitiful worm. At the same time, it shows us the *real* man, who in his suffering bears the image of God.

The scourged man wearing the crown of thorns is driven out by soldiers to the "Place of the Skull", to Golgotha. Jesus carries the heavy cross; he is sweating blood. Three times, he breaks down under the burden. Veronica hands him a cloth; women are weeping; but absolutely no one on the edge of the crowd is prepared to take the cross from him. Presumably because the hirelings are afraid that their prisoner might perhaps break down altogether, even before he is crucified, they make a man by the name of Simon of Cyrene support Jesus under his arms for a little while.

Christian piety has made this Way of the Cross, which one can walk along in Jerusalem, the basic image for the path of human suffering. Certain features of it have arisen through meditation, such as his falling three times or the figure of Veronica. These are things of which people's hearts have become aware through inwardly walking this path with him. After the *Rosary*, the *Way of the Cross* is the second great form of prayer discovered by Western popular piety in the Middle Ages. It is not only a great testimony to an inner depth and maturity, but it is in fact a school for interiority and consolation. It is also a school for the examination of conscience, for conversion, for inner transformation and compassion—not as sentimentality, as a mere feeling, but as a disturbing experience that knocks on the door of my heart, that obliges me to know myself and to become a better person.

The figure of Simon, of course, still makes a great impression. At any rate, Christendom has seen in this an enduring mission. Christ is, so to speak, carrying his Cross throughout the whole of history. He is looking for the hand of Veronica and the hand of Simon, hands that are ready to carry great crosses.

The soldiers abuse Jesus in a way we can hardly imagine. All hatred, everything bestial in man, utterly abysmal, the most horrible things men can do to one another, is obviously unloaded onto this man.

Jesus stands for all victims of brute force. In the twentieth century itself we have seen again how inventive human cruelty can be; how cruelty, in the act of destroying the image of man in others, dishonors and destroys that image in itself. The fact that the Son of God took all this upon himself in exemplary manner, as the "Lamb of God", is bound to make us shudder at the cruelty of men, on one hand, and make us think carefully about ourselves, how far we are willing to stand by as cowardly or silent onlookers, or how far we share responsibility ourselves. On the other side, it is bound to transform us and to make us rejoice in God. He has put himself on the side of the innocent and the suffering and would like to see us standing there too.

Even on the Cross Jesus is mocked. The soldiers offer him wine mixed with gall. They have nailed onto the Cross a board with the inscription: Jesus of Nazareth, King of the Jews (INRI). *The high priests and the scribes call to him: "Did you want to tear down the Temple and build it again in three days? If you are the Son of God, then save yourself and come down from the cross." But Jesus does not climb down from the Cross. He says nothing. Not even when there is darkness from the sixth hour to the ninth. At about the ninth hour, at any rate, he does cry out: "Eli, Eli, lama sabachthani." And that is a remarkable sentence, since it means: "My God, my God, why have you forsaken me?"*

The evangelists offer us two traditions regarding the drink that is offered to Jesus. Matthew tells us about wine that is mixed with gall, which is offered to Jesus at the beginning of his time on the Cross, perhaps as a kind of anesthetic drink. Jesus refuses it—he wants to endure the suffering with undimmed senses. Mark, Luke, and in great detail John tell us about some vinegar that is given to Jesus at the end of his Passion. These evangelists obviously have in mind the saying from a psalm: "They gave me poison to eat, and vinegar for my thirst" (Ps 69:21). We hear the echo of other prophetic passages: I planted a vineyard, and it gave me only sour wine—a complaint that, again and again, applies to Christendom as well.

Then we hear about the mockery that rises like waves around Jesus. We may think about the Book of Wisdom in the Old Testament, where it is said: "The wicked will make mock of the righteous man." They will give him up to death and will say, Now you can show us whether you are God or not. It is their way of making an experiment. And it is their hour of triumph, in which the Pharisees, who perhaps up to now have, in part, still had a bad conscience about this, can see themselves as justified and can clothe their rejection of him in mockery. They make common cause thereby with the banality of evil, as represented by the soldiers.

Altogether, seven sayings of Jesus upon the Cross are handed down to us in the Gospels. The one you have just quoted has in fact a contextual key. This is the first verse of Psalm 21, the great psalm of Israel's suffering, in which Israel, which in the course of history has again and again been trampled down in powerlessness, cried out: "My God, my God, why have you forsaken me?" By beginning his prayer with Psalm 21, Jesus identifies himself with the suffering people of Israel and takes over and internalizes the fate of this people.

But we ought not to forget that this is also a prayer. It is a recognition of God in a cry for help. Jesus dies praying, as someone who upholds the first commandment, to worship God, and God only. The psalm develops into a great declaration of trust, and in a prophecy of the Eucharist it ends with these words: "The poor will eat, and will be satisfied." The food that satisfies the poor, the new manna, comes from the Cross.

In the moment of Jesus' death, the curtain in the Temple tears in two from top to bottom. The earth begins to tremble; rocks split apart; and it says that graves even open up. Artists have attempted, over the centuries, to give expression to this scene. I can particularly recall one picture: The tortured, dying man is leaning his head a little onto one shoulder and looking at the beholder. The crown of thorns has been forced down onto his scalp. Jesus is bleeding. Tears are running down his face. And at the same time, his narrow face, still undamaged despite the onset of death, carries an expression of peace. The tortured man, who would have had every cause for complaint, is smiling at the onlooker. And there is no trace of reproach in him; Christ seems relaxed and quite at ease. And the longer you look at him, the more clearly, paradoxically, you perceive depicted, within the sorrow, a picture of consolation.

The true, great, and unadulterated portrayals of the Cross arise from an inward identification with the crucified Christ, from a meditation, from a prayerful uniting of oneself with him. They do portray the thirst, the misery, the frightful torture and pain, but in this picture they give the last word to peace: "Into thy hands I commit my spirit. It is finished."

Jesus bowed his head and departed. He gave up his spirit and gave back the spirit to the Father, so that the peace of the Crucified One shines forth even in these last words. Pictures of Christ on the Cross can never be merely pictures of cruelty and horror or they would not portray the whole mystery of Christ. If they only show the mockery of man, then they become themselves a subject for mockery.

The Resurrection

Within twenty-four hours, in Jerusalem, the Resurrection was recognized as a fact. Everyone in the city was extremely disturbed that morning. There was first of all the earthquake that had shaken the Temple two days before, then a three-hour sandstorm, then more tremors. When the women were the first to bring the story of the empty tomb, it was treated at first as mere gossip. But by evening there was no more room for doubt, at least among the disciples. Jesus had met with two of them on the road to Emmaus and had made himself known to them. The history of Christianity, as the history of a faith, had begun.

We can leave open the question of how quickly this event became generally accepted in the city of Jerusalem. From the closing passage of the Gospel of Matthew, we know that, even after the great final appearance of Jesus on a mountain in Galilee—the Crucified One had risen and said: "All power has been given to me"—many people still had doubts. At every stage, the message of the Resurrection was accompanied by doubts and was opposed, even though this is the victorious message that overcomes doubt.

Christ departed from this world and from its life in a new manner of corporality, which is no longer subject to physical laws. It belongs to the world of God, from whence Christ shows himself to men and opens their hearts that they may recognize him and touch him. Again and again, we are invited to touch him with Thomas, the "unbelieving apostle", and to recognize his living presence, which he discloses ever anew in history.

And in fact with the Resurrection something new has broken through into this world, and it is starting from the Resurrection that the Church can be built up, the community of those who believe in Christ, the new people of God.

The Cross, the most sacred sign of the universe, as Guardini used to call it, became the sign of Christians. The Cross, with a man being tortured to death—a symbol that gave great offense. Paul already found it necessary to exhort: Do not empty the Cross of meaning, do not make it linear or horizontal, do not turn the plus of God into the minus of the world.

This is in fact a history that has no parallel. That very Cross upon which not only Jesus' message, but he himself, his flesh and blood, were supposed to come to an end became a symbol of salvation, a symbol not of death but, indeed, of life. "The wood of true life", sang Andrew of Jerusalem. A paradox: through the Cross to salvation.

Early pictures of Christ on the Cross show him as the risen Christ, as King. He is shown with his eyes open, so as to make clear that the Godhead did not die, that it is still living and still gives life. From being the stigma of Roman execution, the Cross thus became the sign of triumph of the Son of Man, which not only will appear to us at the end of all time, but which already thus appears to us when he, as Victor, comes to us and seeks us out. With him we start out to meet the living God; in the suffering One, the consolation of God's love, stronger than death, becomes visible.

Thus the Cross has truly become a sign of redemption, the sign of Jesus Christ, the logogram for him, by means of which we symbolically unite ourselves with him.

It must have been a shock for his followers in Jerusalem: the Messiah, who could make the blind see and could raise the dead to life, suddenly allowed himself to be humiliated, insulted, and nailed to the Cross by the hirelings of power. That was absolutely inexplicable: Why should God have to suffer and die in order to redeem his own creatures?

That is the mystery of God, who did not come into the world as someone who was going to set up a just social order by force of power. He came down to our level in order to suffer for us and with us.

We will never be able to understand this mystery finally and completely. And nevertheless, this is the most positive thing that is told us about God: God does not simply rule by power. God uses his power differently from the way human rulers use power. His power is that of sharing in love and in suffering, and the true face of God is shown, indeed, in suffering. In suffering, God bears and shares the burden of the injustice of the world, so that in our very darkest hours, we may be sure that God is then closest to us.

God becomes small, so that we can grasp his nature. So that we men can have set before us that principle, which is the opposite of the principle of pride and the principle of the idolization of self. He comes as someone who touches our hearts.

Part III

THE CHURCH

Cardinal, Jesus Christ promised his apostles and their successors that he would always remind them of his teaching and declare it to them. Do you have any sense of this?

Of course, we must not understand that in a mechanical sense, as if we could retrieve data as we do on a computer. This is a promise that refers to the Church as a whole.

Jesus says, literally: "The Holy Spirit, whom the Father will send in my name, will teach you all things and will remind you of everything I have taught you."

In this he was saying that he would not leave the Church to follow her path alone. That he would not allow her to fall away from him. That he enriches her memory and deepens it, so that she learns to understand those things she did not grasp at first and finds her way into the more profound significance of his words. But that does not mean that each individual Christian can at any time just call upon such a memory for himself, or even that it comes automatically to the Church. She needs living prayer and a living remembrance, through which the Spirit then speaks to her. But I would say that, yes, of course, in some sense I do feel I have this help.

Even so, it is given to many brilliant men and women to receive insights into great coherences and to transmit these complex perceptions in such a way that the masses can understand.

I believe that by belonging to the Church, and living with her faith, one is given a share in the inspiration allotted to this family. The Church can open up horizons for you and deepen your insight into things you could not understand on your own. Then there are, of course, especially gifted men, whom we call saints, who, through their inner closeness to God, penetrate, as it were, more deeply into this memory and bring it before us as a living reality.

Is it love that binds you personally so closely to the Church?

You can certainly say so. She is my home, my extended family, and thus I am bound to her in love, just as one is bound to one's family.

The Church is not some chance product of history, some quirk of history, certainly not by her own understanding of this. Outsiders, on the other hand, often have the impression of an organization with power and possessions, something like a commercial firm, except that in this case the departmental managers run around in long robes. Pope Leo the Great once said that to gain any insight at all into the nature of this Church, even approximately to understand her, you first have to put aside "the darkness of earthbound thought and the haze of worldly wisdom".

Well now, you can experience the Church at many different levels. You can look at her in a purely institutional way, as one of the institutional forces active in the world, or you can take a purely sociological view of her. You can be galled by individual people or particular events. In any case, if you only look at her from an institutional viewpoint, then your view remains superficial.

It seems to me a particular temptation for our very active and rational society to try to make the Church accessible by means of commissions and boards and consultations. People would like to make her handier and more practical, to some extent make her a human construction in which, in the end, some majority or other will decide what we should actually believe or what we cannot believe, and so forth. But we would only distort her by doing this, moving her ever farther away from her true self. She would no longer be a living thing—and certainly not something divine.

If we want to understand the Church properly, then we must look at her, I think, above all from the standpoint of her liturgy. That is where she is most often herself; that is where she is ever and ever again touched and renewed by the Lord. For in the liturgy we must in fact live the Church by starting from Holy Scripture, from the sacraments, from the great prayers of Christendom. And this is the way that, as Leo the Great says, we can gradually clear away the haze that makes the air so thick and the grains of sand that have got in our eyes and can begin to see better.

Then we will see that the Church has far greater depths. That the communion of saints belongs to her, the community of all those who have gone before us and, in particular, the hidden and simple saints. That she lives in so many believing people, who are inwardly bound to Christ, and that her roots above all reach down into Christ himself. Christ is the constant power that gives life to this vine and makes it capable of bearing fruit. In this sense, the reality of the Church is far greater than what you can tabulate in statistics or achieve by decisions. This reality is a living organism, whose life cycle derives from Christ himself.

15. The Spirit

How It All Started

"Blessed are you, Simon Bar-Jona", that is how Jesus spoke to the man whose name the Church has inscribed for herself to all eternity; "you are Peter, a rock, and on this rock I will build my Church, and the powers of the underworld will not be able to overcome it." This saying stands at the very beginning of a quite incomparable success story. Can we say that with this assertion Christ himself founded the Church?

The question of whether the Church was really part of Jesus' intention has given rise to a great deal of discussion. Many say, No, he was only intent on the kingdom of God, or he intended something else, in any case, not the Church. In asserting this, certainly, they are failing to recognize that not only Jesus stands within the salvation history of the Jewish people, but also his intention to renew this people, indeed, to renew salvation history as a whole, to make it broader and more profound—and thereby to create what we call the Church.

There are many actions in Jesus' life that contribute to the founding of the Church. It starts with the selection of the Twelve. We have already seen how they are symbolically the twelve patriarchs of the new Israel. And then it continues with the words he delivers to them, and above all with the Lord's Supper, which is presented to them as a gift, as being at the heart of their new life. It is given greater depth by the commission to baptize, in the missionary mandate, and yet other things. And one of this whole collection of acts is the naming of Peter as the first among the Twelve and the rock of the Church.

After his death, Jesus appears to the apostles in the upper room in Jerusalem. The following words on that occasion are transmitted in the Gospel according to John: "Peace be to you! As the Father sent me, so am I sending you." And after saying this, he breathes on them and says: "Receive the holy Spirit!" Presumably, not one of those present had even the slightest idea of what this was the beginning of.

This dramatic representation of the calling of the Twelve after the Resurrection makes an impressive scene. The apostles become bearers of the Holy Spirit, which carries on in their persons the mission of Jesus Christ himself. At that moment, indeed, no one could imagine what the results of that mission would be. Most of them were thinking about the end of the world, which they expected to come soon. They were convinced that the time was now fulfilled, and history would not run much farther. It was enough for the disciples to know that they now had within them the Spirit of Christ and that they had to carry this peace he had brought them, the new peace he had given them, right beyond the bounds of Israel.

There is a remarkable story that happens in this period after the Resurrection. It was one evening, when Peter and John and a few others were trying to catch fish in the lake of Gennesareth. They cannot have been in a good mood, since the nets stayed empty. When they came back to the shore, in the gray of early morning, they met Jesus. The disciples did not recognize him, even though he spoke to them as good mates. The Master's words were: "Children, have you got anything to eat?" And he called across to them: "Throw out the net on the right side of the boat; that way you'll get something." For whatever reason, they followed his advice, and right away the net was so full that no one could pull it out of the water. "It's the Master", John said, as it dawned upon him. Peter threw himself into the waves, and swam ashore, the disciples following him with the boat. They had caught 153 large fish, and the net wasn't even broken.

This story is richly symbolic and has so many layers of meaning that we cannot explain them all separately here. The marvelous catch of fish. These men had worked all night for nothing, and as experienced fishermen they could hardly expect that they would catch anything now, when daylight had already returned. Nonetheless Jesus sends them out. At his word they go out once more, and they do in fact receive this superabundant gift.

What is meant exactly by the number 153, which John so carefully notes down, not all the learning in the world has yet deciphered. Some would see in 153 a numerical sign for Peter. However that may be, it signifies an enormous quantity. This is a promise that goes beyond the immediate moment. It shows, on one hand, how difficult it is for any human effort to pull fish out of the sea of this world, thus becoming living men for God. And at the same time it promises that, time and again, the improbable will happen, that by means of Christ's net the Church can time and again be pulled out of the ocean of transience, and that in this net of Peter the fisherman she will bring people together in multitudes.

The scene continues. They prepare a meal on a fire; they eat fish and bread together; and all at once Jesus turns to Simon Peter.

"Simon," he says, "son of John, do you love me more than these?" Peter is taken aback and just says: "Yes, Lord! You know that I love you." Three times Jesus asks his number-one disciple the same thing, and three times he gets the same answer: "Yes, Lord, you know that I love you." Finally, a little upset, Peter even says: "Lord, you know everything; you know that I love you." And following on these preliminaries, Jesus gives him, again in three sentences, a remarkable commission: "Feed my lambs", and again: "Feed my lambs", and at the finish: "Feed my sheep." What exactly does this mean?

First of all the disciples catch fish for him, but then *he* gives them something to eat. In the end, then, all human efforts are outstripped by the gifts of Christ. And finally we see here another story of Christ instituting discipleship. Peter's first profession of faith, which we have already talked about, took place at the time when the Galilean successes had ebbed, and it was starting to get lonely around Jesus. Many people deny that the saying about the rock that Jesus pronounced then was spoken by the earthly Jesus; according to them, it belongs among the Resurrection traditions. But the Gospels deliberately locate it at a turning point in the earthly life of Jesus; it is so bound up in this context that we cannot separate it.

In the upper room there was then a new promise to Peter: When you have turned back again, strengthen your brethren. He is commissioned to be the one who strengthens them in the faith. It is significant that all these witnesses to Peter are to be found throughout the various strands of the New Testament writings. Once in the synoptic tradition, then in the Johannine, and then again in the writings of the Pauline tradition, we find the primacy of Peter, so that a knowledge of the special commission given to Peter is reflected in all the various contexts in which the tradition was transmitted.

What is transmitted to us here in John 21 is a ritual of discipleship. Peter now has to take over the care of Jesus' flock. And straight after that, the Lord says to him, in a prophecy of martyrdom, that this is a service that can only be based on love for Christ and can only be carried out in a spirit of readiness to take the path of martyrdom. In that sense, for Catholic Christians, the specific commission to him, in all its many-faceted richness, is marvelously defined with this inclusive theology of Peter that we find in the New Testament—and it is a testament to the Church down all the ages.

The risen Jesus commands the disciples not to depart from Jerusalem until the Holy Spirit has come down, that "power from on high". In saying this, he makes a mysterious reference: "John baptized with water," he says, "but you will be baptized with the Holy Spirit, in a few days' time." What does that mean?

Jesus is announcing the gift of the Spirit, which is then first accomplished at Pentecost. Saint Luke has depicted it in the Acts of the Apostles. He describes how in the midst of the prayer of the 120, who are assembled together with the Twelve and with Mary, there comes the gift of the Holy Spirit. In this way Luke, whose work is composed in most deliberate fashion, refers back to the conception of Jesus, when the Holy Spirit came down and thus the man Jesus was conceived upon earth. Now the Holy Spirit comes again, and thus the Church, the "Body of Christ", is born for the period of history. This happens in the signs of wind and fire —and above all in the sign of the miracle of tongues, which proclaims and anticipates the existence of the Church in every language and tongue. This is the counterpart to Babel. This is the other, new society, which the Lord is now building up by the power of the Holy Spirit, by this flame of God, from now on in the hearts of men.

But can we really picture the scene as being just like that, with flames, tongues of fire, coming down from heaven?

It's up to each person, exactly how he wants to picture it. The Fathers, and especially oriental theology, have developed a most profound interpretation of it. When the Spirit shows himself as tongues, as flames, then that shows how he dwells in a separate and very personal fashion in each single person. These are most important images, in which the mystery of the Spirit, the rebirth of the Church, is portrayed—and with the miracle of tongues, precisely what we call the catholicity of the Church.

The Essential Nature of the Church

Let's stay with this rebirth. What is the Church supposed to be? What kind of body is she meant to be? Her nature is always specified as being apostolic and catholic. What does that mean?

Apostolic signifies the horizontal cross-connection of the Church through all the ages. She is first of all fixed to the historical origin in the eleven men whom Jesus chose (eleven were left, plus Matthias, who was elected to the office). This is not just some mythology or other, an invented piece of ideology, but is truly anchored in the historical events concerned with Jesus Christ and can always at any time be renewed from these apostolic origins. At the same time, this expresses not only fidelity to the witness, to the faith of the apostles, but also a sacramental dimension. Because of this, we cannot simply rethink the Church whenever we like; she stands rather in an unbroken relationship with her origins, in constant continuity with them. The sacrament of ordination to the priesthood expresses this relationship to something we have not ourselves invented and, at the same time, refers to the Holy Spirit as guarantor of this continuity.

And Catholic?

The translation of Catholic is "including the whole"; it signifies "relating to the whole". It is a way of expressing the fact that the Church belongs to the whole world, to all cultures and every age. That is quite essential. For the Church must never shrink to being a national Church. She is always there to ensure that boundaries are transcended. She is to prevent the occurrence of Babel. The Church is there to prevent the confusion of opposition and contradiction from dominating mankind. She should, instead of this, bring the whole wealth of human existence, in all its languages, to God—and should be thereby herself a power for reconciliation among mankind.

There is a quite particular Catholic habit of thought. This is a certain way of looking at events and people and everything that happens on the stage of this world. Can we define this habit of thought in any way?

That is hard to say. Catholicism is fed by the whole of the history of belief, but in its characteristic form it developed in the Western Church. In that sense, much of what we today call a Catholic way of thinking is not beyond the limitations of time, nor is it unchangeable. It may be subject to modification, development, and renewal through the arrival of new peoples or the departure to new historical ages.

Protestants have in their faith, so it seems to me, the rigorous either-or stand, whereas with Catholics a flexible both-and is dominant; what unites is important. So it's a matter, in each case, of Scripture and *tradition, of authority* and *freedom, of faith* and *works. What is the specific difference between what is Protestant and what is Catholic?*

I don't think it's so easy to say what it is, and you certainly can't make it all dependent on one single point. Although the categorical dividing into either-or is indeed deeply rooted in Protestantism. In Lutheran thinking, at any rate, the principle *solus Christus*—Christ alone—is very strongly emphasized, whereas for Catholicism the attempt at a synthesis was more typical. But we should beware of any schematic definition of this difference, above all because Protestantism exists in great variety of forms and because, when it comes down to it, the Catholic Church also has a wealth of different forms—and, over and beyond this, is confronting a range of historical possibilities that are still far from exhausted.

It is of course true that the Catholic Church has always rejected certain *sola* formulae—for instance, that only Scripture counts. The Catholic Church believes that Scripture *and* a living tradition belong together, since it is tradition that is the agent in providing the Scriptures and the agent when the Church interprets them. Another point is that she only allows the *sola fide* in a limited sense. In the sense, that is, that faith is in the first instance the only door by which grace can reach us, but that this faith, as the Letter to the Galatians says, is actively at work in love. The power of justification of the Christian life thus consists in an amalgam of faith *and* love. So here, too, the *sola* must be broken open.

So this tendency to open up, which rejects exclusive categories—whose importance we must not fail to recognize—as liable to be one-sided is one of the essential points of difference.

The Heart of the Church

At the heart of the Church, if I have grasped this rightly, is not the Vatican or the Pope, but a woman. The rediscovery of Mary as "prototype of the Church" is among the most significant developments in theology of the twentieth century. It was the poet Paul Claudel, above all, who realized that there was a new way of looking at this figure and who thereby rescued Marian devotion from a somewhat marginal position in the faith.

Claudel later recounted how this insight was closely connected with a conversion experience, which came during Vespers of Christmas 1886, in Paris. It happened like this: he had gone to this Mass in Notre Dame more out of boredom than anything else, but all at once, during Mary's song of praise, the Magnificat, *something burst in upon him with great force. He was brought to realize that everything that is said about Mary is true of the Church. And, conversely, in Mary the Church can see the perfect prototype of herself. Mary personifies the essence of the Church, he said, since the Catholic principle of the significance of human beings cooperating in their salvation is made visible in her. "The Mother of God", says Claudel, "is for me one and the same with the Church; I have never learned to distinguish between the two."*

The tradition identifying the Church with a woman reaches far back into the Old Testament, where Israel sees itself as the bride whom God wishes to take into his confidence, to make his own, and to unite to himself in eternal love. That was adopted in the Church, which in fact continues the life of the Old Testament. Paul talks about our mother, the Jerusalem on high. He is thus discovering, from within the Jewish tradition, the image of the Church as mother, this motherly city that has given birth to us all and that gives us life and freedom. And so the Fathers took up this idea, which also appears in the Apocalypse—the woman arrayed in the sun—and used it to portray the whole holy being of the Church. Although often they had no thought of Mary in doing this, basically the whole of mariological thought is being expounded here along with ecclesiology. In other words, what the Church is, is made concrete in Mary. And the theological significance of Mary appears in the Church. Both spill over into each other, so to speak: Mary is the Church in person, and the Church as a whole embodies what Mary, as a person, anticipates. In that sense, Claudel did in fact intuitively rediscover, in this conversion experience, the original mother figure and the indivisibility of Mariology and ecclesiology.

In our own century, Hugo Rahner, the brother of Karl Rahner, who was a great patristic scholar, has collected and marvelously presented all the patristic texts so as to show that wherever the Fathers are talking about the Church as a woman, then, as it were, Mary also appears—and that a narrowing of Mariology is thereby overcome. Other people have done further work on this. The Second Vatican Council picked this up by linking Mariology and ecclesiology.

I think that in fact this rediscovery of the interchangeability between Mary and the Church, the personification of the Church in Mary and the universal dimension acquired by Mary in the Church, is one of the most important theological rediscoveries of the twentieth century.

"Anyone who looks attentively at the history of the Catholic Church", one of the popes remarked, "can see at once how the protection of the Virgin Mother of God has become visible in all the most important events in Christendom. Always, whenever error is spreading everywhere to attack the wonderfully unified fabric of the Church and to throw the Catholic world into confusion, our Fathers have always turned confidently to her, and each time she alone has destroyed all errors throughout the world; and the victory won by the holy Virgin has always prepared the way for the return of better times to follow." That sounds somewhat fantastic.

It is perhaps a bit too poetic. Old expressions are used here —Mary the vanquisher of all heresies—dating from the age of the christological disputes. At that time, looking at Mary helped to preserve, on one hand, the full humanity of Jesus, yet also, in the struggle about the status of Mary, his divinity. In the dispute concerning Mary the christological issues became clear, this mystery of the unity of God and man in Jesus Christ. This is the origin of the saying about Mary being the vanquisher of all heresies, which at some periods has been exaggerated into a proper war cry. I think we prefer to see Mary as the consolation of Christendom, to whom we turn for refuge, and of course as the one who will always make Christ accessible for us. She does not take his scepter away, nor does she misappropriate devotion belonging to him. On the contrary, she offers people the opportunity to grasp the mystery of Christ by approaching him by way of her and thus brings this God closer to them as well.

The Task of the Church

The task of the Church is exciting and almost supernatural. Perhaps we can't quite entirely describe it. Paul, in one of his great say-

ings, calls the Church the pillar and the foundation of truth. She is, he says, on one hand, the divinely appointed teacher of the faith and, on the other hand, has also to ensure that nothing of this faith is lost and that no error finds its way into the faith. The Church as strict guardian of the grail—is that what she is?

You are quoting here from the Pastoral Letters, which a majority of modern exegetes say are not by Saint Paul, but that need not concern us here. In any case, these letters stand in the Pauline tradition; and they take Paul's ideas a step farther, at least within the Pauline school. It is already evident in the great Pauline letters that the Church is the living agent carrying the truth of Christ. It is for her to hold fast to this truth, to be, so to say, a pillar upon which it can stand and also to live it out in reality, to hand it on, so that it remains accessible and comprehensible, so that it can develop and unfold. We have also heard how, in all of this, the *Spirit* leads her into the truth, so that fidelity and development go together.

Which some people dispute.

Luther objected that there was no need for an office of teaching in the Church, as Scripture itself was sufficient. A Magisterium, or teaching office, so Luther says, is an imposition; whoever reads Scripture aright will understand it aright, as it is comprehensible in its own terms. Today more than ever we can see that a book on its own is always open to the risk of ambiguity. It belongs without question in the living context of the Church, within which the Word comes to life properly. In that sense, then, a fully authoritative reference for questions of interpretation is necessary, though certainly this agent of reference must be aware that it does not stand *above* the Word of God, but in service *under* the Word, and must be judged by the Word.

At this point, by the way, processes of ecumenical reconciliation are already underway. For, on one hand, the determinative force of Scripture is becoming evident in all clarity even in the Catholic Church and, on the other, the situation of the Word, embedded in the living teaching activity of the Church, as being active in interpreting the Word, is clearly seen today by Protestants. In the course of time, the following conclusion has been drawn from these perceptions: If the Church interprets responsibly, then the support, the promise, must be given her that she is truly interpreting in accordance with the Spirit of God, which guides her. It is in this way that the teaching about infallibility ultimately developed.

Concerning which, there is obviously a great need of further enlightenment.

This doctrine obviously needs to be understood very precisely within its correct limitations, so as not to be misused or misunderstood. It doesn't mean that every word that the ecclesiastical authorities say, or even every word said by a pope, is infallible. It certainly does mean that wherever the Church, in the great spiritual and cultural struggles of history, and after all possible prayer and grappling with the truth, insists that *this* is the correct interpretation and draws a line there, she has been promised that in this instance she will not lead people into error. That she will not be turned into an instrument of destruction for the Word of God, but remains the mother, the living agent, within whom the Word is alive and truly expresses himself and is truly interpreted. But that, as we have said, is linked to certain conditions. For all those in positions of responsibility in the Church, this means that they themselves must, in all seriousness, subject themselves to those conditions. They are not allowed to impose their own opinions on the Church as doctrines, but must set themselves within the great community of faith, and at its service, and must learn to listen to the Word of God. They must allow themselves to be judged and purified by this Word, in order that they may be able to convey it correctly.

The spirit of contradiction and confession is obviously a part of the Church's task. This gives her an aspect of rebelliousness, something radical and unaccommodating. The Church is also, if I'm not mistaken, always in opposition to the dictates of fashion. The Pope, in any case, has specified this as his principal task, to set his apostolic contradicitur *against the world: We contradict, he cries. A protest against the power of mere empiricism, against the excesses of materialism and the insanity of a world without morals.*

There is no doubt that being prepared to contradict and to resist is a part of the task of the Church. We have seen that man always has a tendency to resist the Word that has been given him, to want to make it more comfortable for himself, to be the only one to decide what is right for him, by formulating ideologies and developing dominant fashions according to which people shape and conform their life-styles.

Let's go back to Simeon's prophecy. He says, concerning Christ, this man will be a sign that will be contradicted. And let's recall the saying of Jesus himself: "I have not come to bring peace, but the sword." We can see here that the Church has been given this great and essential task of contradicting fashions, contradicting the power of empirical thinking, the dictatorial power of ideologies. Within this last century, she has had to raise her voice in opposition to the great dictatorships. And today we are suffering for the fact that she did not contradict them enough, that she did not cry out, into the world, "We contradict!" loudly enough or dramatically enough. Thank God when official spokesmen are weak, because of diplomatic considerations, there are martyrs, who suffer this contradiction in their own bodies, as it were.

But certainly, this opposition ought not to arise from a taste for contradiction in principle. Nor indeed from a reactionary attitude, nor from an incapacity to adjust to the contemporary world or to face the future. She must always preserve the capacity to be open to what is good in any period, to whatever new possibilities it opens up—which will always reveal entirely new dimensions of the Word of God. But in all this, faith must not dissolve into something arbitrary, must not lose all definition. It must in fact itself contradict whatever contradicts God—to the point of finding the courage for martyrdom.

It is one thing for faith to contradict the spirit of the age so often. To an even greater extent, the spirit of the age sets itself against belief; and that's hardly new. Guardini once wrote: "Anyone who keeps company with the Church will, at first, experience a certain irritation and impatience with the way she always puts him in opposition to what other people want." The believer will even feel that he's being reactionary, in opposition to the prevailing opinion, which is always in the first instance looked on as being modern. Guardini then said: "But once the blindfold has been taken from his eyes, then he will recognize how the Church always liberates those who live in her company from the power of the contemporary world and puts them in touch with enduring standards; the strange thing is, no one is more sceptical, no one has more inward independence, over against 'what everyone says', than the person who truly lives with the Church."

Yes, and that has certain autobiographical dimensions. Guardini was a student at a time when the heritage of liberalism was very much alive, even in Catholic theology. One of his teachers at Tübingen, he was called Koch, was very much influenced by it. And naturally Guardini, in his youth, was on the side of this teacher. It's obvious that students will support a teacher who says new things, who says them more clearly and boldly, who sets them free from the chains of tradition and, in doing so, crosses swords with Rome.

It was in the course of his time as a student, at any rate, during which he suffered great doubts concerning his faith, that Guardini finally came face-to-face with the real Church, in the liturgy. And without abandoning his particular liking for this teacher, as he himself says, he developed an antiliberal position, because he found that, when it came down to it, the only truly independent mind in this whole story was the Church. And that keeping her company, entering into her, entrusting yourself to her faith—which is allegedly being nothing but infantile and dependent—represents in reality the greatest degree of independence from the spirit of the age and signifies greater boldness than is embodied in any other possible position. Guardini is among the pioneers who got rid of the liberal trend in theology. In doing so they awakened, in that whole period, from about 1920 to 1960, great joy in the Church, in thinking with her and believing with her. For Guardini personally this sprang from this experience of having the scales drop from his eyes, of suddenly seeing that it was really quite different. That is not an infantile dependence; that is courage to contradict and the freedom to go against prevailing opinions, the freedom that offers us a firm footing and which the Church has not invented for herself.

Some astonishing parallels open up . . .

Yes.

God and the Church

It is not always easy to find this courage to contradict in the Church. Many Christian communities act tired. They often lack spirit, the courage to think anything unusual, beyond generally accepted opinions and what is modern, even to make any defense at all of the fundamentals of the faith. Many Christians who embrace the spirit of the age would like to be at best a service industry, which collects information about the needs of its members by an opinion survey. Even bishops give you the feeling that the Holy Spirit left them long ago.

Could it not be that a time will come when we will have to say: Yes, the time of the Church is now really past? And, who knows, why should it be impossible for God to abandon his Church, to become tired of her and withdraw, at least temporarily?

There are times when the Church gets tired, and there is certainly the phenomenon of "lampstands being removed from their place", as the Apocalypse puts it. Just think of the sixteenth century. The monographs on this period show how accommodating the established Church was, how weak the faith of the bishops was. They had just become part of the system, and certainly they were not the kind of people to become living witnesses to the faith, apostolic and capable of being martyred. They were looking to see how best to get through, and in the best cases, they were just trying to avoid anything worse happening. And while this was going on the Church was almost asleep, in a state of almost total decay.

This is the kind of situation that can always arise again. The Holy Spirit then always puts us to shame by bringing the needed renewal from a quite different direction. Then, the powers of renewal for their time rose up in Teresa of Avila and John of the Cross, in Ignatius of Loyola and Philip Neri and quite a number of others. Their new impulse at first took the institution by surprise and frightened it, but in the end it could be seen that this was the outbreak of a true renewal.

There is no doubt that the Church gets tired. The Church can even become tired throughout an entire cultural area and even come to ruin there. The Apocalypse warns, in the letters to the seven churches, which point to an example for the future: Watch out, or I shall take the lamps away. It is in fact the case that not only the flourishing Church in Asia Minor, which was once the vibrant heart of the Church, but also the Church in North Africa vanished entirely beneath the tempests of Islam. Of course, the force applied by the conquerors, the repression of whole classes of society, played their part here; we don't want to make an oversimplified complaint against a tired Church. But still, this can happen.

The promise of Christ—"Behold, I am with you always, until the end of the world"—does not mean, in addition, that each and every diocese has the assurance that it will endure forever. It does mean, on the other hand, that the Church will be, until the return of the Lord, his special sphere of action, his organism, his Body, and his vine.

Perhaps God will never let the Church completely go to ruin, but wouldn't it be a bold idea to start something entirely new? Then there would be an Old Testament, a Middle and a completely New Testament. It's well known that all good things come in threes.

Joachim of Fiore thought all that up in the twelfth century. He said that the course of history would inevitably correspond to the threefold nature of the Trinity. From the age of the Father, the Old Testament, which was the period of the particular strictness of the Law, through the age of the Son, the period of the Church, which is much gentler, to the age of the Holy Spirit, with an entirely new spiritual Church. The spiritual Church would bring about the reconciliation of East and West, the reconciliation of Jews and Christians, and true freedom from the Law. This theory has had great echoes down through history. First of all, part of the Franciscan movement felt a part of this and saw itself as the new spiritual Church. Later the idea was transmuted into the secular sphere and comes right down to Hitler's "Third Reich".

Henri de Lubac wrote two great volumes about the later influence of Joachim. There he shows how this idea aroused considerable theological disputes, on account of one part of the Franciscan movement, which saw itself as the new, true, and spiritual Church over against the worldly papacy. This did at least make clear that there is no threefold development of history. The whole of history is, throughout, the period of a single trinitarian God. The Church as such is God's last Word in history, because Christ is his final and complete Word. She is indeed capable of multiple developments, but there will be nothing further. It really has been promised to her: I am beside you, with you, with this Church, right to the end of the world. Anything else would be self-generated, a human achievement that comes into being and then disappears.

16. Spiritual Gifts

The Primitive Church

No Messiah could ever have left his followers a more heavily mortgaged future than Jesus did. He allows himself to be humiliated; he is tortured and finally put to death. And nothing happens. No rescue squad comes to free him from his tormenters; the alleged Son of God does not come down from the Cross. And there's no way everyone is going to believe the news of his Resurrection. Now his disciples are just sitting around in Jerusalem. They are living partly on charity. It does, at least, say: The spirit of love and brotherhood was at work among the first Christians: "All were one in heart and mind. Not one of their number was left in need." Was that a sort of communistic commune?

The comparison with a commune has been used time and again. Insofar as it's not a matter, here, of the compulsory imposition of something by the state, but of a community built up upon the inner freedom of faith, from the message proclaimed by the apostles at Pentecost, then the term is not applicable.

The Acts of the Apostles shows us how this message, this word, penetrates to men's hearts. How they are touched and transformed by it. They feel this really is that new thing we were waiting for; we must change; we must turn ourselves around. On one single day, three thousand people are baptized, we are told. And so this first, earliest Church, comes into being which lives by the original impulse and enthusiasm of the Holy Spirit, springing directly from the impact of Pentecost.

These people constitute an exemplary—even if it is not universally applicable—realization of the community of faith: there can be no more poor, and they share with one another and are one in heart and mind. In history, this model of Church has repeatedly been a thorn in the side of a respectable Church that has accommodated herself to the standards of the world.

The monastic life, among other things, arose in response to this demand. Saint Augustine made this saying, about a community that was one in heart and mind, the centerpiece of his rule. He wanted in this way to keep alive the flame of the early Church, at least in this little circle, which stood in the middle of his diocese by way of example. As we said, and this rapidly becomes clear as the Church grows, even in the apostolic age, this is not a model that can be imposed upon everyone in this fashion—but it is; and remains, a spur. There really ought not to be any poor in the Church. There ought really to be nobody, among the faithful, who is truly abandoned. And that truly is a demand which, especially today, touches us in quite concrete fashion.

How is it that the Christians, who were after all Jews, gave up the rite of circumcision?

That was the great dispute that Paul, above all other people, had to endure. First of all, people recognize Jesus Christ as the Messiah of Israel. They see in him the new way of living and practicing Judaism. But the question of how far the law still remains valid and, above all, whether a custom such as circumcision, which reaches back long before the Mosaic Law, is still valid has no self-evident answer.

The movement over to the Gentiles happens in stages. There is the meeting of Saint Peter with the Roman centurion, Cornelius. Peter recognizes, in a vision, that the category of unclean no longer exists, that faith is the cleansing power, and not, as was hitherto assumed, the descent in blood line from Abraham. When, finally, Gentiles come into the synagogue in Antioch and hear the message of Christ and want to accept it, then all these questions arise together: Will they now have to undertake what is Jewish if they become Christian? Do they have to be circumcised? And from that point onward the realization begins to evolve—the realization that Paul fully accomplished, above all else, on the basis of his special encounter with the Risen One—that you do not have to become a Jew in this external sense in order to belong to Jesus, but you have to become Jewish in the inner sense of being in fellowship with Christ. Christ himself is the power of cleansing, of purification. And the initiation rite that takes you into this new people of God is baptism. And, further: anyone who is baptized has no need of circumcision.

Paul is not always so progressive as he shows himself to be in the circumcision question. As far as the place of women in the Church is concerned, in his First Letter to the Corinthians he demands that they appear at worship veiled—"as a sign that they are under lordship". And that's not enough, he writes: "Women should be silent in the congregation. It is not appropriate that they should take up the word. They should be subject, just as the Law commands. If there is something they want to know, they should ask their menfolk at home. For it is not seeming for a woman to speak in the congregation." It is probably no exaggeration to interpret this intervention as misogynistic. Was Paul successful in imposing this in the Catholic Church?

Well, on this very point the Pauline writings offer various shades of meaning. On one hand, these bits, of course, trouble women, as you can understand. There have been attempts to remove this passage from the letter on grounds of textual criticism, but that's nonsense. On the other hand, women appeal to Paul in a quite particular way today, because they can see that in his lists of greetings women play a special part and that they stand in particularly close relationship to him. He says about one of them, she has become like a mother to me. He describes others as "yoke fellows" in the service of the gospel with him. In another place, he gives a woman the title of apostle.

Well, yes.

We see that, just as with Jesus, who was understood by women, accompanied and supported by women, in Paul's mission likewise, women play an important part. In Philippi, for instance, Lydia, the dealer in purple dye, who virtually compels him along with his people to stay in her house and thus becomes the starting point for the mission. Paul, then, in no way stands as the "obstinate defender of men's rights" that the text you quoted seems to show him to be; rather, he carries on absolutely the behavior that Jesus Christ had shown.

We can see, of course, that this same Paul, who so boldly achieved the breakthrough from the Jewish Law into the Gentile world, thereby ensuring the universality of the Church, who succeeded, against Peter's opposition, in having the ritual food laws set aside, this same Paul, at other points, considered certain customs important and did not want to let go of them. Each person has, if we may so express it, his conservative side.

All in all, I think, Paul prevailed in two ways. First, in that women were not permitted to preach in the liturgy, but also, on the other hand, in that they have played an important part throughout the history of the Church.

Paul

Let's take a little closer look at this man. Paul was born around ten years after Christ, as Saul, and inherited from his father a family tradition of strict pharisaism. It says he burned with hatred and murderous intent against the early Christians—until, in the course of one of his manhunts, the appearance of a bright light, just before Damascus, brought about his conversion from Saul to Paul. Following this, he went off into the solitude of the desert for nine years, to prepare himself for his new ministry. For the Pharisee's son himself, this was an incomprehensible mystery, that he of all people should have been called to be the "teacher of the Gentiles", as he wrote.

It is quite unusual. He had indeed been an ardent and fanatical Pharisee. Wanting to be zealous corresponded in a way to the fervor of his faith. The concept of zeal plays an important part in the Old Testament tradition. And then the word "zealot", someone who was zealous, had a particular meaning and import in the time of Jesus. Paul is, then, someone who was zealous like them. He wanted to satisfy the entire demand of his faith—and being addressed by the Risen One threw him off track, so to speak, and reshaped him.

Paul now hears the Risen One speaking to him from out of this great light. Thus he is able to say that he, too, has met the Risen One personally, that he has been called, commissioned, and advised by the Risen One himself. In that way he is able to feel of equal standing with the other twelve apostles. And obviously he regarded it as his task, right from the start, to take the message to the Gentiles. With his conversion, a strong and forceful personality entered the service of Jesus Christ, without whose work we would be unable to imagine the Gentile Church.

Paul traveled from one country to another, though certainly he was not always entirely happy with his fate. "The Holy Spirit has born witness to this for me, from town to town," he remarks once, "that bonds and affliction are waiting for me." He was imprisoned, suffered shipwreck on the high seas, finally went to Rome on foot, where he was beheaded by the Emperor Nero in the year sixty-seven. He must have been a disputatious type. On one occasion a high priest complained: "This man is a plague." And the prince of apostles calmly replied: "God will strike you down, you white-washed wall."

But then he worked such miracles that people even took his handkerchiefs and other cloth that had touched him and placed them on sick people, to try to heal them. On one occasion he had his head shaved, in accordance with a vow he had made; another time there was a woman who had been running around behind him all day, and he was so unnerved by it that he commanded the spirit of prophecy to depart from her. Paul ended up in prison, which one can well understand. The woman's previous employers were not overjoyed to see the end of her prophesying.

Here you have touched on the adventurous life of this great missionary. His letters are not well-balanced tracts of apostolic teaching, but are infused with a very personal feeling and style. All the passion of a man engaged in desperate struggles speaks to us through them. And they tell us about all the different things that happen to him. How he is thrown to the wild animals in the amphitheater; how he is imprisoned; how he several times receives the Jewish judicial punishment of forty lashes less one; how he is attacked by robbers; how he suffers both on account of enemies and on account of friends; how he suffers shipwreck; how he was adrift on the high seas, and much more. We can hardly imagine a more adventurous and more human life.

Of course, Paul is not always well-informed. When he arrives in Ephesus, he asks the disciples: "Have you received the Holy Spirit?" The answer is: "We've never heard of a Holy Spirit."

Naturally, he first has to ask about the situation of the Christians he finds when he arrives in any community. As far as his human capacities go, he might appear in many respects unsuitable for his great task. That's what he says about himself: You know that I came with very little ability as a speaker; I'm no public speaker; and people say against me, "He's very strong in his letters, but when he comes he's really very quiet. . . ."

. . . and once, one of his audience went right to sleep . . .

. . . yes, and fell out of the window. Well, that's one thing. He says: "I did not come with great skill in speaking, but with power." And he means by that, with the power of Jesus Christ, which is demonstrated in miracles. It was obvious that the ability was given to him at the right moment really to give a sign of the presence of a more powerful being, of the Lord Jesus Christ himself, and thereby to demonstrate that he was someone who belonged to him. It was not his own ability at work, but the truth for which he stood.

It is said that time and again, in circulars, Peter referred to letters by Paul. How did these two get on with each other?

It's clear there were tensions between the two. In Holy Scripture there are two letters by Saint Peter, although it is true that scholars say he did not write the second letter, which they date much later and which belongs to some kind of school of Peter. At any rate, this Second Letter of Peter, which particularly aimed to keep alive the heritage of Saint Peter (and this is the reason why it was taken into the canon), refers to the misuse of Paul. It says: Our brother Paul has written a great deal, some of which is hard to understand—and which is then misinterpreted. And Peter then exhorts people to make the interpretation of the Scriptures consonant with the Church that interprets them. In this Second Letter of Peter, then, we find both gestures of respect toward our brother Paul, that great teacher, and at the same time a warning that it is possible to misunderstand and misuse this same Paul.

Mission

On one occasion, Pope Gregory the Great gave his missionaries to England the following advice: "You should not destroy the shrines of the idols this people worship, but only the idols themselves that are in them. Then you should consecrate holy water, sprinkle the shrines with it, raise up altars, and bring the relics of saints there." And again: "If the people themselves see that their temples have not been destroyed, they may put aside their error from their hearts, and they may confess and worship the true God." And now the Catholic cunning comes into play. Gregory writes: "Because they are accustomed to sacrifice many oxen for these demons, you should introduce some other festival at which they can do so."

Why was the Christian mission so successful, right across the spectrum of languages and cultures? Because it made a good first impression? Because of particular miracles? Or was it especially because of clever advice such as that given by Gregory the Great, when he suggested how evangelization should be undertaken?

That is a difficult question: Why was the mission so successful and spread right across the empire so quickly? We should not, in any case, form any exaggerated notion of the numbers involved. Even by the time of Constantine, only a few percent of the empire's population were Christians, even if the emperor recognized them as being the decisively important group with the greatest future. What brought about this success? Well, the pagan religion was exhausted and in itself unbelievable. It was by then only a form of political expression; no one believed the stories about the gods any more. It had a certain continuity in the countryside, where, with the processions and everything else that went on, it had become a part of country life, but in society these myths had become increasingly ridiculed. They had served to promote the stability of the empire, but when they were no longer credible, then, of course, they were no longer an effective force for stability.

In this later Roman empire the question was now raised, yes, well, how are things with man and God? At this period there were certain philosophical movements that actually talked about the one God, but this remained, so to speak, God as he was conceived by them, not a God to whom one could pray. And then suddenly a movement sprang up that also proclaimed the one God, but now, indeed, on a religious basis.

We have to interject, at this point: In the course of this search for a rational form of belief, in the period of late antiquity, Judaism in particular had shown itself to be most attractive. As a monotheistic religion, it was seen by many people as *the* religion that could be combined with the Greek tradition of wisdom, a religion that, so to speak, proclaimed *the* God, a God whom the philosopher, the enlightened spirit, could likewise in some sense understand. On this account there had long since developed, around the synagogues, a circle of so-called God-fearers, who were unable to become Jews, but wished to associate themselves as closely as possible with the Jewish religion. It was within these circles that Christianity found its first home. And while this group of sympathizers formed only a secondary ring of associates in relation to Judaism, they could now belong to this God completely. A God who had shown himself and who in Christ had come close to them.

In this way, the ideal of a purified and rationally comprehensible religion coincided here with the religious power of a faith that was indeed not something invented but had been experienced, had been given by God.

Sounds like an absolutely ideal time for it to happen.

The essential elements that make the initial success of the Christian mission understandable I would see as follows: On one hand, there was the integrity of this faith; then its comprehensibility; and finally the moral claims of Christianity, which in the face of a corrupt and decaying world lived out the principles of the Stoic philosophy in a new and purified way. And one quite new factor was above all Christian charity or love, which could be seen at that time as a verification of this faith, so to speak, in a manner that had been unknown hitherto, in turning in love to those who were suffering. It was this that gave complete credibility, you might say, to the face of this God. He thereby appeared as a new God, and yet as the true God.

In the relationship with paganism quite different and varied developments often took place. The mission as a whole was not consistent. There were in fact Christian hotheads and fanatics who destroyed temples, who were unable to see paganism as anything more than idolatry that had to be radically eliminated. People saw points in common with philosophy, but not in pagan religion, which was seen as corrupt.

When, finally, Gregory the Great, through his great human wisdom, sought for the inner continuity of religions and thus new points of contact, paganism was really no longer a serious competitor. Its vital force was long since spent. Nevertheless, with his advice to preserve the continuity of what is seen as sacred, he developed a Christian legitimacy. It is doubtless a profound insight that these religions that preceded Christianity, however many distortions they included, still opened up a vision, offered a way of approaching God, so that one ought not to eliminate these primitive religious feelings but use them as a starting point and then transform them. The continuity of the sphere of the sacred was thus retained, but was given a new content.

In the year 1492 the Genoese Christopher Columbus, with his Santa Maria, *discovered the New World. The first island he landed on, he named San Salvador, the island of the most holy Savior. This was the beginning of a missionary effort without compare, which was in reality not always beneficial, but which did christianize the entire continent of America. But in the north and northeast of Africa, until the nineteenth century, Islam barred the road to*

Christian missionaries. In India and China, too, among the most numerous populations of the earth, the Christian mission did not make real progress. Why was that?

You are quite right that in these two great cultural areas of India and China Christianity could win only partial and temporary successes. In the fifth and sixth centuries there was the Nestorian mission, which reached as far as India and China. This left traces behind and had perhaps a certain influence in the growth of Buddhism, but then it just disappeared. Just why, exactly? My idea—which might be quite wrong—is that it's because there were already highly developed cultures. While the tribal religions in Africa, when they encounter the great civilizations, open themselves up from within to these new elements—precisely because they are tribal religions, which need to develop—here we have highly developed cultures in which religion, national identity, and social order—think of the caste system—are woven into an indivisible whole and have been taken to a high spiritual level.

India and likewise China have highly developed religious philosophies. Any transition into Christianity thus becomes more difficult, because people believe they have already found a permanently valid form of synthesis, in which national identity, philosophy, rational thought, and religion unite to confront what is alien. We would certainly have to add that entering the European scene, since about the nineteenth century, has considerably changed Indian religion. The message proclaimed by well-known figures such as Gandhi or Radha Krishnan is no longer Hinduism as it originally was but as it has been rethought on the basis of Christian elements. What we should note is that Christianity as such could gain no foothold but was merely absorbed by Hinduism as a kind of energy for renewal.

The special case of Korea: the message of Christ came here allegedly without the assistance of missionaries, directly into the heart of the people. How can we imagine that happening?

There were a group of people who had studied in China and had no doubt come into contact with Christian priests there. Having been given this initial impulse, they then studied the Holy Scriptures for themselves in their own country, became convinced that this really was what God was saying, and tried to put this into practice—but always with a desire to make contact with the Church as a whole. At first they found this was not possible, and they had to endure long periods of persecution and martyrdom.

So we have here a remarkable development indeed. On one hand, the initial impulse to become Christian does stem from the living Church, and not just from the book, but this fact of having been touched then becomes a search for themselves. And from their encounter with the Scriptures comes their own conversion, which cannot remain just a notional religion, but means belonging to the community of the living Church.

Is it conceivable that such a great part of the earth as Asia may yet be converted to the teaching of Christ? Or is that field already closed off?

I think we should set no limits to our hopes there. We can already see how, by way of Indian intellectuals, the leaven of Christianity has found a way into Hinduism. The number of Indians who revere and love Jesus is extraordinarily great;

far greater than the number of Christians, even if in this case Christ is simply counted in among a series of other saviors.

As far as Japan is concerned, it has shown itself remarkably closed against Christianity. People like Christian schools, Christian customs; people even like to get married in a Catholic Church; but to go in for it wholeheartedly obviously runs counter to Japanese attitudes. China is dominated by the power of an ideology that sees itself as the only force capable of keeping China together, keeping it true to itself, and enabling it to play its part in the world. But there, too, there are faithful who give themselves to Christ in an extraordinary way, who may be seen as a leaven at work. So we ought not to look at the story as being finished there.

In some parts of Asia, of course, the resistance to Christianity, which is regarded as a foreign religion, has become very strong. We have seen how much enmity toward the Pope is demonstrated, in India for instance, to what extent the concepts of conversion and evangelization are virtually forbidden. The reaction is quite extraordinary. But that helps us to see that people are trying to protect themselves from something that in their experience is powerful. At the present moment, at any rate, we cannot predict the future, but we ought not to be resigned or to think that here the field is already occupied.

Even so, in many countries the persecution of Christians is reaching dramatic proportions, without public concern in the West about it.

Yes, in many countries. We have seen it in China; we come across it in Vietnam, in the whole of Indochina. We see there is a threat of similar developments in India, and how it is only through the witness of blood that the faith can ever open a way for itself.

The Pope

Many people have the idea that the Church is an enormous apparatus of power.

Yes, but you must first of all see that these structures are supposed to be those of service. The pope is thus not the chief ruler—he calls himself, since Gregory the Great, "servant of the servants of God"—but he ought, this is the way I usually put it, to be the guarantor of obedience, so that the Church cannot simply do as she likes. The pope himself cannot even say, I am the Church, or I am the tradition, but he is, on the contrary, under constraint; he incarnates this constraint laid upon the Church. Whenever temptations arise in the Church to do things differently now, more comfortably, he has to ask, Can we do that at all?

The pope is thus not the instrument through which one could, so to speak, call a different Church into existence, but is a protective barrier against arbitrary action. To mention one example: We know from the New Testament that sacramental, consummated marriage is irreversible, indivisible. Now, there are movements who say the Pope could of course change that. No, that is what he cannot change. And in January 2000, in an important address to Roman judges, he declared that in response to this movement in favor of changing the indissolubility of marriage, he can only say that the Pope cannot do anything he wants, but he must on the contrary continually rekindle our sense of obedience; it is in this way, so to speak, that he has to continue the gesture of washing people's feet.

The papacy is one of the most fascinating institutions in history. Besides all the instances of greatness, the history of the popes certainly does include some dramatic and abysmal low points. Benedict IX, for example, reigned, even after being deposed, as the 145th pope, as well as the 147th and the 150th. He first mounted the throne of Peter when he was just twelve years old. Nonetheless, the Catholic Church holds fast, with no exceptions, to this office of the vicar of Christ upon earth.

Simply from a historical point of view, the papacy is indeed a quite marvelous phenomenon. It is the only monarchy, as people often put it, that has held out for over two thousand years, and this in itself is quite incomprehensible.

I would say that one of the mysteries that point to something greater is quite certainly the survival of the Jewish people. On the other hand, the endurance of the papacy is also something astonishing and thought provoking. You have already suggested, with one example, how much failure has been involved and how much damage the office has had to suffer, so that by all the rules of historical probability it should have collapsed on more than one occasion. I think it was Voltaire who said, now is the time when this Dalai Lama of Europe will finally disappear, and mankind will be freed from him. But, you see, it carried on. So that's something that makes us feel: This is not the result of the competence of these people—many of them have done everything possible to run the thing into the ground—but there is another kind of power at work behind this. In fact, exactly the power that was promised to Peter. The powers of the underworld, of death, will not overcome the Church.

We have already talked about the so-called infallibility. Why was this dogma so late in being established?

You first of all have to note that there was a teaching about the office of Peter—and, above all, an exercise of this office—at a very early period. When Pope Clement I, around the year 90, wrote a letter to the congregation at Corinth, which was threatened with schism, we can see in it already the responsibility of the Church of Rome and of the bishop of Rome. That he also has a special responsibility as a focal point for unity is shown quite clearly in the second century, in the dispute about the celebration of Easter. The central position of Rome increasingly develops into a generally recognized standard in the Church.

Finally, at the Council of Nicaea in 325 there is mention of three primates in the Church: Rome, Antioch, and Alexandria. Rome stands in first place, and the two other sees are also associated with Peter. And the delegates of the pope are always given first mention in the list of those who took part in the Council. It is clear that Rome is respected as the so-called *prima sedes*, the first episcopal see, and the Council of Nicaea itself strengthens this system.

In the subsequent history of councils the special function of the pope became ever more clear. He did not exercise a universal government that was always at work, as is the case today, but at critical moments people knew that the bishop of Rome had a special function. In the Arian crisis, in the course of which Arianism almost became the rule of faith, Saint Athanasius saw in the pope the point of reference for the faith, and it went on like that.

Finally, in 1054, came the break between East and West. The East certainly had recognized Rome's special function, even if they saw this as more narrowly defined than it was seen in Rome. After the split, especially with Pope Gregory VII, the idea of the primacy was developed and strengthened. It was given another onward thrust by the appearance of the mendicant orders, which were, so to speak, bound to the pope. Since these orders did not belong to any local Church, their life absolutely depended on there being an organ of universality. For this alone made possible the existence of a priesthood and of movements that spread across the whole Church and thus constituted the precondition for mission.

Practical application and gradual articulation moved along together step by step. By the Council of Florence, in the fifteenth century, but also as early as the Council of Lyons in the thirteenth century, a preliminary attempt at the doctrine of primacy was being worked out. At Trent, since the conflict with Protestantism was already more than enough to occupy them, no one wanted to take up this question and propose a definition, so in fact it was left to be dealt with by the First Vatican Council of 1870, which gave, shall we say, a conceptually austere definition of it, which was a surprise for many people. We know that a whole series of bishops left early, so as not to have to sign it. But even these bishops of the minority group recognized that the essence of the doctrine of primacy is one of the basic constituents of the Catholic faith and that it has a biblical basis in the promises made to Peter by Christ. In that sense, the dogma in its new and more pointed form contributes more precision, but nothing substantially new; rather it gathers together and gives concrete form to what had been shaped, what had been happening, throughout history.

Peter can hardly have suspected that he was bequeathing to his successors what was basically an impossible job: the pope has to keep in mind, as bishop of Rome, the local situation, but as head of state in the Holy See, the problems of states worldwide, and as Holy Father, the difficulties of the universal Church. He must write addresses, encyclicals, and sermons, hold greater and lesser audiences. Then there are the congregations, the courts of the papal rota, commissions, councils, and in addition the great offices responsible for doctrine, liturgy, discipline, education. There are hundreds of mother houses of religious orders, more than a hundred colleges, and so on.

In the college of cardinals the pope does indeed have a first-rate advisory staff at his side, with leading authorities from a variety of cultures, bringing various intellectual backgrounds and political experience, but from the office of secretary of state come boxes full of papers every day, and each sheet of paper represents a problem. Bishops all over the world assault him with queries about more or less impossible problems. And besides this, he is supposed to live an exemplary life of prayer and meditation and be inspired to make a quite personal contribution of his own. The universal Church grows ever larger—can this papacy remain the way it is?

Well, the way in which it actually operates can of course change. In the eighth century it was different from what it was in the fifteenth, and in the fifteenth different again from the way it was in the twentieth. A great deal of what you just listed does not absolutely have to be that way. Let's start with the Vatican State: this is in fact only a provisional arrangement. The pope does not strictly need to have a state—but he does need freedom, a guarantee of secular independence; he cannot stand in the service of some government.

I maintain that the primacy was only able to develop in Rome because the imperial government had moved away to Byzantium with Constantine. Only this could provide the requisite freedom. The idea that it became so effective because this was the seat of government seems to me to be turning things upside down somewhat. In the first three centuries, living a Christian life in Rome offered the surest possible way of being exposed to the risk of martyrdom. This gave the pope a "martyrological" character. Only when the empire moved its seat to the East did there arise in Italy, through the "power vacuum", that kind of spiritual independence that did not subject the pope directly to political authorities. Later on, the Papal States grew out of this situation, bringing with them many disastrous associations, until they were finally lost in 1870—thank God, we would have to say today.

In their place came this artificial construct of a mini-state. Its only purpose is to ensure that the pope has sufficient freedom to carry out his ministry. Whether this could be simplified still further is a question we may ask.

And then many other things you have mentioned are variable. Not all motherhouses of orders, for example, would have to be at Rome. And how many encyclicals the pope chooses to write, how often he wishes to address people—these, too, are questions to be decided in accordance with the situation, and which will always be decided differently, according to the personality and attitude of the various popes. Nevertheless, the question remains whether it is not all far too much. The sheer quantity of personal contacts imposed on him by his relationship with the universal Church; the decisions that have to be made; and the necessity, amidst all this, of not losing his own contemplative footing, being rooted in prayer—all this poses an enormous dilemma.

But aren't there quite new movements today?

We are indeed thinking about the extent to which further relief might be found through decentralization. The Pope himself, in his encyclical on ecumenism, invited further suggestions about what form the papacy might take. And already various people have responded. The emeritus archbishop of San Francisco, Monsignor Quinn, has for example vigorously addressed the problem of decentralization. A lot can obviously be done there. For my part, I see the *ad limina* visits of the bishops' conferences in Rome as being very important, simply so that there is direct contact and a real meeting. They are needed in order to strengthen the internal unity of the Church. Letters cannot make up for actual personal encounter. Talking to each other, listening to each other, seeing each other, and discussing things together constitute a process for which there is no substitute.

In that sense, I should say, these forms of personal encounter, which the current pope has, so to speak, deritualized and made more concrete, will always be of great importance. Particularly because unity, understanding one another—something that cuts straight across all practical problems and cultural differences—is so fundamental that it can hardly grow at all without personal contact.

It is becoming ever more clear today, even on the basis of rational and practical considerations, that a point of reference for unity, as offered by the pope, is truly necessary. Meanwhile even Protestants have said they agree there needs to be that kind of spokesman for Christianity, just such a symbol of unity. And many say that if the institution were reshaped along these lines, then we would be able to declare ourselves in agreement with it.

In any case it is, as you so crudely put it, an "impossible job", which is almost unlivable. On the other hand, it is also one that has to be done—and which can, then, with the help of the Lord, nonetheless be lived after all.

Decentralization—does that mean there are going to be patriarchates in the Catholic Church as well?

Whether this is the form by which great continental units will have to be organized—as I used to think—does in fact seem more and more questionable to me. The roots of these patriarchates lay, after all, in their connection with their respective place of apostolic origin. The Second Vatican Council, on the contrary, has already defined the *bishops' conferences* as the form giving concrete shape to such supraregional units. Continental units have come in, in addition to them. Not only Latin America but also Africa and Asia have in the meantime developed various structures of episcopal association at the continental level. Perhaps these offer possibilities better adapted to the current situation. There have to be supraregional structures of cooperation, in any case, that remain more of a loose association and do not degenerate into great bureaucracies or lead to domination by officials. But there is no doubt that we need such supraregional associations, which can then take over some of the work from Rome.

Can you imagine the pope being one day recognized again by the Protestant, the Orthodox, or the Anglican Church?

There is an official theological dialogue with Orthodoxy, which thus far has not dared to grasp this particular nettle. On one hand, the idea of papal primacy is not entirely foreign to Orthodoxy, because Rome has always been recognized as the First See. On the other hand, the papacy contradicts their structure of autocephalies (autonomous units of the Church), so that there are very many historically sensitive factors opposed to recognition, which will make it difficult. There are perhaps areas here and there where it is less complicated. We ought not to hope for any early success, but we still have to strive for it.

The Anglicans, in response to the Pope's encyclical on ecumenism, have outlined a vision of how they could understand the papacy. That is a step toward Rome. And there is also the dialogue on "Authority in the Church", for which this question is part of the background. There are also steps to rapprochement here, though there are barriers, stemming from the historical origins of Anglicanism. We shall see.

Protestantism is an extremely complex entity. On one hand, there are the traditional Protestant Churches—Lutheran, Reformed, Methodist, Presbyterian, and so on—who are to a great extent facing a crisis in many parts of the world. Here there has been an observable shift in Protestantism from the classic historical Churches to the Evangelicals, to the Pentecostals, to the fundamentalist movements, in which we see a new vitality arising in the Protestant faith which is recasting to some degree the historical emphases. The Evangelicals and fundamentalists always used to be typical leaders of the opposition to the papacy. But there have been astonishing changes there, because they can see that the Pope is actually the Rock who asserts before all the world exactly what they confess in opposition to modern versions of watered-down Christianity. So, from a certain point of view, they see the Pope as their strong ally, even though their old reservations have not been cleared away. So the whole picture is moving and changing. What we dare to hope for we should await confidently, but with great patience.

The Network of the Church

The Catholic Church has a classical, clear arrangement: people—priests—bishops. And the pope is enthroned over all as the universal head. Is the hierarchy—the word means "sacred lordship"—already there in the gospel, or was it rather established in a tightly structured organization that was intended to be as efficient and as powerful as possible?

I would certainly dispute the well-known translation that gives "sacred lordship" as the meaning of "hierarchy". I am persuaded that the word means "sacred origin". It means that the Church does not spring from any decisions of ours, but only ever anew from the Lord himself, from the sacrament. Seen in that light, the priesthood looks quite different. We are not talking here about a ruling class that enforces strict discipline in the Church. The priesthood is, on the contrary, what connects the Church with the Lord. It is the way in which the Church transcends herself, not taking her origin from meetings, decisions, learning, or the power of organization, but always and only ever owing it to Christ. In that sense, priesthood is also beyond anyone's control. Accordingly, if there are no more vocations to the priesthood, then we have to ask the Lord for them and cannot simply force them ourselves.

The Church is often described as the "pilgrim people of God", and her faithful are called "God's flock". Many people also say they are just like a flock of sheep, that's to say, a great mass who have no rights and are only there to believe and to obey.

I would not set the concepts "people of God" and "flock" against each other. The Jewish religion developed in a pastoral culture, so that the image of a flock has always retained a quite special significance and passed from there into the New Testament. We should not therefore judge it on the basis of the pejorative sense of being sheep like, but on that of the relationship of trust between the shepherd and the flock, in which the same thing is expressed as in the saying about the "people of God" that is traveling on, that follows its path through history.

In Italy, after reconciliation with the secular state, Pius XI exhorted the Catholic laity to develop a new manner of living the lay life, even being Christ in the world, and thereafter he founded the lay apostolate. As far as I can see, the anticlerical emphasis, the feeling that lay people had first of all to secure their own rights in the Church, did not develop until after the Second Vatican Council.

Meanwhile, this idea has grown into a proper anti-Roman war cry, into a dogma of liberal bourgeois thought.

In my opinion this emphasis rests on a false basis. It assumes that the Church now has to be run as if there were two classes that, as it were, must both be represented and that arrange between themselves what the Church is. So that, in the first place, the laity set up their own representation —which extends up into the central committee of German Catholics—and speaks to a certain extent on behalf of the lay members of the Church. And then the clergy, on their side, form their own groups; which is complete nonsense. What are the clergy there for at all? But above all the notion has formed that we have to determine together what it is possible to believe today, what kind of Church we should construct. And in doing this we would, so to speak, have to deprive the clergy of their power and to ensure that the laity have their due say.

That's what many people think.

If the clergy understand their role correctly, they do not prescribe what the Church is, but stand in obedience to God, which is guaranteed by the pope. Then their task is precisely to ensure that people do not shape the Church in accordance with their wishes, but rather that she remains in the hands of the Lord. That is what the sacrament of priestly orders, the derivation from an origin we have not made ourselves, really means. And then it is not dishonorable to be a layman, but the normal form of being a Christian; the normal form in which the gospel is lived out in this world and brought into the daily affairs of the world. That Christianity takes hold of the world and reshapes it, that is the true apostolate of the laity.

A separate state in the Church, people who have committed themselves to following Christ in the most radical way conceivable, is constituted by monks and nuns. What is the task of the religious orders, particularly for the Church of the future?

There have to be various levels of discipleship, and not everyone has the same task. There are also essential and irreplaceable forms of discipleship in which to live out one's faith fully in ways precisely suited to whatever one's particular calling may be, whether in politics, in science or research, in trades, in the most ordinary occupations. But we do also need those who dedicate their whole life to the faith, who represent the central reserve of faith for proclamation and for the spiritual life of the Church.

I believe this complex network will be very important for the future of the Church. There always have to be places to which people can withdraw, where they can live the life of prayer throughout the day, where prayer marks the whole rhythm of the day. These are reserves of strength, places where faith can be lived and experienced anew, and from which it then radiates. We are experiencing this, right here, in our conversation, in the original monastery of the Benedictine order, here in Monte Cassino. Or, think of the women's contemplative orders, the Carmelites, for instance, the Poor Clares. These, too, are oases that many people look to and from which they receive enrichment and renewal.

Monte Cassino is reckoned to be the most famous monastery in the Latin Church. People say there is no other of comparable age or status. That very year 529, when this little city on the hill was being built for the monastic community led by Benedict, was the same year the Platonic academy closed in Athens.

I find this temporal coincidence of the closing of the Athens academy, which had been the symbol of classical culture, and the start of the monastery at Monte Cassino, which then became, as it were, the academy of Christianity, to be of great significance. The Roman empire was in decline; it had already broken into fragments in the West and no longer existed as such. There was, of course, the danger that an entire culture might be lost, but Benedict more or less preserved it and gave it new life. And therein he was entirely consistent with a Benedictine motto: *Succisa virescit*—ever again pruned, it grows again. The breakdown became in a certain sense a new departure.

And, obviously, the foundation of European civilization.

The Benedictines, following in monastic tradition, intended at first to be simply a place of prayer. What was important here was that manual work, turning the earth into a garden, and the service of God are fused together and become a whole.

The saying *ora et labora*, work and pray, expresses this structure of Benedictine community life quite clearly. Worshipping God always takes priority. This has the very first place, because God himself is the most important. It pervades the whole day and the whole night; it marks and shapes their time; and thereby it develops into culturally high and pure form. But at the same time, it's a matter of cultivating and renewing the earth in the ethos of worship. This also involves overcoming the ancient prejudice against manual labor, hitherto regarded as fit only for slaves. Manual labor now becomes something noble; on the basis of the Gospel of John, it is seen as being, so to say, an imitation of the Creator's work.

Along with the new attitude toward work comes a change in our ideas about the dignity of man. Anyone entering a monastery comes into a sphere in which the ideas of slave and free man, which are still dominant in the rest of society, are set aside. And on the basis of the freedom God gives, all are equal before the common task of bringing God to the world and lifting the world up to God.

With all this, Monte Cassino brought an end to the culture of antiquity but, at the same time, rescued it. This is where manuscripts were copied; this is where knowledge of languages was cultivated. The French monk Dom Leclerq once showed how love of grammar and love of God were inseparably united. Because they had to understand the sacred words, then the whole business of reading was so to say a ministry. That in turn conditioned the way in which, to take just one example, philology developed, and the Word was cultivated in every shape and form. The other side of the coin was that agriculture led to a need to learn about the things of the earth. All in all, we can say that out of this new ethos, "worshipping God and working", *ora et labora*, truly a new culture, the European culture, arose.

Benedict's great legacy was the rule he developed. This little work is quite certainly one of the great guidelines of Western culture, and its practical message—for a "regular" life, so to speak—is influential even today and can always be rediscovered. "In itself, Holy Scripture is sufficient as a guide for human life", Benedict remarked. But in order to make the path of life accessible for beginners, too, as it were, he says he has written an aid for anyone "who loves life and wishes to see good days".

The great characteristic of the rule is keeping good measure. Many monastic rules have erred in being too strict. In the enthusiasm of conversion people often attempted a monstrously radical program, which one person, who is truly seized with enthusiasm, can keep, but which cannot in the long term sustain a common life. Benedict found the right relation between consideration for human nature, what is collectively possible, and the requisite austerity, the necessary strictness. And besides this, what he prescribes is flexible, because the abbot has a great deal of freedom in how he applies it all. He is allowed to judge what is really appropriate in this situation. Nonetheless, the rule does not remain without obligation, but gives a quite clear, strong framework—above all in the structure of worship that orders the day and permeates it, but also in the structure of mealtimes and the obligation to work. In addition to manual work there was—as we have seen—cultural work, the love of letters, which was promoted by the worship.

In a certain sense, Benedict has been looked on as a kind of Moses, who gives the rule of life. Yet Benedict gives the rule from the viewpoint of Christ, who brought the Law of Moses to its new and final stage, so that it could be turned into a concrete and practical rule of life. In this sense, he became at a high level the lawgiver of the West, and finally this multicultural entity really did develop into a new continent—Europe—a culture that has reshaped the world.

If our culture is on the verge of being out of balance, as we can see, then it is because we have in the meantime moved very far from this. Time and again, our world could so easily find its corrective in the Benedictine rule, since it offers the fundamental human attitudes and virtues needed for a life of inner balance, those that are requisite for social life—and for the maturity of the individual.

Let's stay with this most important resource for just a moment. The first word of the Rule of Saint Benedict is "listen": "Listen, my son, to the counsel of the Master", and Benedict adds: "incline the ear of thy heart."

Yes, it's an invitation to listen, and that is basic for man. Man ought not to try to be self-sufficient, and he must have the humility to learn, to accept something—"incline thy head". He must find the way to follow the call into listening. And listening means not just giving ear to whatever is going the rounds, but also listening to the depths, or to the heights, since what the Master says is basically the application of Holy Scripture, the application of this fundamental rule of human existence.

Listening and responding, so Benedict believed, should be like breathing in and out. And a man should also learn to accept him-

self; he should "live within himself", should keep silence, hearken, find peace. The rule has obviously lost nothing of its immediacy in the course of fifteen hundred years.

We can see here, in the Rule of Saint Benedict, how nothing that is truly human ever becomes old-fashioned. Anything that really comes from the depths of our being remains a counsel of life that is always relevant. You can comment on it; you can try to find the various ways in which at any time it may be applied; but as a rule, as a fundamental structure, it remains relevant. Today especially we can see how turning to the earth, respect for its own laws, the conservation of the created order, is an essential ministry of which we have need.

And perhaps we are beginning to see again that freedom from work, that freedom which is a gift of God's service, stepping outside the mentality of mere achievement, is what we need. That listening—for the service of God is to a great extent a matter of letting God in and of listening—must be a part of life. Just as discipline and right measure and order belong together, just like obedience and freedom, so, equally, tolerating each other in the spirit of faith is not merely a basic rule for any monastic community, but all these things are, when you come down to it, essential elements for building any and every society. This is a rule that springs from what is truly human, and it was able to formulate what was truly human because it looked out and listened beyond what is human and perceived the divine. Man becomes really human when he is touched by God.

One person we really must not forget here. His real name was Giovanni Bernardone. They called him Francesco, the little Frenchie, because he liked French songs. His calling makes a most moving story. Can we say that Francis saved the Church from collapse?

I should say that the Church would never have collapsed completely, but in a major crisis he did take decisive action to uphold her. We all know about the Pope's dream, when he saw the Lateran basilica collapsing over his head, and then along comes a man who holds it up. Innocent III saw this dream as referring to Francis and welcomed him. He, the great politician, recognized that this completely unpolitical man, living out the radicality of the gospel, was exactly the force that could provide the Church with something that all his political skill could not give for her. The Church needed a charismatic renewal from within, a new flame of faith, and not merely the capability and strategy of administrative organization and political order.

I think we have to see how fruitful, how productive this saying of Christ, "Follow me", follow me in a radical sense, has been. How it has given rise over and over again to so many new impulses and new solutions. And it is the hope of the Church, now as ever, that wherever she becomes ordinary and is in danger of falling, new awakenings will come from within, by the power of the Holy Spirit. Awakenings that no one has planned but that spring up from people blessed with grace and that bring forth new fruits from the ever-fruitful gospel.

Francis was just such a man. After a gay and frivolous youth, he was suddenly gripped by a radical calling and lived it out with enthusiasm and joy. He had no thought of founding a new order; he thought the monastic life was sufficient. In this situation in which Christianity had become leaden, heavy, and lackluster—and entirely covered with the gray patina of everyday selfishness—he simply wanted to proclaim the gospel anew and to gather people for the Lord. He wanted to preach just the gospel itself, the Sermon on the Mount, and stir people up and bring them together to Christ, both inwardly and outwardly.

And then, almost against his will, this movement grew out of his preaching, a movement that, likewise rather against his wishes, acquired the legal status of an order. The Pope correctly perceived that this new presence of the gospel, which is what Francis had in view, needed its own instruments, and that the whole thing therefore needed to be a juridical structure. That, in the final analysis, has remained the inner drama of the Franciscan order: the impulse to live and preach the gospel in a radical way, which explodes the institutional framework and would prefer greater freedom, greater poverty—and, on the other hand, the necessity of finding some form in which the whole thing can take its place in a normal human society. But it is precisely in virtue of this inner flame, which has repeatedly leapt beyond the confines of what is merely institutional, that the order has perceived its function within the Church in the long term.

In fact, the Church herself lives in this dilemma, that we all ought to be greater, we all should, in a more radical way, get out of the compromises of our lives. But then, if we must still continue to live out these compromises in the world, as we now have it, then we ought at least to carry within us the goad of this disquiet and to open up our lives and that of the world to the full greatness of the gospel.

Francis was never willing to become a priest. Why?

He was a very humble man. In his case, the word retains its original sense. He wanted to be among those who are little before God, concerning whom the Lord said that they will understand the gospel in a special way. In the class system of his time, priesthood was for him something that belonged to the world of rank and privilege, which he, in his conscious attempt at simplicity in service, did not seek. He wanted to remain the simple evangelist, singing and proclaiming God. According to tradition he was in any case a deacon and thus authorized to proclaim the Gospel in the liturgy. He wanted to be an evangelist. Obviously, the office of deacon [*Dienstamt*], which means "office of service", the sacrament of service, seemed to him to be the form that was suited to his life.

17. The Sacraments

The Design for Life

Now, as in former times, many people make use of Christian expressions, although they are no longer familiar with their content, let alone live according to them. Let us consider the seven sacraments. You once said about them that within them was contained the design for the whole of our life. And Johann Wolfgang von Goethe, who was brought up as a Protestant, maintained that the sacraments of the Catholic Church were not only "the highest expression of religion" but, further, the "sensible symbol of an extraordinary divine favor and grace".

Before we come to the individual sacraments—I ask myself: What is the real value of these sacraments? Confirmation, for example, gives no guarantee that young people will not look for salvation in a drugged ecstasy, and conferring the sacrament of marriage does not prevent the partners deceiving each other and lying to each other and even separating again within a year.

I believe that the seven sacraments truly hold in place the structure and the great events of human life. For these important moments, for birth and death, for growing up and marrying, we need some kind of sign, to give to this moment its full stature, its true promise, and thus also the dimension of being shared together.

In any case, if we look at the sacraments too much from the viewpoint of efficiency and regard them as a means to impart miraculous powers to man and fundamentally change him, then, as it were, they fail the test. Here we are concerned with something different. Faith is not something that exists in a vacuum; rather, it enters into the material world. And it is through signs from the material world that we are, in turn, brought into contact with God. These signs are therefore an expression of the corporal nature of our faith. The interpenetration of sensual and spiritual dimensions is the logical extension of the fact that God became flesh and shares himself with us in earthly things.

The sacraments are thus a kind of contact with God himself. They show that this faith is not a purely spiritual thing, but one that involves community and creates community and that includes the earth, the creation, which in this way, together with its elements, becomes transparent.

The essential point is that the communal aspect, the corporal dimension of faith, expresses itself in the sacraments and that it is made clear, at the same time, that faith is not something produced within us but comes from a higher authority. Certainly, they are entrusted to our freedom, like everything God does; and—like the gospel as a whole—they do not work in a mechanical way but only in company with our free response.

Enlightenment

At the beginning stands baptism, which in the primitive Church was also referred to as enlightenment. *It is a most dignified and most moving ceremony, which in great texts takes up the main lines of life. When, in the baptismal liturgy, the sign of the cross is given to the person being baptized, the following words are pronounced: "I sign you with the sign of the cross, that you may know that Jesus loves you.—I mark your eyes with the sign of the cross, that you may see what Jesus does.—I mark your ears with the sign of the cross, that you may hear what Jesus says.—I mark your mouth with the sign of the cross, that you may reply to Jesus' call.—I mark your hands with the sign of the cross, that you may do good as Jesus does." This formula is referred to as a "symbolum", as a "symbol". What does this mean?*

Symbolon means in translation "what falls together". The symbol was originally a way of identifying oneself. It worked like this: two people each had one piece of something, perhaps a seal, and they could identify themselves by putting the pieces together. Symbol then comes to mean in an extended sense the representation of something invisible in a visible and perceptible form, in signs and things that signify something beyond themselves.

A whole array of symbols are brought together in the conferring of baptism. The basic steps of the catechumenate, as it then existed, were incorporated in the way it was celebrated. This signified that baptism demands a catechumenate, that is, fellowship on the road, which is also a fellowship of learning and of life. The various stages of the catechumenate are here summed up. The opening of the eyes, of the mouth, of the ears. This is the word, "Ephphatha", that Jesus says publicly to the mute man and that opens his ears and his mouth and finally makes him hear and speak properly. Thus also our own muteness and deafness toward God is to be overcome through baptism and through the fellowship of life into which it introduces us. For if we cannot properly hear God, then we cannot speak properly, we have nothing to say to him, we cannot pray. The opening of ears and eyes in the baptismal celebration was supposed to signify in advance that in the fellowship and the life of faith we can learn to hear and to speak properly, that we perceive the transparent presence of God in creation, and that this unites us to God in the sign of the Cross.

In the ancient Church, baptism was a tremendous mark of distinction. As a precondition for it, besides having completed the catechumenate, the person to be baptized needed two guarantors, who would stand surety for his trustworthiness. Are you, by the way, against infant baptism?

Baptism also serves the purpose of giving a meaning to man's life, above and beyond biological life, so that this life is justified. In an age like today, when the future looks dark, the question can arise of whether it is moral at all to bring someone into the world and thus perhaps to impose upon him a future in which it is no longer possible to be truly human. And indeed, if we no longer know if it makes sense to be human, then this gift of life can only be justified if I can give the new person more than mere biological life. If I can give him, along with it, a meaning that I know to be stronger than all the darkness of history. That is what baptism is, which takes him up into fellowship with Christ.

In that sense, infant baptism is clearly justified. It does become a different matter, of course, when in a dechristianized society baptism no longer evolves within the catechumenate. If many still cling to baptism only because it somehow provides the beginning of life with its celebration, with its requisite ritual expression, so to speak, then, at any rate, baptism is called into question from within. Baptism is, in fact, much more than a ritual conferring membership in a community, as many people conceive it nowadays. It is a process of birth, through which a new dimension of life opens out.

In canon 849 of Church canon law it says: "Baptism . . . [is] necessary to salvation in fact or at least in intention." But what happens, when a man dies unbaptized? And what happens to the millions of children who are killed in their mothers' wombs?

The question of what it means to say that baptism is necessary for salvation has become ever more hotly debated in modern times. The Second Vatican Council said on this point that men who are seeking for God and who are inwardly striving toward that which constitutes baptism will also receive salvation. That is to say that a seeking after God already represents an inward participation in baptism, in the Church, in Christ.

To that extent, the question concerning the necessity of baptism for salvation seems to have been answered, but the question about children who could not be baptized because they were aborted then presses upon us that much more urgently.

Earlier ages had devised a teaching that seems to me rather unenlightened. They said that baptism endows us, by means of sanctifying grace, with the capacity to gaze upon God. Now, certainly, the state of original sin, from which we are freed by baptism, consists in a lack of sanctifying grace. Children who die in this way are indeed without any personal sin, so they cannot be sent to hell, but, on the other hand, they lack sanctifying grace and thus the potential for beholding God that this bestows. They will simply enjoy a state of natural blessedness, in which they will be happy. This state people called *limbo*.

In the course of our century, that has gradually come to seem problematic to us. This was one way in which people sought to justify the necessity of baptizing infants as early as possible, but the solution is itself questionable. Finally, the Pope made a decisive turn in the encyclical *Evangelium Vitae*, a change already anticipated by the *Catechism of the Catholic Church*, when he expressed the simple hope that God is powerful enough to draw to himself all those who were unable to receive the sacrament.

Maturity

Confirmation, according to the belief of the Catholic Church, is the "sacrament of growing up in the supernatural life". How are we supposed to imagine this—and just how does confirmation work?

The essential sign is, first, the anointing; another is the laying on of hands. The laying on of hands is the sign of being sheltered and protected by God and the sign of the presence of the Spirit. The anointing unites us with the Anointed One himself, who is Christ, and becomes a sign of the Holy Spirit, who inspired and lived in Christ. Confirmation is the completion of baptism; if baptism primarily emphasizes our being united with Christ, in confirmation the emphasis is more on our fellowship with the Holy Spirit.

What is also expressed therein is that the confirmed Christian is now a fully active and responsible member of the Church. Thus, for some time now, people have liked calling it the coming-of-age sacrament. The "slap" that used to be given does indeed remind us of coming-of-age rituals in earlier times. This disappeared after the Council. In our own area, the idea of its being a coming-of-age sacrament has led to a desire to celebrate it later and later, at around the age of sixteen or eighteen. But there is a quite different way of looking at it. The Eastern Churches combine it directly with (infant) baptism. The reasoning that underlies this is that one should really only be admitted to Communion after having received the two initiation sacraments of baptism and confirmation and having thus been fully received into fellowship with Christ in the Holy Spirit.

Confirmation is also a kind of initiation, by which young people celebrate the step they take into more mature adult life. In the Middle Ages, the Augustinian monk Thomas à Kempis wrote a book called The Imitation of Christ, *in which there are rules intended to show us the way toward the* right *way to live. This collection became the most widely read book in the world, after the Bible. Some things in it seem a little strange to us. But even a Marxist philosopher like Ludwig Marcuse found in it the "art of coming to terms with oneself". "The most important task each person has", the monk writes, "is to learn to know themselves inwardly and truly." And, again, "To see oneself as unimportant, and always to think of others as good and noble, requires great wisdom and a degree of perfection."*

Interiorization is still important today. Undoubtedly one significant aspect of confirmation is that it means to turn us away from what is merely exterior, from preoccupation with success and achievement, and says to us, you have an inward aspect. And think about it; let the inner man, as Paul puts it, grow strong within you. The stifling of the inner life by practical cares has become one of our greatest problems. In this sense, confirmation can truly stand as a counterpoise to mere externalizing and thus help to keep the business of being human in a proper balance.

Material success has meanwhile become the value above all values in modern civilization. "Anyone can do it" is what a whole army of motivation gurus promise us. This attitude almost has the effect of fostering the desire.

It's catching. When I see someone else with it, then I want it too. When parents see how other people's children are all dressed up and how paths are opened up for them, they quite justifiably want the same for their own. I think when that happens we are only looking in one direction. People want to have as much as possible, want to be something in an exterior sense. But how necessary in our lives the cultivation of our inner selves is, is something we forget.

People are certainly now attempting, by methods of meditation, to build up some kind of inner life again. But generally speaking these attempts to cultivate meditation often only end up in improving our external performance. Or they are no more than techniques for emptying oneself, which do not in the end give a person any real inner strength. In fact we do need, and I would like to repeat this, to discover a new way of cultivating our inner life, to learn anew how the "inner man", as Paul calls him, can grow along with the outer one and can acquire the strength for us to be sufficiently mature to confront the external events we encounter.

The Most Sacred Action at the Most Sacred Place

Around the year 150 after the birth of Christ, a learned man by the name of Justin presented the Roman emperor Antoninus Pius with a tract in defense of the Christians. We owe to this a very early description of the celebration of Mass: "On what is called the day of the sun," it says, "all those who live in the city and in the country gather together. Then the memorials of the apostles or the writings of the prophets are read out to everyone, as much as there is time for. When the reader has finished, then the person presiding urges people to imitate all the good things they have heard. After that, we all stand up and pray. After the prayer, bread, wine, and water are brought up; the president offers up prayers and thanksgivings with all his might, and the people utter their assent by saying Amen. Then there is the distribution. Each person receives his share of what has been consecrated; but the deacons take it to those who are absent. Now, this feeding is called the Eucharist. Only those people who accept our teaching as true, who have been purified by the bathing for the remission of sins, and who live in the way that Christ demands are allowed to take part." This ceremony seems to have remained just the same for two thousand years, right up to today.

Yes, the basic structure of the Eucharist is outlined here, even though particular parts of it have of course developed since then.

Perhaps we need a certain time in order to understand that beneath all these things is hidden something more than just some arbitrary ceremony. The wonderful pictures in church windows can be seen properly only when you look at them from the inside. Can you, please, explain for me a little the structure of a Holy Mass?

The first part is the Liturgy of the Word. We gather together under the Word of God, just as the original community did at Sinai, to hear and to receive. In the text we heard just now, there is talk about readings, about prophets and evangelists. This has taken on a particular structure within the service, so that we hear *prophet, apostle, and Christ*, as they say. Under the heading of *prophet*, we understand the whole of the Old Testament; under that of *apostle*, the apostolic letters; and under that of *Christ*, the Gospel. In that way we hear the Word of God, which is, so to speak, divided into three sections. We are now told that the exhortation follows, that is, the Word needs to be expounded, because it comes to us, in a sense, from afar off and needs to be brought nearer to us so that we can understand it.

This basic foundation for the Mass, being gathered together under the Word that renews us, teaches us, and enlightens us, is followed by the actual service of the Eucharist itself. This in turn is made up of three parts. First of all the gifts are provided, bread and wine. This is an image of our bringing to the Lord the whole of creation. Then follows the prayer of thanksgiving. That is to say, the bishop or the priest joins in the prayer of thanksgiving offered by Jesus on the evening before he died. This is the great act of praise of God. It includes both our thanksgiving for Christ and our remembrance of his words and actions in the last hours of his life—and thus also the transubstantiation of the bread and wine, which are now no longer our gifts but the gifts of Jesus Christ, in which he gives himself, in accordance with his words at the Last Supper.

Justin, an ancient writer, talks of the gifts being, as he puts it, "eucharistified". In other words: bread is no longer bread, but is the Body of Christ. And wine is no longer wine, but the Blood of Christ. The gifts, therefore, are changed into a living Word, into the Word of Christ, the Word of thanksgiving of the Lord.

Justin also mentions certain conditions for the sharing of Holy Communion that follows. This is the worship of those who are believers, he says. Just as the Lord gathers together the Twelve at the Last Supper, so likewise the Eucharist is the gathering together of those who have become believers in Christ, who by baptism have become the Church. To that extent, both the structure of the celebration and the conditions for admission to it have in fact become quite clearly developed, already in this early stage, and have remained determinative to this day.

The Eucharist is seen as the most sacred action in the world, carried out in the most sacred place in the world. The Body, the Blood, the Soul, and even the Godhead of Jesus, it is said, are present in this sacrament. Let me ask again, quite particularly: Is it true that a new miracle happens each day in this action? The transformation of bread and wine into flesh and blood—surely that can only be meant as a symbol.

No. The Church believes firmly that the Risen One truly gives himself here, wholly and entirely. To be sure, at various periods in the Church's history there have, again and again, been disputes about this. The first great dispute cropped up in the early Middle Ages, the second in the sixteenth century. Luther held out in favor of transubstantiation here, with great emphasis, while Calvin and Zwingli, in their different ways, were in favor of a symbolic understanding, so that from this developed the great division within the Reformation movement.

While Luther, in any case, held the view that this presence of Christ was necessarily associated with the moment of the celebration, the Catholic Church believes that the presence of Christ within these gifts continues. For if bread and wine have truly been "transubstantiated", that is, if the gifts of the earth have really become the gifts of the Lord, then the Lord has thereby irrevocably taken possession of them. And of course in our own century there has been renewed debate about this. But even if exegetes have found themselves divided on this question, nonetheless non-Catholic exegetes such as Käsemann have strongly defended the Real Presence. It is clearly stated and described, they say, in the words of Scripture themselves. And indeed, Scripture—and likewise the whole of the primitive tradition of the Church—is unequivocal: Christ does not just give us symbols; he truly gives himself. That means that Communion is an encounter between one person and another. That Christ enters into me, and I may enter into him.

But anyone can see that the wine remains wine . . .

But this is not a statement of physics. It has never been asserted that, so to say, nature in a physical sense is being changed. The transformation reaches down to a more profound level. Tradition has it that this is a metaphysical process. Christ lays hold upon what is, from a purely physical viewpoint, bread and wine, in its inmost being, so that it is changed from within and Christ truly gives himself in them.

If, then, someone has received Christ in this way—how will this most holy sacrament then take effect upon a person? Or, at least, how might it take effect?

There, too, we must leave aside all thought of what is miraculous and magical. This is a personal process. The Risen One, who is now present—the expression "Body and Blood" always refers to the entirety of the incarnate Lord, who now continues to live in bodily form in the new world of the Resurrection—is not a *thing*. I don't receive a piece of Christ. That would indeed be an absurdity, but this is a personal process. He himself is giving himself to me and wants to assimilate me into himself.

Once, in a sort of vision, Augustine thought he heard these words: "Eat me; I am the bread of the strong." Jesus is saying here that it is the opposite to how it is with ordinary food that your body assimilates. That food is lesser than you, so that it becomes part of your body. And in my case, it is the other way around: I assimilate you into me. I am the stronger; you will be assimilated into me. This is, as we said, a personal process. Man, if he abandons himself in receiving this, is in his turn received. He is made like Christ, made to resemble Christ. And that is what is really happening in Communion, that we allow ourselves to be drawn into him, into his inner communion, and are thus led finally into a state of inner resemblance.

How should we prepare ourselves to receive Holy Communion?

It is right when I truly enter into its form and its reality. When I allow myself to be touched, to be spoken to, by the Word of God. When I direct myself toward Christ in the prayers shaped in the primitive tradition of the Church. True sharing in the prayer and the celebration of the Eucharist means that I listen, receive, and that the door opens up within me, so to speak, through which Christ may enter into me. And, on the other hand, that my own self becomes so free and open that I can begin to enter into HIM.

How should we actually receive Holy Communion?

In a way that is appropriate for the presence of the Lord. The signs of reverence we use have changed in the course of time. But the essential point is that our behavior should give to inner recollection and reverence an outward bodily expression. Earlier, Communion used to be received kneeling, which made perfectly good sense. Nowadays it is done standing. But this standing, too, should be standing in reverence before the Lord.

The attitude of kneeling ought never to be allowed to disappear from the Church. It is the most impressive physical expression of Christian piety, by which, on one hand, we remain upright, looking out, gazing upon him, but, on the other, we nonetheless bow down.

"Man is never so great", said John XXIII, "as when he is kneeling."

And that is why I believe that this attitude, which was already one of the primitive forms of Old Testament prayer, is something essential for Christians.

Communion in the hand, or directly in the mouth?

I wouldn't want to be fussy about that. It was done in the early Church. A reverent manner of receiving Communion in the hand is in itself a perfectly reasonable way to receive Communion.

After receiving the sacrament, what can we meditate upon?

We should first seek to turn our inner gaze upon Christ. There are aids to prayer, which help us to turn ourselves in this direction and to turn toward *him* from within. In doing this, I should place my day in his hands and ask him to let his presence take effect in me. It is important to entrust oneself to him, which may be expressed in quite particular kinds of prayer, according to one's situation.

Is the circle of those who have the right to receive Communion as clearly defined as it was before?

Yes. From the earliest records on—we can see it in the First Letter to the Corinthians—that is quite clear. It is a problem of our own day that we take part in Communion rather as a kind of rite of socialization, by which we ensure, so to speak, our mutual solidarity. There is a danger, then, that it might become simply a sign of friendship and belonging. And that is much too little. In this way, not only do we lose sight of the holy and essential thing that is offered us here, but the necessary inner cleansing never takes place within man.

Saint Paul warns of the danger of no longer distinguishing this transubstantiated bread from any other. Today we have somehow lost our grasp of the distinction—and that makes for a multiplicity of problems. Then divorced people who have remarried, for example, feel they are the only ones excluded, and then that rightly looks like an unfair discrimination. I think we all ought to look at ourselves more critically; we ought to distinguish the Body of the Lord and to know that we are all, again and again, in need of penance before we receive Holy Communion. There are conditions for being admitted to this. We have no right to the Lord on our own account, but through the rules of the Church he shows us when we may receive him.

And is that the difference between a Catholic Eucharist and an ecumenical Lord's Supper fellowship?

Yes. The Catholic Eucharist is always associated with membership in the community of faith of the Catholic Church. And the Eucharist itself, we are convinced, should only ever be celebrated by an ordained priest. The Protestant celebration of the Lord's Supper, on the other hand, is subject to different rules. We know that people can also meet the Lord here, but we cannot allow the fact to be obscured that the question of apostolic succession and of priesthood—as of the Catholic faith and teaching in its entirety—marks a boundary here.

The Liturgy

The Eucharist takes its great solemnity, its dignity, from that sublime masterpiece of Catholic spirituality, the liturgy. In the liturgy, each phrase and each gesture seems to have its own meaning, almost, indeed, its own particular mystery. The Second Vatican Council likewise considered that in this earthly liturgy the faithful take part and experience in anticipation the "heavenly liturgy".

And that is a very important point. The liturgy is never a mere meeting of a group of people, who make up their own form of celebration and then, so far as possible, celebrate it themselves. Instead of that, through our sharing in Jesus' appearing before the Father, we stand both as members of the worldwide community of the whole Church and also of the *communio sanctorum*, the communion of all saints. Yes, in a certain sense this is the liturgy of heaven. That is its true greatness, that heaven is torn open here, and we are incorporated in the great chorus of praise. And that is why the Preface ends with these words: With all the choirs of angels in heaven, we join in singing. And we know that we are not alone, that we are joining in, that the barrier between earth and heaven has truly been torn open.

Saint Basil the Great, Father of monasticism, stated that the Mass is just as great a revelation as Holy Scripture. He deduced from this a strict rule that one should distort the liturgy neither by explana-

tion and interpretation nor by reformation. If the liturgy is indeed something not made by man, something in which, as it were, the divine glory may be able to be experienced by men—would we not have to regard the old Gregorian Mass as having been handed down from on high and as something never to be changed?

East and West have in certain respects followed different paths in this question. The Byzantine Church, for instance, was given the shape of her liturgy in the fourth and fifth centuries by Basil and by John Chrysostom. She sees in it, as likewise do other Eastern Churches, a divine gift that one should not alter: we enter into it; we do not make it (even though in details there have of course always been minor fluctuations).

The West, on the contrary, has always had a far stronger sense of history. Here, too, the liturgy was understood in its essentials as a gift, but also as something that is set within the living Church and that grows with her. We can certainly make a comparison with Holy Scripture. This too, is not a Word of God that simply drops down vertically from above, but a Word of God that is offered and given into a history and has been able to grow within it. Thus the Western Church has indeed preserved untouched the liturgy as a whole, both in its essence and in its form, but at the same time has cautiously allowed it historical growth.

The Roman Canon probably also originated around the fourth century, just as with the Eastern Church. In the subsequent period various types of liturgy developed in the West, too. The Gallican, the Spanish, and then German influences came in, and so on. Each of the nations that came into the Church was able to contribute something, while Rome kept watch on this and pruned back any overgrowth. It was at Rome that the liturgy was most strictly preserved in its archaic form, I should say even in a somewhat earlier form than in the East, at least with respect to its theological type.

In this way the liturgy is always alive within a historical process—so that new material, and in particular new saints, can come in—but has in its essentials remained ever constant. That is why the Western Church was able to consider reforming the liturgy. Certainly, reform could not be simply a break with the past, but had to treat living growth with respect, just as you always care for a living thing and thus keep it alive. Pius X, for instance, trimmed back the overgrowth of saints' days. He also returned Sunday to its privileged position and pruned away overgrown parts. Pius V had already removed the great superfluity of sequences that had crept in. The Second Vatican Council set itself in line with them. This was right, because further growth without sclerosis is a part of the liturgical tradition of the Church. But I would say the distinction is between whether I am caring for something living and growing, and thus know that this life as such is not given to me to dispose of—I must serve it and respect the inner laws of the living being—or whether I regard it as something that has been made, that works, so to speak, in the same way as a machine, so that I can take it apart and set it up differently.

The Second Vatican Council undoubtedly had in mind organic growth and renewal. But we have to see clearly that today there are widespread tendencies toward conducting simple dismantling and reassembly—and they are thereby doing something that cannot be reconciled with the nature of the liturgy. You cannot simply devise in professorial commissions what will be better in pastoral practice; what will be more practically effective, and other such things; rather, you must look, with great respect for what is carrying the riches of the centuries within it, and see where it is necessary and possible to supplement or to prune back in a way that is meaningful.

And that should really be a serious exhortation to everyone who has anything to do with the liturgy. They should perform their ministry in a spirit of service to this living and growing entity that brings to us the faith of all the centuries, and not want to invent and manufacture something better, like experts who are almighty in and of themselves.

No one can now fail to hear the criticism of contemporary liturgy. For many people it is no longer sufficiently sacred. Do we need a reform of the reform, in order to make it holier again?

We do at least need a new liturgical consciousness, to be rid of this spirit of arbitrary fabrication. Things have gone so far that Sunday liturgy groups are cobbling together the liturgy for themselves. What is being offered here is certainly the work of a few clever and hard-working people who have made something up. But what I encounter in that is no longer the Wholly Other, the Holy One being offered to me, but rather the cleverness and hard work of a few people. And I notice that that is not what I am looking for. It's too little, and it's something else.

The most important thing today is that we should regain respect for the liturgy and for the fact that it is not to be manipulated. That we learn to know it again as the living entity that has grown up and has been given us, in which we take part in the heavenly liturgy. That we do not seek self-fulfillment in it but rather the gift that comes to us.

That, I believe, is the first thing we need, so that this peculiar or unauthorized fabrication may vanish again, and the inner sense for holiness be reawakened. In the second stage we will be able to see in what area, so to speak, too much was pruned away, so that the connection with the whole history may become clearer and more alive again. I myself have talked in this sense of a *reform of the reform*. But in my opinion this ought in the first place to be above all an educative process, which would put a stop to this trampling all over the liturgy with one's own inventions.

For fostering a true consciousness in liturgical matters, it is also important that the proscription against the form of liturgy in valid use up to 1970 should be lifted. Anyone who nowadays advocates the continuing existence of this liturgy or takes part in it is treated like a leper; all tolerance ends here. There has never been anything like this in history; in doing this we are despising and proscribing the Church's whole past. How can one trust her present if things are that way? I must say, quite openly, that I don't understand why so many of my episcopal brethren have to a great extent submitted to this rule of intolerance, which for no apparent reason is opposed to making the necessary inner reconciliations within the Church.

But when will this second stage of which you were speaking, this reform of the reform, really come about?

I would say that just as the Liturgical Movement that led to the Second Vatican Council was something that grew slowly—and that then very quickly became a flood—so here, too, it is a matter of an impulse emanating from people who celebrate a living faith. That there are exemplary centers where the liturgy really is celebrated in the right way, where people can experience what liturgy truly is. If out of this a kind of movement develops from within and is not simply imposed from above, then it will come. And I believe that here in the new generation there is already a move in this direction.

A true, a divine liturgy, a liturgy for the future of the faithful people and of the Church—what might this look like, in your view?

Basically we would once more receive the forms that have been given us and would inwardly penetrate them. When I think about the time of the Liturgical Movement, in which I indeed shared, it was simply marvelous gradually to learn how the Lenten Masses developed, to understand the structure of Lent, the whole structure of the missal, and so much more. It was just a matter of finding one's way into this treasury of things that had developed and grown, and thereby into the glory that is offered to us there from God. I think it comes down to this: learning once more the spirit of listening—"Listen, my son", says Benedict—and understanding ourselves less as those who make than as those who receive.

Should Masses be said in Latin again?

That is no longer going to be possible as a general practice, and perhaps it is not desirable as such. At least it is clear, I would say, that the Liturgy of the Word should be in people's mother tongue. But otherwise I would be in favor of a new openness toward the use of Latin.

Latin in the Mass has come meanwhile to look to us like a fall from grace. So that, in any case, communication is ruled out that is very necessary in areas of mixed culture. At Avignon, for instance, so the parish priest at the cathedral told me, suddenly there were three separate language groups who came on Sundays to celebrate Mass. He suggested using a Latin canon in common; then everyone would be able to celebrate Mass together. All three groups said straight out: No, each group must have something for itself. Or let's think of tourist centers, where it would be lovely for people to recognize each other in something they have in common. So we ought to keep such things alive and present. If even in the great liturgical celebrations in Rome, no one can sing the *Kyrie* or the *Sanctus* any more, no one knows what *Gloria* means, then a cultural loss has become a loss of what we share in common. To that extent I should say that the Liturgy of the Word should always be in the mother tongue, but there ought nonetheless to be a basic stock of Latin elements that would bind us together.

The writer Martin Mosebach once told a little story about a Holy Mass. It is set many years ago on the isle of Capri. One day an English parish priest turned up there who still dressed as a priest, something that had become rare even in southern Italy. When they heard that the man in the soutane wanted, quite seriously, to celebrate Holy Mass every day, then after some hesitation they offered him a chapel on a steep cliff overlooking the sea, Monte Tiberino, where the Villa Jovis, one of the "planet villas" of the emperor Tiberius, once stood. This chapel used to be opened just once a year, on the eighth of September, for the Feast of the Nativity of Mary. The rest of the year the mice just ran about the deserted building and gnawed their way into the chest of drawers in the sacristy.

Well, the English priest, who was a practical man, no great theologian, set out. He climbed up the steep head, with its wide view over the whole gulf. At first he found it hard to unfasten the rusty lock of the chapel. Then, accompanied by a ray of sunshine, he entered the musty room. The leaden door of the tabernacle was standing open, the candles were burned down to stumps, the chairs were knocked over, and the sacristy looked as though it had been left in a great hurry. Dirty flower vases, a soiled altar cloth, a decorated chalice in poor taste, items of altar linen stuck together with damp, a disintegrating missal. Yes, even the crucifix was bent and twisted.

The priest had a good look at everything and did not waste much time on reflection. He opened the window, picked up a straw broom from the corner, and began to sweep everything out first of all. Then he took the crucifix, kissed it, and set it on the cupboard in the sacristy. He cleaned out the chalice and set the candlesticks upright. When he found the bell rope, he got up on a ladder outside and fastened it to a bell. Now the spell had been broken.

The priest put on a spotted violet satin stole; then he poured out some water, which he had brought with him in a plastic bottle, into a little pot, started to pray, added some salt, made the gestures of benediction and poured the water into the little marble shells beside the entrance, so that one would almost have thought to hear the stone awake and sigh. So, then, when the bell rope was pulled, the faithful came from a distance, one by one, women and children, and soon filled the whole chapel.

The service could now begin. The priest bowed before the altar and began with these words: Introibo ad altare dei.

And to an observant bystander it seemed as if, while the man in the soutane had been cleaning the place of sacrifice, while he was lighting the candles, consecrating the water, wiping away the dust, and sweeping the mouse droppings into the corner, something strange had been happening. For, just like Abel and Noah, he first built an altar before he offered sacrifice. And like Moses he was marking off the place for the tabernacle. This was a preparation and a marking out of the holy place.

That is of course a very poetic piece by Mosebach, though on the whole things are not so desperate in Capri as you might suppose from that. But let's stay with the point that of course outward and inward things belong together. Even the mission of Saint Francis begins with that. He hears those famous words from the Cross—"You must rebuild my Church"—and supposes at first they refer to that ruined church building, the Portiuncula church, which he restores and rebuilds

—and then realizes that he is meant to do more; he must rebuild the living Church.

But this initial physical laboring is also part of it. This concern that the place must always be made ready again, so that the Church, the sacred, may be felt anew and be recognizable, both inwardly and outwardly, is most important. We have, thank God, to a great extent such glorious church buildings in the world, which we should learn to love again in their sacred aspect. The light before the holy of holies helps us be aware that there is always a silent presence here. If, nowadays, churches are often more like a concert hall, where we see the beauty of the past as being, so to speak, just a theatrical setting for our own thing, then we are suffering in fact the inner loss of our sense for what is holy. Recovering this, preparing and making room both inwardly and outwardly, is a precondition for being able to enter into the celebration in such a way that we indeed encounter the Holy One there.

Guilt and Reconciliation

The sacrament of penance: some say it puts a person in an impossible situation and basically produces only anxiety and guilt feelings. Others maintain that if there were no such thing as confession, then we would have to invent it.

There is no doubt that, in the course of its history, confession has been subject to greater changes in its external manifestation than has any other sacrament. For the very reason that this is such a personal thing, it has, in the midst of varying constellations of human individuality and cultures where one is open or reserved, had to take on a variety of forms. After the Second Vatican Council people tried to create new possibilities of this kind, among which one seems to me very good, that is, the shared examination of conscience, which can be of help for individual confession.

The second thing was the creation of confessional rooms, where confession can take place in conversational form. That, too, can be a great help to people in opening themselves up, in crossing the threshold that for each one of us lies before confession. Of course, it can also result in confession dissolving in conversational commonplaces and mere psychologizing, and in its losing its own particular strength and character. Collective absolution has become very widespread, but this cannot be a proper form of confession—since that is essentially personal—and it only makes sense, and ought only to take place, in quite exceptional circumstances.

A quotation from Cardinal Ratzinger: "Being incapable of acknowledging guilt is the most dangerous form of spiritually arrested development one can imagine, because this in particular makes people incapable of improvement."

People talk about Christianity having burdened people with guilt and having tried to use this as a lever to oppress them. Well, of course, such a misuse of guilt feelings may occur. But it is worse to extinguish the capacity for recognizing guilt, because man then becomes inwardly hardened and sick. Just think a stage further, to an intensified form of the inability to recognize guilt. That was what was intended in Nazi education. They thought they were even able to commit murder, as Himmler expressed it, and still remain respectable—and thereby they were deliberately trampling on human conscience and mutilating man himself. The capacity to recognize guilt can be tolerated, and properly developed, whenever there is also healing. And healing, in turn, can only exist when there is absolution. Psychotherapy can indeed do a great deal to help us perceive defective connections in the psychical structure, and to help us put them right, but it cannot overcome guilt. At that point it has passed beyond the limits of its own capabilities, and that is why it so often fails. Only the sacrament, the authority from God, can truly overcome guilt.

We must admit, in any case, that in our individualistic age it has become enormously difficult for people to cross the threshold of personal confession. But where the spirit of faith is leading us, then it can be learned anew. Above all because this is not an admission of guilt before men, but before God, and because it ends with the word of forgiveness —and perhaps also with advice that will help us to overcome the aftereffects of guilt.

As children we used to have to go to the confessional by classes. "In sorrow and humility I confess my sins", we used to start off. It was never entirely simple, but then it did indeed work like a sort of spiritual washing machine, and afterward you felt you were somehow cleansed. I've noticed that the Church still offers us today, in the hymnbook, a so-called "mirror of conscience" for preparing ourselves for confession, a kind of checklist. I'll quote a few questions from it: "Do I seek to be close to God?—Do I show gratitude and love toward my parents?—Am I inclined to gossip and slander and to say hurtful things?" Or, again: "Do I shift my work onto other people?—Do I respect the individual character of others?—Do I try to bring my children up well?—Am I lazy? Or mean? Or a spendthrift? Pleasure-seeking?—Have I committed adultery?—Have I lied?—Do I try to seem better than I really am?" We can see that the Church is no stranger to anything human.

I believe that helping the conscience to become articulate is most important. In this respect we are obtuse, if only on account of original sin, and want to draw the veil of forgetfulness over it if we behave unsuitably toward our neighbor. We are maybe inclined to swallow lies easily, and so on. This dulling of our conscience is the greatest danger to us. It degrades man. Because of that, being trained to listen to our conscience is quite essential. It is therefore the task of the Church to recognize the sins particularly prevalent in any age and thus help to prevent society from becoming deadened and decayed in this essential area of its existence.

To interrupt with one little question: Are necessary lies permissible, for instance when getting someone to say on the telephone that you are unavailable?

These are quite practical questions on which even moralists are divided. There is an important school of thought, represented by Kant, that holds that truth has a value in itself and that it is therefore never appropriate to trespass against it. It's quite understandable that someone should want another person to say on the phone that he is not there. But you should at any rate keep very careful watch on yourself here; once you open this little door you very quickly slip farther and farther. But I would not want to condemn straightaway such an attempt to protect oneself—because I do it, too.

One derivative of the sacrament of confession is the so-called "indulgence". The first indulgences were granted by the popes for taking part in the crusades, and the proliferation of the practice of granting indulgences ended in offering the practical occasion for Luther's protest and, thus, led to the Reformation and to schism. I think there are few people today who would still have any idea what to make of this teaching.

That is a very difficult chapter in Church history. In the Bull for the Holy Year 2000 the Pope tried to offer a new interpretation. There is the old distinction between sin and the punishment for sin. According to that, the sins are remitted by absolution, but the *punishment* for the sins remains. That strikes us as very mechanistic. The Pope reinterprets it by saying that even when guilt has been overcome, there remains what I have brought about by sin, that is, the hurt I have done to my neighbor, some kind of damage at any rate, the effects of whatever it was I said or did. And within me there remains, you might say, a repercussion, a twisting or distortion of my being.

It is therefore a matter of dealing with the existential consequences of sin. Dealing with this can, in turn, only be undertaken together with others, because sin always reaches out beyond my own self. Indulgence then means that we enter into the resources of the communion of saints, where there is an exchange of spiritual goods, in which we make a gift of our own and receive what others have to offer. Understood in this sense, as a clearing of existential debts, as a sharing of support and of being supported, indulgence can continue to be a perfectly meaningful image.

Marriage

Young people in multitudes are thinking about whether they really ought to get married or should live together in a somewhat looser form of association. On the part of governments there are efforts to put associations outside marriage as well as homosexual partner-

ships on the same footing as marriage. The question arises: Why should marriage be the only acceptable form of living together?

For one thing, it happens that only a stable sphere of trust is worthy of the dignity of this intimate human association. And not only so far as the responsibility toward each other is concerned, but also concerning the future of the children who come forth from it. In that sense, marriage is never just a private matter, but has a public and social character. The basic way in which any society is built depends on marriage.

And finally we can now also see it in the way that life partnerships outside of marriage are granted certain legal forms. These associations are supposed to be less binding, but they, too, cannot escape some public responsibility, being tied into the common life of society. And that alone shows the inescapable necessity of a form of association that is legally and, thus, socially and publicly regulated, even if people now believe they need to introduce lesser versions of this.

A second aspect to which we must pay attention is this: Wherever two people give themselves to each other and, between them, give life to children, this touches the holiness, the mystery of human existence, which goes beyond the realm of what I can control and dispose of. I simply do not belong to myself alone. There is a divine mystery within each and every person. That is why the association of husband and wife is regarded within the religious realm, within the sphere of the sacred, of being answerable before God. Being answerable before God is a necessity—and in the sacrament this is planted deep and given its proper foundation.

Hence, all other types of association are deviant forms,

which in the end are seeking to evade responsibility toward each other and also toward the mystery of human existence —and which, at the same time, are introducing into society an element of instability that will have further effects.

The question of homosexual partnerships is a different matter altogether. I think that when it is no longer considered important to have a man and a woman in a marriage, in a family, when, on the contrary, homosexuality is given equal status with this relationship, then the basic structural pattern of human existence is being violated. In this way, in the long term, a society will run up against serious problems. If we listen to the Word of God, then we should above all be prepared to be enlightened by the perception that the association of husband and wife and children is something sacred. And we can successfully build a society in the right way if that society sees the family, and thus the kind of association blessed by God, as the right way of ordering sexual relations.

The marriage vow is as follows: "I, N., take you, N., to be my wife/my husband. I promise to be true to you in good times and in bad, in sickness and in health. I will love you and honor you all the days of my life." That all sounds very good, but why should marriage last a whole lifetime, "till death us do part"?

Because that is determined by the irrevocability of human love, and in the irrevocability of the responsibility that is being assumed. We ought not to try to demonstrate the rational ground for everything, down to the last little dot on the "i". The great wisdom of tradition comes to us with this, supported in the end by the Word of God itself. Only if I give myself entirely, without keeping any part of me back or being involved just until further notice, until, so to speak, I find something better, does this fully correspond to human dignity. Human life is not an experiment. This is not a commercial contract, but a surrender of myself to another person. Only in the form of a love that is entire and unreserved is the self-giving of one person to another commensurate with the essence of man.

We have already talked about sexuality several times; obviously the Church feels that this involves a great mystery. Otherwise it would be inconceivable why she has such strict notions about these things, even within marriage. Is it a different understanding about life, about people, that makes the Church forbid contraception?

Indeed, the Church sees sexuality as a central reality of creation. Here man is brought into the closest proximity with the Creator, into the highest degree of responsibility. He himself is allowed a responsible share in the source of life. Each single person is a creature of God—and he is at the same time the child of his parents. For this reason there is to some extent an intermingling of divine creativity and human fruitfulness. Sexuality is a powerful thing; we can see that in the fact that it also involves the responsibility for a new person, who belongs to us and yet does not belong, who comes from us and yet not from us. From that viewpoint, I think, it's understandable that it is at the same time something sacred to be able to give life and, in return, to have responsibility for it beyond its biological beginning. For all these various reasons, the Church had to expound what is important here and what is basically being said to us in the Ten Commandments. She has always, again and again, to bring this as a responsibility into human life.

Can you be a good Christian if in questions of sexual morality you are always running counter to the Church's ideas of what is right?

The other side of this is that we always fall short of the great things that the Church, in expounding the Word of God, proclaims man to be capable of. If, at any rate, one wants to stay on the path, if one retains a basic recognition of the sacred nature of this co-creation with Christ, then one does not cease to be a Catholic simply on account of failure. Then, in our very searching, we remain, if you want to put it like that, a "good Catholic".

The Italian bishops have asked people to have more courage in begetting offspring. For a society that is afraid to beget children is, they proclaim, becoming "less human".

Wherever love for children is extinguished, then really a great deal is lost. Italians used to be famous for their love of family and children. Today, some regions of Italy have the lowest birthrate in the world. Here, something fundamental has changed with newfound wealth. This is in fact a great temptation for Western societies, to see children as competitors who take away from us something of our living space, something of our future. In just the same way, children are then regarded at best as a possession and as an image of oneself. People are not, in the end, ready to accept them in their own right, with all that must be given them in terms of time and the whole of one's life.

An Italian bishop once said to me that poor people invest in life; they look on children as their future; rich people invest in things. I don't want to exaggerate what he meant by that, but it is obvious with us the investment in things, insuring oneself by the value of things, which are a multiplication of our own self, is stronger than our readiness to stand at the service of another life. Even if we take the problem of population growth quite seriously, we still have to recognize, on the other hand, the problem of an aging society that is robbing itself of its own future.

The catchword population growth. The Church is accused of aggravating serious problems in some parts of the Third World with her strict policy of forbidding the use of contraception, to the point of real misery.

That is of course complete nonsense. The misery is the result of a breakdown of the moral sense that once gave order to life in tribal societies, or in the community of believing Christians, and that thus prevented the great misery we can see nowadays. Reducing the voice of the Church to no more than a prohibition against contraception is utter rubbish, based on a completely distorted picture of the world, as I will explain in a moment.

The Church still teaches above all the sacredness of marriage and faithfulness in marriage. That is her true voice. Where people listen to this voice, then children have a sphere of life in which they can learn love and self-restraint, the discipline of the right way to live, in the midst of any poverty. Where the family is functioning as a sphere of fidelity, people have patience and consideration for each other, providing the necessary preconditions for the practice of natural family planning. The misery comes, not from the large families, but from the irresponsible and undisciplined procreation of children who have no father, and often no mother, and who, as street children, have to suffer the real distress of a spiritually distorted world. We all know, besides, that in Africa today the opposite danger has long since arisen, through the rapid spread of AIDS: not a population explosion, but the dying out of entire tribes and the depopulation of the countryside.

When I think, besides, that in Europe they pay farmers subsidies to kill off their livestock, to destroy grain crops, grapes, all kinds of fruit, because we supposedly cannot control overproduction, then it seems to me that these knowledgeable managers ought still to reflect on how, instead of destroying these gifts of creation, we could make good use of them all.

The misery is not produced by people who bring up children to learn faithfulness and love, respect for life and self-restraint, but by those who try to talk us out of morality and who see man only in a mechanistic way: the condom seems to them more effective than morality, but when they think you can replace the moral dignity of man with condoms, so as to make his freedom no longer a danger to him, then they have stripped man of all dignity, down to his most basic self, and have produced exactly what they claim to be preventing: a selfish society in which everyone lives his own life and is responsible for nothing and no one. Misery comes from demoralizing society, not from moralizing it, and the condom propaganda is an essential part of this demoralizing, the expression of an attitude that despises people and that in any case thinks people capable of nothing good whatsoever.

Priests

Every world religion has men who are particularly designated to be responsible in society for the rites and the rules of that faith. In what way is a Catholic priest different from these others?

Well, first of all, the Catholic priest is there in response to the mission of Jesus Christ, in the authoritative pattern of the apostles. So he is not the figure of priesthood as seen in the general history of religions. The standard for this class, if we may call it that, derives from the figure of the apostle, as created by Christ. Christ gives him the task of proclaiming his Word, proclaiming himself, proclaiming the promise he has given us. And within the framework of this proclamation—which is always a task of love, of building up the Body of Christ, of service to the poor—the proclamation of his death, which we call the Eucharist and which is a sacrament, is central.

If they have been called by Christ himself, why are there bad priests? Why are there even bad bishops? In the case of some of those he has chosen the Lord obviously seems to have made a mistake.

It certainly can happen that people slip through, as it were, without really having received a call. But there are also "failed callings", that is, callings that are not truly lived out. The strange thing is, as we have already discussed, that God entrusts himself to such fragile vessels. That he has taken such a horrible risk with the Church. He has put himself into hands that betray him time and again. And he has left us the opportunity of falling and of being corrupted, so that he still has to support the Church himself again and again through these very tools that have proved unsuitable. It is a consolation, on one hand, that the Lord is stronger than the sins of men, but, on the other hand, a great challenge for all those who have turned toward this calling and who believe they have received it to let it truly mature in fellowship with Christ.

Jesus Christ commanded his apostles: "Go out into all the world and preach the gospel to all creatures." And just as the apostles regarded the office of preaching as one of their chief tasks, so again and again great men of the religious orders—the Dominicans were even known as the "preaching friars"—gathered vast crowds around them. With his penitential sermons, Savonarola made all Florence tremble. And it is said of Augustine that his sermons became ever shorter; each sentence was charged with power and went to the root of the matter; every word had weight and meaning. "He took no rest from this", one of his biographers wrote, "until sheer applause, or the tears in everyone's eyes, allowed him to believe that the last element of resistance against truth and grace had been broken down in the souls of his hearers."

Being able to preach is a gift, a special grace, and Saint Augustine always had great respect for the simple pastors who need a book in order to work out what to say in a sermon. He said: It is not originality that is important, but humble service. If another person's book helps someone to preach the Word to men, that's very good. We will be thankful when God raises up a great preacher, but we should also learn to be humble enough to listen to a lesser preacher.

Recently a parish priest in a large German city told me that he had come to his vocation by the particular agency of a priest who was actually bereft of all exterior gifts. He was a hopeless preacher, a dreadful singer, and so on, and yet under his care the parish really blossomed. In the end four or five priestly vocations were awakened in this city parish, something that happened neither under his predecessor nor under his successor, both of whom were far more capable. We can see here how the humble witness of someone who does not have the gift of persuasive speech can itself become a sermon, and how we should thank God for the variety of gifts.

Dying

At the end of our lives, Mother Church provides us with a good exit from this world. She offers her children the holy sacrament of the dying. It used to be called "the last rites" . . .

And if you asked anyone whether he would like to receive it, he probably refused, because he didn't want to think he was already about to die.

The term "last rites", which had come to hold such terrors for sick people, has long since been replaced, deliberately and quite rightly, with "anointing of the sick", so that for the patient the arrival of the priest with this sacrament is no longer an announcement that he is finally about to die.

In fact the anointing of the sick is meant to help with a spiritual process that in some circumstances can become a process of healing. This is the Church's sacramental help in the situation of illness. It's less a matter of the moment of death. In that case, the true Viaticum is the Eucharist. And in the prayers for the dying, the benediction of the dying, and the supplementary absolution, the Church has in readiness specific consolations. These strengthen people for their difficult passage, over this terrible threshold into a dark that seems to have no light at all.

The anointing of the sick is more a help toward the acceptance of suffering. It is meant to help me, by lifting up my pain and suffering into Christ, to enter into sacramental fellowship with him. This is not necessarily a matter of physical healing. For illness can indeed heal me spiritually; I may even have spiritual need of it. Christ, by teaching me how to suffer and by suffering with me, may truly become my doctor, who overcomes the deep spiritual sickness within my soul.

It is said that in the hour of death people are inclined to have a radical change of mind. The most hardened atheists become at the very last minute, as it were, meek and pious lambs. Elisabeth Kübler-Ross, who made a special study of dying, found in her investigations into people's experience just before death that "Most of them change completely. They change all their values round. Their values are no longer so materialistic, no longer so aggressive and contentious. They become much more spiritual." Does that mean that when it's a matter of self-preservation, a man can suddenly recognize quite clearly what really counts in life?

At any rate an extreme situation like this can help him to see that the material goods he has amassed or the honor, respect, and influence he has had are not, despite everything, what is finally real. It can lead to a rethinking of his values —but not necessarily. The soul can become dulled or hardened, so that it no longer sees clearly. In extreme situations like this, only something that is still there within a person can in fact break through and make its appearance. In that sense we ought not to rely on the last hour but should, as it were, not let the supply of goodness within us run out completely, so that there is still oil in our lamp, to recall the Lord's parable, when the bridegroom knocks at the door.

There is an old piece of Catholic wisdom: A man's day of death will be like his Sunday.

That touches on the same point. If God has vanished from one's life completely, along with Sunday, there is nothing in reserve to make its sudden final appearance. Even if God's grace is inexhaustible—I should still heed the warning not to let these quiet reserves within my soul run out, so that in the hour when I have need of them I may not find myself standing there quite empty.

According to the belief of the Church, we ought actually to be glad to die: "Life is death, death is life." After all, eternal life is waiting for us.

Yes. But then, human temperaments are different. When Augustine was lying on his deathbed, all his sins came back before him. Augustine therefore had the penitential psalms fixed to the wall, so that he could constantly absorb them. He even excommunicated himself for a while, and placed himself, so to speak, in the state of a penitent. In doing this, he thought of his spiritual father, Ambrose, who died with great inner peace and resignation, and he said: He who had this great dignity received it as a gift; I am someone else; it has not been given to me; I need to be humbly penitent, in the hope that the Lord will accept me in spite of all.

But I would certainly say that one of the tasks of Christian education and preaching is to give people confidence that by way of death we are entering upon true life. This can help us to overcome our fear of the unknown, or at least the purely physical fear that attacks us, and to grant us peace in dying.

How is it with you? Are you afraid of dying?

Well now, since I, too, know all about my insufficiencies, I have necessarily before my eyes the thought of the judgment. But at the same time the hope that God is then greater than my failures.

Do you give time to preparing yourself?

Of course, since the older you get, the closer it comes.

Is it permissible to have dead bodies cremated, or is that just a heathen ritual?

The Jews, in distinction to other Mediterranean cultures, did not practice cremation. For them, the burial of the body was, so to speak, like sowing the seed in expectation of resurrection. And that became the Christian custom. In burial, there was a silent expression of faith in the resurrection and in hope, and there still is. Right up to the Second Vatican Council, cremation was subject to penalties. In view of all the circumstances of the modern world, the Church has abandoned this. Faith in the resurrection does not have to be proclaimed in that way, because God will in any case give us a new body, so that cremation is permissible in the meantime.

I have to say that I am old-fashioned enough to regard burial as still being the proper Christian expression of respect for the dead, for the human body, and of the hope that it will be given a future.

You were saying that in the world to come God gives us a new body—does that mean that none of us will be exactly the same as he was?

In one respect, the resurrection at the last day is a new creation, but it does preserve the identity of a man as composed of body and soul. Saint Thomas says on this point that it is the soul that gives shape to the body—it is the soul that forms a body for itself. Identity means, therefore, that the soul, which through its resurrection has been given anew its power to shape, will build from within an identical body. But to speculate about just exactly what resurrection corporeality and substance might look like would, it seems to me, be quite useless anyway.

A quite particular question: My brother died at the age of just fourteen. Where is he now?

He is with God. I think at this point we have to abandon our purely material categories of location. Just as we cannot think of God as residing on some particular cloud on high, likewise the dead person has a different relationship to material existence. God's relationship to the material sphere is that of ruling it throughout. We have already talked about degrees of closeness to God, which are not determined by spatial location, and we also said that the soul, the spiritual principle within man, is not located in a specific place like a physical organ, but represents, in its turn, a formative principle of the whole. In a similar way, the dead person shares in God's different kind of relationship to space, which cannot be determined within geographic categories.

A good many people have even said that the dead stay near their graves, which I would see as being rather frightening. No, they have left this sphere of material existence and have entered into a different kind of spatial relation, which is based on God's being above and beyond any spatial relationship. We sometimes experience the way, even though separated by an ocean, people can be intimately united in their thoughts. So we can sense something about this being above and beyond space, about this further stage in spatiality, which is spiritual proximity. We should in any case rid ourselves of the idea that the dead person has to be located at a certain geographical place. Instead of that, we ought rather to say: He is with God—whereby he is inside the reality of the universe in a new way and is thus close to me, too.

We humans are curious; we would like to know just a little bit about what Paradise is like. Does Scripture tell us anything about what is awaiting us?

Even the Scriptures can only talk about it in images. They try to suggest it, for instance, with the image of the heavenly liturgy. The new sphere of existence is thus this transcendance of the actual liturgy, and singing and flying also appear as images.

But all that can be seriously misunderstood. We know the story about the Bavarian who comes to Paradise and then cannot stand the eternal singing of Alleluias. What seems important to me is that not only spatial relations are different but also temporal relations. If we imagine Paradise as an immeasurably long time, the idea inevitably arises that it will eventually be too long. But being removed from our normal time sequence, away from hour after hour, day after day, which are linked to the revolutions of celestial bodies, being in a new type of personal companionship, also means that this kind of eternal sequence of things disappears—and that it all becomes one great moment of joy. We should therefore imagine eternity rather in terms of the fulfilled moment, which is beyond all time.

Can it be that you are an organ donor?

Yes, even though I assume that my old organs will not see much further use.

An exciting prospect: an African Moslem in Paris with the heart of Cardinal Ratzinger . . .

. . . It could happen.

Elisabeth Kübler-Ross, who made a study of dying, had a quite clear opinion on the question of whether we ought to prolong life artificially. She said: "One hundred percent, No. We should not shorten life or prolong it. There is a right moment for everyone, when it is time to die." That, she said, had something to do with certain unfinished business. And this doesn't even depend so much on the particular person, since in the end there is "a bigger boss, who has something to say in the matter".

Well now, there are ways of prolonging life, or trying to, that I, too, see as outrageous interference and that I would oppose. But cures are, of course, in themselves always a way of prolonging life. Illnesses are treated today that used to be incurable. And if medical science develops further, then I would not see that as an artificial prolonging of life.

The question is, then, to what extent organ donation may be one of those means that we would regard as a normal and logical extension of medical technique, of the means of healing. I think when it's a matter of transplanting one of a pair of organs, like kidneys or eyes, we see no great difficulty, although this does of course mean a great sacrifice for the donor. It is more difficult with something like a heart, which can only be taken from someone clinically dead but must be taken so soon that the organ itself is still "living". The question of when someone is dead—and the organ itself, on the other hand, must still be living—is already a critical question, which we have to argue out most responsibly. The criterion of brain death has been worked out with great care, but I think it still needs to be subject to critical examination from time to time. There is above all the temptation to apply the criterion too early. In that sense, heart transplants are in fact an extreme instance of healing. Nonetheless, I would not go so far as to exclude them entirely. I think there are still legitimate instances when it may be regarded as falling within the sphere of proper healing.

18. The Future

National Church or Minority Church?

Many years ago, you made a prophetic statement about the Church of the future: The Church, you said at that time, will "become small, and will to a great extent have to start over again. But after a time of testing, an internalized and simplified Church will radiate great power and influence; for the population of a entirely planned and controlled world are going to be inexpressibly lonely . . . and they will then discover the little community of believers as something quite new. As a hope that is there for them, as the answer they have secretly always been asking for." It looks as though you are going to be right about this. But how are things going to develop in Europe?

First of all: Is the Church really going to get smaller? When I said that, I was reproached from all sides for pessimism. And nowadays nothing seems less tolerated than what people call pessimism—and which is often in fact just realism. Meanwhile, most people admit that at the present stage of things in Europe the number of baptized Christians is simply dwindling. In a city like Magdeburg, only 8 percent of the people are still Christians—and mark you, that's all kinds of Christians, put together. Such statistical findings show the existence of trends that are indisputable. In that sense, the extent to which church and society are seen as synonymous in some cultural areas, with us in Germany, for instance, will diminish. We simply have to face up to this.

What does that mean?

The traditional Church can be very lovely, but this is not something necessary. The Church of the first three centuries was a small Church and nevertheless was not a sectarian community. On the contrary, she was not partitioned off; rather, she saw herself as responsible for the poor, for the sick, for everyone. All those who sought a faith in one God, who sought a promise, found their place in her.

The synagogue, Judaism in the Roman Empire, had surrounded itself with this circle of God-fearers, who were affiliated with it and thereby achieved a great opening up. The catechumenate of the early Church was very similar. Here people who didn't feel able to identify with Christianity completely could, as it were, attach themselves to the Church, so as to see whether they would take the step of joining her. This consciousness of not being a closed club, but of always being open to everyone and everything, is an inseparable part of the Church. And it is precisely with the shrinking of Christian congregations we are experiencing that we shall have to consider looking for openness along the lines of such types of affiliation, of being able to associate oneself.

I have nothing against it, then, if people who all year long never visit a church go there at least on Christmas Night or New Year's Eve or on special occasions, because this is another way of belonging to the blessing of the sacred, to the light. There have to be various forms of participation and association; the Church has to be inwardly open.

But isn't the traditional Church the highest achievement of religious civilization? Is she not the truly universal Church, accessible to everyone, able to shelter everyone under her many-branched roof?

Can the Church really abandon the claim to be the Church of the people, and thereby the Church of the majority? This is, after all, an achievement won at the cost of enormous effort and sacrifice.

We will have to accept losses, but we will always remain an open Church. The Church can never be a closed and self-sufficient group. We will have to be missionaries, above all in the sense that we keep before the eyes of society those values that ought to form its conscience, values that are the basis of its political existence and of a truly human community.

In that sense, the struggle for what the traditional Church used to be—and what she will continue to be in certain countries and will yet become in others—will certainly go on. The Church will have to intervene in the law-making process and to keep before people's eyes the great and unchanging human elements that go to build up the society of men. For if law no longer has any common moral basis, then it is no longer valid as law.

Seen in this way, the Church always has a responsibility for society as a whole. Missionary responsibility means in fact that, as the Pope says, we really have to try to reevangelize. We cannot just calmly allow everyone else to relapse into paganism, but have to find ways of bringing the gospel into the spheres of life of those who do not believe. There are already models for this. The Neo-Catechumenate has one model, and other groups are trying in their own various ways. The Church will have to develop a great deal of imagination to help the gospel remain a force in public life. So that it may shape the people and pervade their life and work among them like yeast. It was to a very small community at the time, the disciples, that Jesus said that they had to be the yeast and the salt of the earth. That assumes they are small. But it also assumes they have a responsibility for the whole.

John Paul II

John Paul II was the firm rock of the twentieth century. The Pope from Poland has left his mark on the Church more clearly than many of his predecessors. His very first encyclical, Redemptor Hominis *(The Redeemer of Man), laid out his program: Men, the world, and political systems had, he said, "strayed far from the demands of morality and justice". The Church must now offer the alternative to this, he said, through clear teaching. This fundamental thesis is to be found in all the papal encyclicals. As against the "culture of death", the Church must proclaim a "culture of life". Has John Paul II left the Church the requisite foundation for her to make a good start in the new century?*

The true foundation is of course Christ, but the Church always stands in need of new stimulation; she always has to be built up again. Here you can certainly say that this pontificate has left an unusually strong imprint. It was occupied in dealing with all the basic questions of our time—and over and beyond this, it gave us a running start, a real lead.

The pope's great encyclicals—first *Redemptor Hominis*, then his trinitarian triptych, where he depicts the image of God, the great encyclical on morality, the encyclical on life, the encyclical on faith and reason—set standards and, as you have said, show us the foundations on which we can build anew. And for the reason that in this world, which has changed so much, Christianity must find a new expression.

In just such an epoch-making way as Thomas Aquinas had to rethink Christianity in the encounter with Judaism,

Islam, and with Greek and Latin culture, so as to give it a positive shape, just as it had to be rethought at the beginning of the modern age—and in that rethinking, it split apart into the Reformed style and the basic outline given by the Council of Trent, which dominated the shape of the Church for five centuries—so today, at the great turning point between epochs, we have both to preserve undiminished the identity of the whole and at the same time to discover the ability of living faith to express itself anew and to make its presence known. And the present Pope has certainly made a quite essential contribution to that.

The Universal Church in the Future

While, fifty years ago, the industrial nations still made up one-third of mankind, within two generations about 90 percent of the population will be living in developing countries. By the middle of the twenty-first century, both China and India will probably each have more inhabitants than the whole Western world put together.

And the universal Church of the future will likewise be sharply differentiated from that of the present day by the change of gravity in population distribution. Today the congregations in what used to be the Third World have outstripped the parishes of central Europe, not only in terms of numbers. If, for example, at the beginning of the twentieth century there were just 1.7 million Catholics in Africa, at the beginning of our new century there are already 110 million. Can we already foresee, today, the ways in which the outward shape of the Church might change, perhaps both in liturgical and pastoral forms?

I think we ought not to extrapolate too far here, because there are always so many surprises in the course of historical development. Every futurology comes to grief over this factor of surprise that makes its appearance in history. No one, for instance, had dared to predict the collapse of the Communist regimes, which brought an entirely new historical constellation. It's quite right that the picture of world society as a whole will change quite fundamentally. What this numerical reduction of the Western world, which is still a dominant factor, will mean then, how Europe will change as a result of immigration—for these empty spaces are being filled up—how the balance will change in various ways, which civilizations and which forms of society will be predominant—we simply cannot imagine any of that.

In that sense, we have to be extremely cautious in trying to picture the future. It is at least clear, at any rate, that the population that will potentially make up the Church will be quite differently constituted. The Western type of man, with his attitude toward the world, will no longer be able to be so dominant as before. Other temperaments, other spiritual gifts, will come to the fore and make their mark on the face of the Church.

For this reason, *essentializing*—one of Guardini's words—is in my opinion what is fundamental. This is not so much a matter of making imaginative constructions of something in advance, which will then turn out to be quite different and not something we could have constructed artificially, as of turning our lives toward what is essential, which can then be embodied and represented anew. In this sense, a kind of simplification is important, so that what is truly lasting and fundamental in our teaching, in our faith, can emerge. So that the basic constant factors, the questions about God, about salvation, about hope, about life, about what is fundamental in ethics, can be made visible in their basic elements and be available for the construction of new systems.

And I do not think it would be helpful if one were to

construct liturgies for the technical world or for who knows what other civilizations. Those are all stunts cut to the measure of oneself. The greatness of the liturgy lies in that it comes from the beginning and has grown as a living thing. It must be treated by us with reverence and treasured. Thus it is great and speaks to men of various civilizations—while at the same time the wealth of the various rites has long been in existence. It will then become apparent which will show the greatest vitality in the various civilizations.

Let's take another look at America, which is particularly interesting. It is beyond dispute the leading nation in the world. It has left its mark on the politics, the science, economy, and above all the life-style of our age. What does American Catholicism contribute to Christianity worldwide?

American Catholicism has nowadays become one of the determinative factors in the universal Church. The Church in America is very dynamic. She is, of course, also characterized by tensions. On one hand, there are groups who are critical of the Church and advocate a more rational and more democratic Christianity. But above all else there are quite new and vital religious manifestations, new religious communities are being formed who quite consciously aim at a complete fulfillment of the demands of religious life. They live this out of a great joy in their faith, also particularly intending to read again the Fathers and Thomas Aquinas, and to form their lives on what they read. This is a Church that is very strongly bringing to bear the vital element of religion: the courage to give one's life to and out of faith, in the service of faith. This is a Church that takes great responsibility in society through her considerable system of education and through her hospitals.

In our Congregation, for instance, we do things in this way: in questions of medical ethics, which are multiplying with the development of medicine, it is not we who make the central decisions in the first place. The Americans have this great network of Catholic hospitals. So they have nowadays a great wealth of experts, of specialists, of lived experience in practicing modern medicine. So we have these questions discussed in the institutions that they have created for the purpose. Guidelines are then worked out there, which we talk about with them. These things remain partial at first, are for the time being American, so that, as it were, other experience can be brought to bear, and the door is not closed. Yet they are already model decisions, which have an effect on medical ethics in other parts of the Church and at least give some direction there.

So I believe that both through the great sphere of worldly experience that the Church has in America as well as through her faith experience, decisive influences can be passed on to European and also to African and Asian Christianity. It used to be said that what happens first in France then happens in the rest of the world. Nowadays it is more the case that America, on one hand, provides secular fashions and slogans that spread throughout the world yet, on the other hand, also offers ecclesiastical models. What is certainly surprising about this is that these models do away with a Christianity that is seemingly modern but at the same time too rationalistic, insufficiently saturated with faith, and replace it with genuine impulses of faith and also typical forms of the life of faith.

So is there an "American way of life" for Catholic, Christian life, too?

In the sense that it is truly permeated with Catholicism, and is not just "American", there is. I believe that it is particularly in the American sphere that people are taking up Catholicism as a whole and trying to relate it anew to the modern world.

In which country today is a groundbreaking theology or Church being developed? Who is leading the way here?

Well, there is no single leader in the classical sense. There is rather a polycentric activity.

First, Latin America posed a challenge to the whole of Christendom with liberation theology. That is gradually becoming a thing of the past. What remains from that is the call to faith to be socially and politically responsible. In Latin America nowadays, in the encounter with native cultures, there is some passionate thinking about questions concerning inculturation.

America certainly heads the list for debates, simply through confrontation with the demands of the modern age. And it has made new breakthroughs in exegesis, in overcoming the one-sidedness of the historical-critical method by so-called canonical exegesis, that is, by reading the Bible as a whole. In that sense, American theology is making a most important contribution nowadays. But in Europe, too, even in Germany, there really is still a great deal of theological potential. Simply through our system of faculties, through the means at our disposal, there is still intensive spiritual work going on, which also bears fruit. Certainly there is a threat from a new kind of rationalism, which is seen as obligatory in academic work. This kind of theology is unfruitful because it questions its own basis. I believe that the new generation of theologians can again see more clearly that theology must above all originate in faith and cannot be purely academic. In any case, Europe has certainly remained a storm center of theology.

In Asia, it is at present India that is setting the tone, by the exemplary work being done to shape the debate with the world of other religions and the question of the standpoint of faith in this world. Africa nowadays stands for traditional values. Think of the weight that Africa carries nowadays in the World Council of Churches, where Western Protestantism has really been floundering with ethnic questions, while African Christianity has brought to bear once again, with some emphasis, its basic sensitivity for fundamental and enduring values. Naturally, questions concerned with the social structure—how can Christianity be a power for peace, a power for reconciliation—are worked through in painful particularity. Perhaps not so much in terms of theory, but then, that much more so with passion and with suffering, which nonetheless have something to say to the Church as a whole.

Christian Unity

Right at the end of the last century, the so-called "Joint Declaration on the Doctrine of Justification" was signed by theologians of the Protestant and the Catholic Church. According to this it is obviously taught now that it is not so much a matter of a man's deeds as such, but that the man is justified solely by the grace of God, irrespective of how well or how badly he has lived his life. Is that truly a significant step in the direction of ecumenism? Is it not necessary, however much there is in common, to hold on to the specific elements of faith with all strictness, so that it runs no danger of losing its intrinsic identity?

We have unfortunately been unsuccessful in really getting across the content of this declaration of consensus, simply because nowadays no one can imagine what is meant by "Doctrine of Justification". In Luther's time that was an important theme, which stirred people up, even though the advance of Protestantism did not come entirely from that, but also, for example, from the self-interest of the German princes, who thought they could expect some advantages from it. Today, even within Protestant Christianity, it is no longer a truly operative issue. Thus, with the public the notion has remained that now everyone says that a man's deeds (his life) do not count before God, but only his faith. That is not merely a very crude simplification of Luther. Above all, in saying that, we fail to recognize the real questions that men are putting to Christianity today. And in the end, in the five hundred years that have passed since the Reformation, the whole of Christendom has undergone new experiences and has passed through an epoch-making change. I can't describe all that here. Only this much: In the joint declaration it was first of all reasserted that the beginning of a man's life with God is really determined by God. We are not capable of hoisting ourselves over to him; rather, only he can fetch us to himself. The beginning that sets a man on the right path is faith. And faith, in turn, is the expression of God's initiative, which we can neither obtain nor earn for ourselves.

In the process of working out this consensus, the Catholic Church laid great emphasis on the fact that we fully recognize this first initiative taken by God, but that it should then also be recognized that now God is at work in me. That God includes me in, that he gives me responsibility, that there is then cooperation and the bearing of fruit—and the judgment, which relates to my shared responsibility. This is the second aspect of this declaration, of which however the public consciousness obviously no longer seems to be aware.

To put it another way: God does not want to have slaves, whom he simply renders righteous and whom he himself does not take at all seriously. It is, rather, a matter of his making men into genuine partners, into real conscious agents, who then, on the basis of this beginning that he has given them, become capable themselves of cooperating and who are also responsible in this cooperation. I should say those are the two things that matter here. They include the things that, in Luther's experience, truly corresponded to Scripture. At the same time, however, what the Catholic Church could never renounce is brought into balance with the other element.

The Church prays for Christians to be reunited. But who ought to join up with whom?

The formula that the great ecumenists have invented is that we go forward together. It's not a matter of our wanting to achieve certain processes of integration, but we hope that the Lord will awaken people's faith everywhere in such a way that it overflows from one to the other, and the one Church is there. As Catholics, we are persuaded that the basic shape of this one Church is given us in the Catholic Church, but that she is moving toward the future and will allow herself to be educated and led by the Lord. In that sense we do not picture for ourselves any particular model of integration, but simply look to march on in faith under the leadership of the Lord—who knows the way. And in whom we trust.

Are there any potentially spectacular reflections on that?

No, since the unity of Christians cannot be restored by some kind of political coup or by cutting the Gordian knot with a sword. It's a matter of living processes. And neither a pope nor a World Council of Churches can simply say, Dear friends, let's do it this way! Faith is something alive and deeply rooted in each one of us and is answerable to God. The Pope, as we were saying, has no totalitarian or absolute powers but is serving the obedience of faith.

In faith you cannot simply order someone to do something, as certain ecumenical projects have assumed, so that now the leadership of the Church says to everyone, Friends, we're going to leave a bit out here and add something on there—that won't work. Either we have believed in the Lord—and then you can't say, tomorrow we'll do it differently. Or, it was from the beginning a human construction—and then everything is null and void in any case. No, faith is something living, and in it we have entrusted ourselves to the Lord, and it can never, through any possible political manipulations, be brought to some kind of formula of compromise.

We can only humbly seek to essentialize our faith, that is, to recognize what are the really essential elements in it—the things we have not made but have received from the Lord—and in this attitude of turning to the Lord and to the center, to open ourselves in this essentializing so that he may lead us onward, he alone.

New Dangers for Faith

In connection with the loss of Christianity's importance in a secularized society, you have pointed to a new and wholly underrated danger for faith, namely, that of a subtle, anti-Christian manipulation of public opinion. This manipulation of public opinion would find only an accommodated and streamlined Christianity, that is, a "nice" Christianity, acceptable, while discrediting those who pass on the authentic faith as "hardliners" or fundamentalists.

That is, I believe, a very real danger. Not that they would openly persecute Christians; that would be too old-fashioned and unsuitable. No, they are most tolerant; they are of course open to everything. But then there are all the more definite things that are excluded and that are then declared to be fundamentalist, even in the case of true faith.

And I think the situation may absolutely develop here in which there must be resistance against the dictatorship of this apparent tolerance, which eliminates the scandal of the faith by declaring it intolerant. Here, in fact, the intolerance of the "tolerant" really comes to the fore. Faith does not seek conflict; it seeks a sphere of freedom and of mutual support and bearing with each other. But it cannot allow itself to be formulated in terms of standardized labels supposedly suitable for modern life. Faith is committed to a higher loyalty to God and thus has to anticipate situations in which there is a quite new kind of conflict.

A Renaissance of Spirituality

Young Christians are looking for a religion that is more informed by feeling. They want to get back to the Church's beginnings, to the origin of the mystery, and are demanding a renewal of spirituality, so that the neglected aspects of Christian tradition may be brought to life again. Does the Church need to be given a jolt that might make the silent Christian symbols speak again?

She does certainly need outbreaks of living spirituality. Forms of that kind, in which a new passion for faith emerges that is not politically contrived but has developed from within, have been important for the Church in every age. We have seen how in the sixteenth century the renewal did not come from institutional authority but through people who were gripped by God and created new movements. This is happening again today in a great variety of forms—the charismatic movement is one of them—and this is, you might say, the consolation that the Lord sends us by showing that the Holy Spirit is still present and still powerful.

Catholicism in fact can never be merely institutionally and academically planned and managed, but appears ever again as a gift, as a spiritual vitality. And it, in the process, also has the gift of diversity. There is no uniformity among Catholics. There can be "Focolare" or Catechumenate piety, Schönstatt, Cursillo, and CL spirituality, and so on, as well as a Franciscan, Dominican, and Benedictine piety. The treasury of faith provides many dwelling places within the one house. And we should preserve this dynamic openness.

Nowadays, particularly among the most modern representatives of Catholicism, there is a tendency toward uniformity. Whatever is alive and new, anything that does not conform to the academic outlines or to the decisions of commissions or synods, is regarded with suspicion and is excluded as being reactionary. Of course, there are always dangers, distorted developments, narrowing of vision, and so on. All that always has to be put right by the gardener, the Church, but at the same time has to be welcomed as a gift.

I believe that a great deal of tolerance is required within the Church, that the diversity of paths is something in accordance with the breadth of Catholicity—and that one ought not simply to reject it, even when it is something contrary to one's own taste. In Germany, for instance, people only have to hear mention of "Opus Dei" or "European Scouts", or whatever it might be, in order to feel they must show their indignation; otherwise they just wouldn't be a good German Catholic. There are in fact things that run somewhat contrary to "normal" taste, or, let us say, the "German" taste. In those cases tolerance is in order, accepting the breadth of Catholicism.

The others must then, of course, be likewise ready to adapt themselves to the service of the Church, to allow themselves to lose something of their peculiarities or of the factors that tend to shut them off. And that is exactly what the office of pope, and the office of a bishop, is there for, to guarantee the breadth, on one hand, and, on the other, to open up what is closed, what could lead to sectarianism, and to integrate it into the whole.

Honesty

Augustine took trouble with the great treasures of the Church, the poor, the widows, and the orphans. His way of life as a Christian convert made all his words credible, true to life, and winged with flame. Would an honest Christian example not have far more influence on society than any speeches, however soothing, or the most extravagant gathering of academics?

Of course you can only say Yes to that, and thanks be to God there are these as well. I think, for example, of how Cardinal O'Connor in New York has founded a new religious order for the care of AIDS sufferers and gives up an hour every week to this work himself. Or I think of the new community of "Sisters of Mercy", in America, who are simply living out again this honesty of purpose in educational work and in providing various kinds of healing services. Or let's take the example of Mother Teresa and her religious order. Thank God there is this witness to faith, lived out in radical, simple fashion, which does have an effect.

The French writer Georges Bernanos once wrote: "Holiness is an adventure, in fact the only one there is. Anyone who has understood that has penetrated to the heart of the Catholic faith."

In our Creed we confess that the Church herself is "holy". Not that we think everyone in the Church is holy. Not that everything in her is good, but in the sense that she is touched by the Lord and saints are forever growing within her. It is important that we should take the concept of holiness in a sufficiently broad sense, for there, too, there is no uniformity. And when the figures of the saints come before us, we can see how many shapes and fashions of sanctity there are. From a doctor who does his work unselfishly, to a scholar, to simple folk, founders of religious orders, and lay people who live their lives in this world.

What is important for me is to see the many inconspicuous saints, simple people like the ones I got to know in my childhood, like kind old farmers, kind dutiful mothers, who have given up their lives for their children, for their family, for the Church, and always for the other people in the village as well. It really doesn't have to have anything of the heroic about it, no, it can just be a matter of simple and humble things.

And then again there are always exciting things. Here in Italy, the figure of Padre Pio kindled great enthusiasm, and he, by the way, is supposed to have been really grim as a confessor. He was far from dealing kindly with his penitents, but he was obviously, in his entire person, a guarantee for people that this is genuine, that the Lord himself is talking to you here, and that, when necessary, he can give you a thrashing. And, on the other hand, help you when you need it. Just as we see in the Gospel, with the figure of Jesus, that he can be quite hard, yet at the same time he is kind and helpful, so people perceived the same thing on the scale appropriate to a priest of this century. So there are things that everyone can see and that are signs that tell us, yes, sanctity is here, and it gives people renewed strength. And there is also simple, humble sanctity that no one writes about and yet is so essential for the life of the Church.

Again and again it can happen that overnight some current, hitherto completely unknown, can alter the course of the rudder. What is particularly noticeable at present is a worldwide renaissance of Marian devotion. What do you think: Can Mary once again become the great gateway by which millions of new Christians find their way into the Church?

You can never predict in advance how things will turn out. Anyone who is extrapolating the decline of the Church in academic, statistical fashion from the situation in Europe is failing to recognize the unpredictable nature of human history in general—and in particular, God's power to take the initiative by intervening, as he is always able to do. There is no doubt that there are quite unexpected new departures and a worldwide Marian movement. Among them, of course, there are many forms of false phenomena and messages. We need to be very cautious, therefore, and not be too ready to believe that there is a supernatural power at work.

But on the other hand, we ought not to allow this critical attitude, which is both genuine and correct, to become an impenetrable shield against the reality that is there. Initially, it was possible for people to think, with respect to Lourdes, that this little girl had fantasized something. And then it turned out after all that she herself was really there, the Mother—Mary. It is certainly not by chance that people are nowadays turning again to Mary, in whom Christianity becomes lovable again and close to us, and we really do find the door again through the Mother.

What we said about Latin America, where Guadalupe represented a breakthrough, so that the Indians could see that this was not the religion of the conquerors but the religion of the kindly Mother and of the God who suffers for us—and Mary truly became the gateway to Christ—that is equally true today. Even today, it could happen, far beyond the bounds of Latin America, to a Christianity that has become tired and rationalistic—and to humanity, exhausted by a cold, technical world—that precisely there in the sign of the Mother they would find again the living Christ himself. Confident in this, we can go forward to the future.

Pope John XXIII could say: "I belong to a Church that is alive and young and that is carrying her work on fearlessly into the future." Can Joseph Cardinal Ratzinger say that, too?

Yes! I can say that with joy. I can indeed see many old and dying branches in the Church, which are slowly dropping off, sometimes quietly, sometimes loudly. But above all else I can see the youth of the Church. I am able to meet so many young people, who come from every corner of the world; I am able to meet these new movements, meet with an enthusiasm of faith that is making its appearance here anew. And this enthusiasm cannot be shaken by any of the criticisms of the Church—which always have some basis—because their joy in Christ is just simply greater than that. In that sense I occupy a place where there are many troubles and yet still more encounters with the fact that the Church is young. And that we can move on into the future consoled by the fact that the Lord will quite obviously not abandon her.